BRISTOL ROVERS
THE BERT TANN ERA
A Personal Memoir

DESERT ISLAND FOOTBALL HISTORIES

CLUB HISTORIES	ISBN
Aberdeen: A Centenary History 1903-2003	978-1-874287-57-5
Aberdeen: Champions of Scotland 1954-55	978-1-874287-65-0
Aberdeen: The European Era	978-1-905328-32-1
Bristol City: The Modern Era – A Complete Record	978-1-905328-27-7
Bristol City: The Early Years 1894-1915	978-1-874287-74-2
Bristol Rovers: The Bert Tann Era	978-1-905328-37-6
Cambridge United: The League Era – A Complete Record	978-1-905328-06-2
Cambridge United: 101 Golden Greats	978-1-874287-58-2
Carlisle United: A Season in the Sun 1974-75	978-1-905328-21-5
The Story of the Celtic 1888-1938	978-1-874287-15-5
Chelsea: Champions of England 1954-55	978-1-874287-94-0
Colchester United: Graham to Whitton – A Complete Record	978-1-905328-35-2
Colchester United: From Conference to Championship	978-1-905328-28-4
Coventry City at Highfield Road 1899-2005	978-1-905328-11-6
Coventry City: The Elite Era – A Complete Record	978-1-874287-83-4
Coventry City: An Illustrated History	978-1-874287-59-9
Derby County: Champions of England 1971-72, 1974-75	978-1-874287-98-8
Dundee: Champions of Scotland 1961-62	978-1-874287-86-5
Dundee United: Champions of Scotland 1982-83	978-1-874287-99-5
History of the Everton Football Club 1878-1928	978-1-874287-14-8
Halifax Town: From Ball to Lillis – A Complete Record	978-1-874287-26-1
Hereford United: The League Era – A Complete Record	978-1-874287-91-9
Hereford United: The Wilderness Years 1997-2006	978-1-905328-22-2
Huddersfield Town: Champions of England 1923-1926	978-1-874287-88-9
Ipswich Town: The Modern Era – A Complete Record	978-1-905328-24-6
Ipswich Town: Champions of England 1961-62	978-1-874287-63-6
The Old Farm: Ipswich Town v Norwich City	978-1-905328-12-3
Kilmarnock: Champions of Scotland 1964-65	978-1-874287-87-2
Leyton Orient: A Season in the Sun 1962-63	978-1-905328-05-5
Luton Town at Kenilworth Road: A Century of Memories	978-1-905328-10-9
Luton Town: The Modern Era – A Complete Record	978-1-874287-90-2
Luton Town: An Illustrated History	978-1-874287-79-7
Manchester United's Golden Age 1903-1914: Dick Duckworth	978-1-874287-92-6
The Matt Busby Chronicles: Manchester United 1946-69	978-1-874287-96-4
Motherwell: Champions of Scotland 1931-32	978-1-874287-73-5
Northampton Town: A Season in the Sun 1965-66	978-1-905328-01-7
Norwich City: The Modern Era – A Complete Record	978-1-874287-67-4
Peterborough United: The Modern Era – A Complete Record	978-1-874287-33-9
Peterborough United: Who's Who?	978-1-874287-48-3
Plymouth Argyle: The Modern Era – A Complete Record	978-1-874287-54-4
Plymouth Argyle: 101 Golden Greats	978-1-874287-64-3
Plymouth Argyle: Snakes & Ladders – Promotions and Relegations	978-1-905328-34-5
Portsmouth: The Modern Era	978-1-905328-08-7
Portsmouth: From Tindall to Ball – A Complete Record	978-1-874287-25-4
Portsmouth: Champions of England – 1948-49 & 1949-50	978-1-874287-50-6
The Story of the Rangers 1873-1923	978-1-874287-95-7
The Romance of the Wednesday 1867-1926	978-1-874287-17-9
Seventeen Miles from Paradise: Saints v Pompey	978-1-874287-89-6
The Southend United Chronicles 1906-2006	978-1-905328-18-5
Stoke City: The Modern Era – A Complete Record	978-1-874287-76-6
Stoke City: 101 Golden Greats	978-1-874287-55-1
Potters at War: Stoke City 1939-47	978-1-874287-78-0
Swansea City: Seasons in the Sun	978-1-905328-02-4
Third Lanark: Champions of Scotland 1903-04	978-1-905328-03-1
Tottenham Hotspur: Champions of England 1950-51, 1960-61	978-1-874287-93-3
West Bromwich Albion: Champions of England 1919-1920	978-1-905328-04-8
West Ham: From Greenwood to Redknapp	978-1-874287-19-3
West Ham: The Elite Era – A Complete Record	978-1-905328-33-8
Hammers Through the Looking Glass	978-1-905328-23-9
Wimbledon: From Southern League to Premiership	978-1-874287-09-4
Wimbledon: From Wembley to Selhurst	978-1-874287-20-9
Wimbledon: The Premiership Years	978-1-874287-40-7
Wrexham: The European Era – A Complete Record	978-1-874287-52-0

WORLD CUP HISTORIES	
England's Quest for the World Cup – A Complete Record	978-1-905328-16-1
Scotland: The Quest for the World Cup – A Complete Record	978-1-897850-50-3
Ireland: The Quest for the World Cup – A Complete Record	978-1-897850-80-0

MISCELLANEOUS	
Blinded by the Lights: A History of Night Football in England	978-1-905328-13-0
Red Dragons in Europe – A Complete Record	978-1-874287-01-8
The Book of Football: A History to 1905-06	978-1-905328-00-4
Football's Twelve Apostles: The Making of the League 1886-1889	978-1-905328-09-3
Football's War & Peace: The Tumultuous Season of 1946-47	978-1-874287-70-4
Freestaters: Republic of Ireland 1921-39	978-1-905328-36-9

Bristol Rovers

The Bert Tann Era

A Personal Memoir

Series Editor: Clive Leatherdale

Edward Giles

DESERT ISLAND BOOKS

First published in 2007
by
DESERT ISLAND BOOKS LIMITED
7 Clarence Road, Southend-on-Sea, Essex SS1 1AN
United Kingdom
www.desertislandbooks.com

British Library Cataloguing-in-Publication Data
A catalogue record for this book is available from the British Library

IBSN 978-1-905328-37-6

Printed in Great Britain
by
Biddles Ltd, King's Lynn

Photographs kindly supplied by the Mike Jay Historical Archive

Contents

Author's Note

During my fourteen years on the sports staff of the *Bristol Evening Post* I kept a detailed record of the activities of both of Bristol's Football League clubs, and this has provided me with the basis for looking back on the Bert Tann era, from 1948 to 1972, of the Bristol Rovers story.

I have been grateful, however, to have access to other sources, especially the *Pirates in Profile* compiled by Bristol Rovers historians Mike Jay and Stephen Byrne that has provided extra career facts about the players – the great majority of them local born – who carried the club to FA Cup glory, the club's first-ever promotion, and the brink of the old First Division during the years of the No Buy, No Sell policy.

The *Rothman's* (now *Sky Sports*) *Football Yearbook* – the game's equivalent of *Wisden*, the 'Cricketers' Bible' – and *The Football Grounds of Great Britain* by Simon Inglis have also been of great assistance. In addition, I have had the benefit of articles of reminiscence written by Bill Pinnell, known to his *Post* readers as 'The Traveller', and interviews that another former colleague, George Baker, conducted with Rovers' star man Geoff Bradford, John Atyeo (Bradford's opposite number over in the City camp) and Bert Williams, the Rovers' long-serving trainer.

On a personal level, I am greatly indebted for their assistance and patience to David Foot, a freelance journalist who used to be with the *Bristol Evening World*, Peter Godsiff and Robin Perry, who reported for the *Post* on City and Rovers, respectively, for most of my time with the paper, and Jack Rollin, editor of the *Rothman's* and *Sky Sports Yearbooks* with his daughter Glenda. Jack was on the sports staff of *The Sunday Telegraph* during some of the years when I was with *The Daily Telegraph*. Mervyn Baker, a delver into Bristol soccer statistics, merits a mention too, for again being ever-ready to answer an appeal for aid. Mike Jay assisted in providing photos from his extensive archive and proof-reading my manuscript.

Last, but certainly not least, many thanks to my wife Joan for the usual forbearance she has shown during the hours I have spent working on my computer.

EDWARD GILES

Dedication

To the memory of the late George Baker, John Coe and Bill Pinnell, highly respected colleagues in Bristol sporting journalism.

CHAPTER 1

'Prince,' the Manager Showman

Bert Tann was an inspired, though not obvious, choice as manager of Bristol Rovers. His footballing background was modest compared with those of some of the men who had gone before him. Indeed, he had more limited experience of League play than any other former player-turned-manager up to that time. Yet he guided the club to and through the most prosperous and eventful period in their history.

Born on 4 May 1914 in the Plaistow district of London, one of eleven children of a ship's painter who worked in London's dockland, Bertram James Tann grew up in an atmosphere of street football, close family ties, and his father's keen trade unionism. He played soccer for London Boys, West Ham Boys and the Essex FA, also excelling at cricket and athletics, then was an amateur with Clapton Orient and Romford before joining Charlton Athletic in the February of 1934. A wing-half or inside-forward, in the terminology of those days, he was mainly a reserve at the Valley, and he had made only nineteen League appearances, scoring two goals, when his playing career was ended by injury shortly before the outbreak of the Second World War in 1939.

Instead of going back to following his father in painting and decorating, at which he had started his working life at the Dorchester Hotel in London, he stayed in football with the Kent club Erith & Belvedere – first as coach, then, in September 1945, as manager. He became an FA staff coach, and it was as chief coach that he was first taken on to Bristol Rovers' staff early in 1948. His reign as their manager began almost exactly two years later – first, in January 1950, in an acting capacity, then confirmed in the appointment at the beginning of March. In lasting for just over eighteen years, up to April 1968, it was second only for length with Rovers to that of their first holder of the post, Alfred Homer. Homer had been in office from 1899 to 1920 as the club progressed from being founder members of the Bristol & District League in 1892 to joining the Birmingham & District League, Western League and Southern League.

Both stayed on in another role – Homer as secretary until 1928, Tann, who also received a Football League long-service medal, as general manager and secretary until his death on 7 July 1972. He was then 58, and died a few days after being admitted to hospital with a heart strain. He was the longest-serving manager with one club in the League at that time.

Alf Homer filled his first footballing post as assistant secretary to George Ramsay at Aston Villa, after giving up the diamond cutting business because he found it too great a strain on his eyesight. He was followed by Ben Hall, a former Grimsby and Derby centre-half, as Bristol Rovers' manager for their entry into the Football League as members of the inaugural Third Division in 1920.

Two of the club's six other managers before Bert Tann were former Scottish internationals Andrew Wilson and David McLean. His most colourful predecessor in the post was Captain Albert Prince-Cox, a flamboyant character steeped in show business but with no previous experience of running a football club. He was chosen from some two hundred applicants after turning up for his interview in a two-seater sports car distinctive for its red wheels.

On a salary of just £10 a week, plus expenses, 'Prince' piloted Rovers to three successive finishes in the top half of the Third South table, wiped out an overdraft of £16,000, and was never more in his showman element when Arsenal, fresh from their completion of a League title treble, were the visitors for a 1936 FA Cup-tie. For an hour Rovers had hopes of repeating the shock victory Walsall had gained over the mighty Gunners three years earlier. Profiting from an early penalty miss by Cliff Bastin, the free-scoring winger who gained all the honours soccer then had to offer by the time he was 21, Rovers took the lead through Harold ('Happy') Houghton, a former clubmate of Bastin's with Exeter City. Although they were then swept out by a five-goal onslaught as Arsenal readjusted their forward line in the second half, Rovers had the consolation of knowing that Tom Whittaker, then the London club's trainer and later their manager, described it as 'our stiffest hurdle on the way to winning the Cup'.

Many years afterwards, Whittaker revealed that before that match he had one of his few serious disagreements with manager George Allison. 'I did not fancy his forward line,' he said, 'with little Bobby Davidson standing in at inside-left for the injured Alex James, but George let the team stand. At half-time I went straight to the dressing room and locked the door, so that nobody, not even the manager, could get in. Then I ripped into the lads, and they sat there gaping as the usually peaceable Tom told them a few home truths. Then, before I unlocked the door to send them out again past the anxious Allison, I told Bastin and Davidson to switch places. Arsenal clicked from the restart.'

Albert Prince-Cox gave his Rovers players a sense of greater importance by having them stay at the better hotels on away trips and eat in the smarter restaurants. 'I don't want any more eating fish and chips out of newspapers,' he said. He also took them on close-season trips to the Continent and came up with a typically audacious and literally high-flown idea in having the amateur Viv Gibbins – one of several former internationals he introduced into the team – brought by plane from London, where he continued to live, for several midweek matches. The first of those trips, at a cost of £40, was to Southend, where Gibbins made a scoring debut in a 3-1 win after Prince-Cox had got him to the ground only just in time after a hurried car journey from the airport. A Football League ban on teams flying to and from matches in Britain prevented similar excursions until it was lifted in March 1957. Chelsea were the first to benefit in being given permission to travel back to London by air from their Good Friday game at Newcastle.

Another notable Prince-Cox initiative was to change the club's colours. Rovers had first worn black shirts with a yellow ribbon sash after being formed as the Black Arabs at a meeting in the Eastville area of Bristol in 1883. The wife of one player is said to have used the yellow ribbon to trim their daughter's hat. While Rovers' home ground was at Purdown their colours were quarters of green and yellow, and as Eastville Rovers – to which they changed their name in their second season – they wore shirts with blue and white Badminton hoops, at a time when one of the Dukes of Beaufort was the club's president. Since becoming Bristol Eastville Rovers in 1897, when they turned professional, and then adopting their present name the next year, they have mainly sported blue and white shirts – but sometimes blue and black – either in stripes or, more regularly, quarters, with white shorts and blue stockings. After the 1914-18 War they were briefly known as the Lilywhites on switching to white shirts and black shorts, before David McLean decided on blue shirts with white cuffs. Prince-Cox brought in the blue and white quarters.

When 'Prince' left after six years to promote boxing and show jumping, and become a circus ringmaster, he was succeeded by Percy Smith, a strong disciplinarian. So was Joe Palmer, a former Bristol City trainer and manager who had been given charge of Rovers between the reigns of Wilson and McLean. Smith had guided Tottenham back to the First Division, but had resigned in acrimonious circumstances after relegation amid claims that his team selections had been overridden by the directors. Within a year Smith was jettisoned by Rovers in the wake of a 1-8 home defeat by Queen's Park Rangers in the FA Cup. Into his place from Barnsley in January 1938 came Brough Fletcher, who had both played for and managed the Yorkshire club.

Fletcher had two spells as a player at Barnsley, split by spending almost the whole of 1926 with the Wednesday. Whereas the Hillsborough club allowed him only a couple of League appearances, he made more than 300 for Barnsley, scoring over 70 goals. He turned to coaching at Oakwell in 1929 and a year later became Barnsley's first manager without secretarial responsibilities. With little money to spend on new players, he was unable to prevent the club's relegation in 1932 from the Second Division for the first time since their election to it in 1898, but he got them back there within two seasons, besides taking them to a Cup quarter-final.

With war intervening, Fletcher had only one full season with Bristol Rovers before League football went into limbo for seven years, and they finished it by having to seek re-election for what remains the only time (though there was soon to be a narrow escape when the game returned to its peace-time format). Beaten 3-6 by Brighton at Hove in their final match of 1938-39, Rovers failed to escape from the foot of the Third South. They and Walsall, who had a superior goal-average, had the same number of points, two behind Clapton Orient. Fortunately, Rovers' application for re-election was successful.

After finishing the first post-war season in a comparatively respectable mid-table position, Rovers fell away again to such an extent in 1947-48 that they were two points behind in last place with only two games left following an eleventh home defeat at the hands of Bournemouth. From 13 September, when they defeated Brighton 4-1, they went through six home League games without a win until Port Vale were narrowly beaten with the aid of an own-goal on the Saturday before Christmas, then promptly lost at Eastville again, to Torquay United, on Boxing Day.

Another bleak spell of six successive defeats set in following a 3-1 win at Northampton on 21 February but, after scoring only four goals in nine hours of football during that period, Rovers suddenly erupted with seven in one Easter Monday home match with Aldershot. Centre-forward Vic Lambden scored four, three of them in nine first-half minutes, the other two minutes from time. It was his second hat-trick in four days, the first one for the Reserves at Eastville. And he might have had another goal in the 7-1 win that avenged a Good Friday defeat at Aldershot, for he was poised to score in the second half when upended in the penalty area. Jackie Pitt scored from the spot – and nearly twenty minutes later Pitt did so again after a handling offence, thus converting his fourth penalty in two consecutive games. The two others were slotted home in the space of seven minutes two days before, but not enough to avert yet another reverse at Eastville, inflicted by Newport County.

Defeat by a lone goal at Southend came in the wake of the Aldershot avalanche, keeping Rovers next to the bottom of the table – a point behind Brighton, who had three games in hand, and one ahead of Norwich, who had played two matches fewer. Hope stirred anew as no goals were conceded in taking four points from Notts County and Swansea, lifting Rovers out of the two re-election positions, only for that setback against second-placed Bournemouth to plunge them to the last place they had hitherto just managed to avoid that season.

At that point their situation looked hopeless. Their remaining two games were both against Ipswich, who had risen to fourth place after being beaten only twice in their last ten outings. The form book, however, went out of the window. A midweek win at Eastville, gained with the help of another own-goal – and despite Pitt's rare failure to add to his penalty account – hoisted Rovers on goal-average above Norwich, who lost on the same evening at home to Notts County. On the final Saturday, Rovers also squeezed above Brighton, but again only through having the better goal figures, by completing an emphatic double with a 4-0 win at Ipswich.

So Brough Fletcher's men, thankful for their superior goal-average, finished 1947-48 on 34 points, along with Norwich, who, after some slip-ups, won their last match at Bournemouth, and Brighton, who ended with a scoreless draw at Swansea. But Rovers, not Brighton, would have had to seek re-election with Norwich if another penalty had not been missed by a player who normally put them away without too much trouble. The goal Brighton required for safety eluded them when Tony James, who was to round off his League career at Eastville, failed to live up to his reputation as one of the Third Division's spot-kick kings.

For their big win at Ipswich, Rovers were mainly indebted to their shortest and tallest players, winger George Petherbridge and goalkeeper Harry Liley. Petherbridge, restored to the side in place of 'Josser' Watling, scored twice and made the fourth goal for Jimmy Morgan after Bryan Bush had also got onto the scoresheet. Liley brought off a succession of fine saves as Ipswich strove to get back into the game.

The signs were again ominous for Rovers when they plunged straight to the bottom of the table in losing their first three matches of the 1948-49 season, but what a transformation there was to follow. By a freak of the fixture list, they had to start from where they had left off the previous May by once more facing Ipswich, and this time, though at home, they let in six goals – with only one in reply. In midweek they were beaten by an only goal at Bournemouth, but conceded four more, again scoring just one themselves, away to Notts County the next Saturday. Yet only eight games later they were up to second place, one point behind Swansea, and during the remaining months of the season they were to drop no lower than sixth.

Fielding a team of Weare; Bamford, Fox; Pitt, Warren, McArthur; Bush, Hodges, Lambden, Morgan, Petherbridge, Rovers began that remarkable rise with 4-0 revenge against Bournemouth, scoring three times in the first 26 minutes. Soon afterwards, by which time Petherbridge had switched back to the right wing with Watling returning on the left, another three-goal spurt put paid to Bristol City. A few weeks after that, four of their five goals at Aldershot came before half-time – one of them direct from a corner kick.

Rovers' only defeat in a dozen games after that shattering start was inflicted by Crystal Palace, who were destined to have to seek re-election with Aldershot, but the 0-1 result was quickly and exactly reversed in the return at Eastville. There was then a blip of two more League defeats, one of which would have been heavier than 0-3 but for a penalty save by Weare from Norwich's long-serving defender Bernard Robinson, and an immediate Cup exit at Walsall. Second place, however, was regained in early February, and held on to until the second day of April when struggling Aldershot were themselves avengers, most unexpectedly, at Eastville. Of their remaining seven games, Rovers won only two, both by 4-1 at home to Reading and Port Vale, but they finished fifth despite failing to win any of the last four.

That was still a big improvement on previous post-war seasons, yet Rovers were down to seventeenth when Brough Fletcher left them midway through the following, 1949-50 season, having gained only nineteen points from 23 games. That left them seventeen points behind leaders Notts County – who were firmly on course for promotion under the free-scoring leadership of Tommy Lawton, the former England centre-forward who had caused such a sensation in forsaking the First Division for the Third. Rovers were only six points ahead of Ipswich, who were then in last place but not destined for relegation.

The unfeeling manner in which Fletcher was dismissed in January 1950, coinciding with an on-going FA investigation into the club's affairs, created a situation that was far from encouraging for the aspiring Bert Tann's takeover. More about that in due course. Fletcher was to have only one more managerial appointment in the League, with Walsall. It ended, ironically, with the Saddlers at the foot of the 1952-53 season's Third Division South table from which Rovers emerged as champions. That brought down the curtain on a career Fletcher had started as a robust forward with his home club Shildon Athletic in County Durham.

With Bert Tann now in charge, Rovers ended the 1949-50 season in ninth place, fifteen points adrift of the champions and eleven better off than the bottom club, Millwall. They scored as many goals as they conceded, 51, and although their nineteen wins were only one more than their defeats, the ratio was eleven to six under Tann's leadership. The family spirit fostered by the club's No Buy, No Sell policy was beginning to have the beneficial effect that would take the club to heights they had never before scaled.

CHAPTER 2

No Buy, No Sell

Bristol Rovers had good reason to be very proud of the No Buy, No Sell policy they adopted after the Second World War, until it inevitably perished with the abandonment of the maximum wage.

No Buy, No Sell put paid, at least temporarily, to the drain of outstanding talent away from Eastville. There had been particular cause to regret the loss of a Bristol-born full-back who played just once for the Reserves before deciding to gee up the horse that pulled his milk float to driving a coal cart owned by one of the Eastville club's directors, who offered him that job in addition to £8 a week as a professional footballer. Off Eddie Hapgood went to Kettering Town, whose right-winger George Charlesworth, a former Bristol Rovers player, persuaded him to sign for the Northamptonshire club, even though their weekly terms during the playing season were half those he could have had at Eastville. It was not long before Hapgood was snapped up by Arsenal, with whom he won a bundle of League and Cup honours, and also turned out for England – whom he captained – more times than any other player between the two world wars.

Three others who played for England had been released by Rovers through the club's worsening financial position. Ronnie Dix, the stocky, fair-haired Boy Wonder who, at fifteen years and 180 days became the youngest scorer in a Football League game on his second first-team appearance, remained a 'Rover' in moving to Blackburn, then went to Aston Villa, Derby, Tottenham and Reading; Cliff Britton was transferred to Everton, Phil Taylor to Liverpool, both rising to management with their Merseyside clubs.

Roy Bentley, scorer of nine goals in his dozen games for England, and captain of Chelsea's first League champions in 1955, also eluded Bristol Rovers. Shortly before the Second World War he was an office boy at Eastville, and then on the club's books as an amateur, before signing for Bristol City. Newcastle did not see the best of Bentley after his £8,500 move from Ashton Gate, but Chelsea's £12,500 outlay proved a real bargain when he prospered as an unorthodox centre-forward at Stamford Bridge. He later excelled again on switching to centre-half with Fulham.

Bristol Rovers' decision to scorn the transfer market and rely on home-grown talent, with a blending of more experienced players signed without payment of a fee to other clubs, led to a sudden blossoming into one of the Third Division South's most attractive sides of the 1950s. There was also a rarity of some FA Cup glory, followed by elevation to the Second Division for the first time – and then to the fringe of promotion to the First.

But it was a policy not without controversy. One of its most outspoken critics, at the outset at any rate, was the man who then reported on Rovers for the *Bristol Evening Post* – John Robert Tudor Coe (never pronounced as anything but 'Coey', with an umlaut over the 'e'). John, as I got to know as one of his colleagues with the paper, was a delightful, if exceedingly eccentric person, one who would not normally look upon anything with gross disfavour. With Rovers and their 'closed shop' mentality, however, he was quite prepared to make an exception. Before its success eventually compelled him to adjust his views, the scorn he expressed so infuriated the directors that they threatened reprisals and litigation which would have daunted less courageous writers. After that he revelled with the rest in the club's boom years of the 1950s before the abolition of the maximum wage blew an irreparable hole in the Rovers' bold policy with the lure of bigger pay packets elsewhere. John Coe was the last reporter who had to pay to be taken onto the *Evening Post*'s editorial staff and trained. It cost his parents, well-to-do rubber planters in Malaya, £1,000 pounds – a lot of money in those days of the mid-1930s – but the whole amount was repaid when the management came to realise what a remarkable and versatile journalist they had acquired. Coverage of soccer was just one string to his amazing bow. In his 42 years with the *Post* he was also drama critic, medical correspondent and reporter on Council affairs.

Coe developed his love for soccer from the day when, as a little lad at Clifton Preparatory School, he was taken to see a Bristol City match one afternoon in 1926 and afterwards had a cup of tea with George Jenkins, the club's chairman. Thus began an association with City that lasted into the 1960s, but it was with the less fashionable Rovers that he had his most eventful, and demanding, times as a shrewd commentator.

Incredibly, for seventeen seasons Coe reported on every *away* match, some 700 overall, played by Bristol's two Football League clubs. Incongruously, their home games during that period were covered by 'The Traveller', a *nom de plume* Bill Pinnell had adopted as John's predecessor at the grounds of opposing clubs, while Harry Slater Stone, who wrote under the name of 'Half-Back', stayed in Bristol. So when I knew him 'The Traveller' did not travel very far.

When Bill Pinnell and John Coe finished reporting on Bristol's Football League clubs during the Bert Tann era, the *Evening Post* was fortunate to have two very capable and resourceful young men to take their place. For many years Peter Godsiff, who eventually became Sports Editor, covered the Bristol City scene, and Robin Perry reported on Rovers. Peter, who had a real eye for a good story, came up from Poole, where he had worked on newspapers at Poole and Bournemouth along with Ian Wooldridge, later a highly respected member of the *Daily Mail* staff. The dapper Robin, who hailed from Wiltshire, crossed over from the local morning paper, the *Western Daily Press*.

Bill Pinnell, a dear old chap who was so kindly a critic that he preferred to ignore a player who had a poor game, rather than point out his short-comings, was said to have reported on 1,500 City and Rovers matches, some 600 of them away from home, by the time he retired, aged 69, at the end of 1956. He had started out with the *Bristol Times & Mirror* in 1919, then been with the city's *Evening Times & Echo* before becoming Sports Editor of the *Evening Post* from its first day of publication in 1932 – an appointment he held until only a few months before his retirement. The promotion of his deputy, Bob Cooper, caused the vacancy I was brought in from the *Derby Evening Telegraph* to fill.

The *Evening Post* arose from the Bristol public's revolt at the loss of some of their local papers. A controversial agreement between Allied Northern Newspapers Limited, whose chairman was Lord Camrose, and Northcliffe Newspapers Limited, chaired by Lord Rothermere, ended the costly competition to attract provincial readers that had been 'bleeding them white'. Allied took over the copyright and goodwill of Northcliffe's *Newcastle Evening World*, which was incorporated in the *Newcastle Evening Chronicle*, but the opposite applied in Bristol and Derby. Allied's *Bristol Evening Times & Echo* was merged with Northcliffe's *Bristol Evening World*, and Allied's *Derby Daily Express* with Northcliffe's *Derby Daily Telegraph*.

With the *Bristol Times & Mirror* incorporated with the *Western Daily Press*, whose sister paper the *Evening News* went out of existence altogether, the first shots across Rothermere's bow were fired with the appearance of *The Bristol Paper* – subtitled *Bristol's Own* – and the *Bristol Sentinel*. Something more substantial was required, however, to compete properly with the financial clout that the Northcliffe group could bring to bear, and that was why the *Bristol Evening Post* Limited was formed with a share capital of £100,000 to which the public were invited to subscribe. The first edition of the *Post* was published on Monday, 18 April 1932, bearing the slogan 'The paper you have so eagerly awaited'.

When I joined the staff nearly a quarter of a century later, ironically from Northcliffe's Derby paper, the line immediately below the masthead had for some time read: 'The paper all Bristol asked for and helped to create.' It was then firmly established – more prosperous, indeed, than the *Evening World*, which lost circulation to such an extent that it went out of business in 1962.

As a schoolboy, Bill Pinnell helped Eastville win the Bristol Schools League Shield, which they claimed for three successive seasons. That team also included Billy Gerrish, an inside-forward afterwards with Bristol Rovers before being transferred with Arthur Cartlidge to Aston Villa in 1909.

One story Bill Pinnell was fond of telling was of the time, during the 1922-23 season, when he very nearly also got to play for Bristol Rovers. He was a useful player in his youth, though not up to Gerrish's standard. It was therefore to his great surprise, and not a little trepidation, that he was told by manager Andrew Wilson to get ready to turn out in a match at Watford when Rovers had only ten men available with the kick-off looming. The missing player, centre-half John ('Jock') Rutherford, was delayed by fog on his journey from his home in Cardiff. After failing to report with his team-mates at Bristol's Temple Meads railway station, he had still not caught up with them when they stopped in London for lunch.

Concern grew on the rest of the way to Watford, with fears of a fine for being a player short. 'You will have to sign, so I will get you registered by wire or phone,' Wilson told Pinnell, who was then in his mid-30s. 'You can surely get a Watford reporter to cover the match for you.' Much taken aback, Bill asked 'Are you really serious?' To which Wilson replied 'Yes, never more serious in my life. I'll put you in one of the wing positions.' So off Bill dashed to get someone to report the match and phone his office to obtain approval. Back in the dressing room he found kit laid out for him. What a story, he thought to himself. But that story was never written. Rutherford, having caught a later train, arrived just in time to get changed and help Rovers to a 1-0 victory.

Bill Pinnell combined his journalism with work behind the Gloucestershire football scenes that earned him an FA gold medal for services to the county over half a century. For seventeen years he was secretary of the Bristol & Suburban League, with which he was first associated as a club secretary in 1903. He was a life vice-president of the Gloucestershire FA and senior vice-chairman of the Council, to which he was first elected in 1909. All this gave him an encyclopaedic knowledge of local soccer, and the detailed records he kept never left him short of material for the columns of reminiscences he continued to churn out for the *Post* until only a few years before his death at 89 early in 1977.

John Coe retired as a full-time journalist, very reluctantly, in the year of Bill's death. Far from being ready for a rest after doing so much soccer travelling – and also spending three or four nights a week, for more than twenty years, reviewing amateur and professional theatrical productions – he took only four months to settle into a new post. He became public relations officer for the Bishop of Bristol, the Rt Rev John Tinsley, bringing out the diocese's monthly newsletter. Not until his health began to deteriorate just over a year before his death did he finally have to ease up.

When John died late in 1983, in his 71st year, he was described in his obituary as 'a highly individual, slightly eccentric, and easily lovable friend'. The Archdeacon of Bristol, the Venerable Anthony Balmforth, who had worked closely with him, told the many who attended the funeral service at St Peter's Church in the Bristol district of Henleaze: 'Drama, sport and medicine must appear to most of us as strange bedfellows, yet he managed to be an authority on them all with understanding, responsibility and courage.'

For eleven years John was the Western Area's representative on the National Executive Council of the National Union of Journalists, and for a record 26 years he was the Father of the Chapel at the *Evening Post*. He had some extremely difficult situations with which to contend in that latter role as disputes arose with the management over pay and conditions. One of these gave rise to a momentous branch meeting at which he uttered the most memorable of the many startling remarks he made in my hearing. As we anxiously leaned forward to learn of the latest developments, he declared with his great sense of drama: 'Gentlemen, to put it in plain English, we are presented with a *fait accompli*.'

That language mix-up ranked for *bon mots* with the lament of the night news editor of *The Daily Telegraph* in Manchester that we in the sports department could not help overhearing as he and one of his colleagues passed by our corner of the editorial room on their way to the gents. Complaining about one of his sub-editors, he was heard to say: 'I've told him all I know, and he still knows nothing.'

CHAPTER 3

Life Membership for Ray Warren

Two of the five players Bristol Rovers called upon in the first team either side of the Second World War would, between them, surely have exceeded 1,000 League appearances but for the loss of those seven seasons from 1939 to 1946. As it was, their combined total went beyond 700, Wally McArthur clocking up 261 and Ray Warren 450. Then there were FA Cup-ties and other competitive games, some of them during the war, also to be taken into consideration. With those included, McArthur's number of appearances rose to near 300, Warren's well in excess of 500.

McArthur, a Yorkshireman, played for Denaby United, his home club, and Goldthorpe United before being signed by Albert Prince-Cox on 2 February 1933, after just one trial game. He made his first-team debut, at centre-half, in a friendly at Eastville with Blackburn Rovers, in which Frank Britton, a former Rovers player, scored four goals for the Lancashire club. Soon afterwards Wally played his first League game against Brentford, that season's Third South champions (they climbed into the First Division two years later), and was in the team that lost 2-4 to Bristol City in the Gloucestershire Cup final. He offset that disappointment by winning his first medal with Rovers as they beat Nottingham Forest with goals from George McNestry and 'Doug' Lewis in the final of the Allan Palmer Cup at Trowbridge. Lewis, whose given forenames were Dudley Reginald James, left Rovers the following season for Exeter City, with whom he revisited Eastville in a remarkable 5-5 draw.

McArthur had only one League chance in each of his first two seasons with Rovers, but he collected another medal as a member of the winning team against Watford in the Third South Cup final of 1935, and firmly estab-lished himself by playing in all but two of the club's 84 League matches in the last two full pre-war seasons. He took over as captain for what were to be Rovers' only three Third Division games of 1939-40, following the trans-fer to Ipswich that summer of centre-half Matt O'Mahoney. O'Mahoney, an Irishman, was the most-capped player with Rovers until Neil Slatter was called up for the eighth time by Wales (one of them as a substitute) to play Norway in Bergen in 1985, in which he unfortunately contributed an own-goal to a 2-4 defeat. Since then, Vitalijs Astafjevs has won 31 of his 133 Latvian caps while with Rovers.

After the war, Bristol Rovers' captaincy passed to Raymond Richard Warren, one of the most loyal and resourceful players the club have ever possessed. He was the first player, in April 1957, to be made a life member of the club, in recognition of his magnificent service over some twenty years. At that time only four other life members were still living – Jim Bissicks, George Humphreys, Eric Lloyd (former directors) and W P Channing. Arthur Hoare, another former director and life member, had died only a few months before. Others honoured with life membership had included James Machin, whose connection with the club dated back to the days of Eastville Bristol Rovers, and Lew John, who had shouldered the responsibility of running the reserve side for many years.

Ray Warren, who on retirement received an inscribed gold wristwatch from the Supporters' Club, was born near Bristol City's ground. He excelled as a forward in schools' soccer, playing for Bristol Boys and amassing 175 goals in three successive seasons, 1930-33, before having a spell in the Bristol & Suburban League. It was at inside-right, filling the vacancy left by Phil Taylor's transfer to Liverpool, that he made his League debut against Queen's Park Rangers at Eastville on 14 March 1936. That was the day on which Billy ('Hartillery') Hartill, having swapped clubs with Taylor after having made his name with Wolves, was introduced into the side at centre-forward.

It was not until during the war, in which he was engaged on top-secret work on amphibious tanks, that Ray Warren was converted into a centre-half. He then became the rock at the heart of Rovers' defence in playing almost 420 post-war games spread across ten seasons. Five times he was a League ever-present, equalling the club record set by Jesse Whatley, the goalkeeper who had an unbroken run of 246 games in the Third Division from August 1922 to April 1928. And the ever-present record would have been Warren's alone but for his being kept out of one match, through injury, in the 1953-54 season. He was absent on only five other occasions, all in 1951-52 and again because of injury, in the course of the 258 League games the Rovers played in six successive seasons from 1948 to 1954.

Warren got into that regular groove straight from the resumption of normal peacetime football in August 1946, having kept in trim by playing as often during the war as his work allowed. In the 1942-43 season he turned out several times for Leeds United while employed in that part of the country, and he also guested for Bristol City and Bath City besides adding nearly 40 wartime matches to his Rovers total.

Not only as a defensive stalwart – once, at Cardiff, as an emergency goalkeeper – did Warren serve Rovers so nobly. He was also quite a penalty expert, scoring most of his 30 or so goals from the spot. In 1948-49, when Vic Lambden (fourteen) and George Petherbridge (eleven) were the club's only other players to get into double figures, seven of his eleven goals were penalties.

After having deservedly been awarded two benefits, Warren finally reached the end of his long League road with his 450th appearance during the 1955-56 season in which Rovers went desperately close to reaching the First Division for the first time. Although by then no longer an automatic choice, he had derived great satisfaction from having led them into their hitherto uncharted territory of the Second Division only three years earlier. Life for Warren after his retirement from professional football at the age of 38 was for many years as a publican at Downend, a suburb of Bristol where the cricketing legend William Gilbert Grace was born. Grace ended his days in Kent, but Warren remained faithful to his roots and was just a few months from his 70th birthday when he died in his home city in March 1988.

The scorer of Bristol Rovers' first goal when the Football League started up again after the Second World War was a player they had sold to Bristol City to ease their serious financial position. An appeal for cash by Rovers to their supporters brought in nearly £1,000, but more was needed urgently. So in 1939 the Eastville club's directors sounded out their opposite numbers at Ashton Gate, who were known to fancy the man in question, Frank Curran, an inside-forward who had been regularly scoring goals since his schooldays. The response was immediately favourable and, in the middle of May, Curran, valued at £200, crossed over to the other side of the city along with full-back Alex Millar. The combined fee was £300, which went straight to reducing Rovers' overdraft at the bank.

Millar, who had been signed from Margate two years before by a Rovers director while manager Percy Smith was on holiday, soon faced his former team-mates in one of the Jubilee Fund games that were played before the 1939-40 season, but Curran's debut for City was delayed until their opening League match a week later. Rovers won that Fund match 4-0, and they were also undefeated in each of the six other meetings between the clubs that season, scoring 24 goals against thirteen. And there would have been another meeting if the final of the North Devon Hospital Cup, in which they had agreed to meet at Barnstaple, had not been cancelled. Those other games included friendlies and encounters in the regional competitions that were organised after the Division Three South programme had to be abandoned because of the war, along with the other sections of the Football League, when there had been time for only three fixtures to be fulfilled.

In the confusing circumstances of wartime football, Bobby Caldwell, of City, guested for Rovers, and Albert Butterworth and Jack Preece, of Rovers, turned out for City, in one of the regional games. It ended 4-4 and was played at the Aero Engines (later Douglas) ground in the Kingswood district of Bristol. In one of Eastville friendlies, drawn 5-5, Jack Milsom, a tall and slim Bristolian who had been with Rovers before scoring more than 200 goals for Bolton Wanderers, did the hat-trick for City.

Frank Curran, a Tynesider, first joined Bristol Rovers in the summer of 1938 on a free transfer from Accrington Stanley – after the Football League's management committee had erased the fee placed on him – and he rejoined them in May 1946 after adding ten goals in some twenty wartime matches for Bristol City to the one had had scored in their last three League games before the war. Two of those City goals were netted against Rovers – one in a friendly in 1940, the other in the Gloucestershire Cup final of 1945. He had scored about 200 goals as a centre-forward in schools football, and just over 100 more at the junior level before becoming a part-time professional with Washington Colliery in the North-Eastern League. From there he first played in the Third Division North with Southport, against whom he made his Accrington debut in a 6-3 victory eighteen months later.

In exactly 50 appearances shared between those two clubs in the League, Curran scored seventeen goals. In his only pre-war season with Bristol Rovers he was top scorer with 21 in 27 games, becoming, against Swindon Town, their fourth player to net four goals in one League match (there have since been half-a-dozen more). The first to that feat, in a 5-0 win against Exeter City in 1921, was Sid Leigh, one of the players who followed manager Ben Hall from Derby County. It was a big blow to Rovers when Leigh, the leading scorer in both their first two seasons in the Third South, had his career ended by torn ligaments suffered in an Easter Monday match at Watford in April 1922. Curran's two other predecessors as four-goal men were Jonah Wilcox, with the aid of two penalties in the last ten minutes of a 7-2 defeat of Bournemouth on Boxing Day 1925, and Bill Culley, in a 4-1 victory over Queen's Park Rangers in March 1927.

The goal with which Frank Curran reopened Bristol Rovers' account on the opening day of the Football League's first post-war season – on 31 August 1946 – was scored in the first half against visitors from Reading. The weather made it a stormy start for several clubs (even pumping by the local fire brigade could not save Newport's flooded home game with Southampton), but more than a million fans welcomed back the resumption of peacetime fare. Almost 12,000 of them were at Eastville, where Rovers had to step up the tempo to salvage a point after goals from McPhee and Glidden had given Reading an interval lead. The 2-2 draw was gained by Vic Lambden, a wartime find who was to follow Curran as the scorer of four goals for the club in one game – and to surpass him and the others by doing so twice.

Lambden had a trial with Notts County before signing part-time professional forms for Rovers in October 1945. A prolific scorer in the Bristol & Suburban League with the Oldland club in the village near Bristol in which he was born, he travelled up to Nottingham with Ernie ('Ginger') Peacock and Bobby Allen, who were both later with Bristol City. Lambden played in his usual position of centre-forward in the first half of his trial against Leicester City Reserves, but during the interval Major Frank Buckley, then the Notts manager, told him to switch to the right wing. Consequently, he was unable to do himself full justice, and he heard nothing more from the Midlanders.

Allen, a full-back from Shepton Mallet, and Peacock, a Bristol-born wing-half or centre-half, were taken on, but both were transferred to Bristol City soon after the return of League football. After taking part in a number of wartime games, Allen played in only one Third South game for both Notts and City. Peacock, though a frequent choice in the first half of the transitional 1945-46 season, did not get into the League side at all while on the staff at Meadow Lane, but he went on to give the Ashton Gate club exceptional service, helping them into the Second Division in the course of making more than 350 appearances before becoming Weymouth's player-coach in 1959.

In one match for a motor works team, Lambden scored eight goals, and he finished the 1943-44 season only four short of 100 for Oldland in the junior section of the Suburban League. It was after seeing him play against the Bristol Aeroplane Company team around that time that Brough Fletcher, then employed at the Filton works but still Rovers' manager, signed him as an amateur. Lambden continued playing for Oldland before accepting an invitation from Fletcher to turn out for a Rovers XI against RAF Melksham during the Easter of 1944. Although on the losing side, he scored three goals, displaying the speed off the mark that had made him capable of running the 100 yards in 10.3 seconds.

Lambden became a regular member of the Rovers side in the 1945-46 season, in which they were runners-up to Bournemouth in one of the regional competitions. He saw his first hat-trick for the club fail to bring victory as Reading battled back from three down to grab a point in the closing minutes of what was complicatedly termed a Third South (South Region) match. For that season the clubs belonging to the First and Second Divisions of the Football League when war broke out were split into League North and League South; the members of both the Northern and Southern sections of Division Three were divided into four geographical regions – North, South, East and West.

Only Wilfred Whitfield, who liked to be known as 'Baggy', played more games for Rovers than Lambden that season (just two more). Lambden ended it as their leading scorer, if with only thirteen goals, and, having become a full-time professional he got off to a great start to his Football League career by finding the net in each of the first four games. Injuries, however, soon afterwards became his bugbear, and, in being limited to fewer than twenty appearances in the 1946-47 season, he added only one goal to the five of his early spurt – and that was Rovers' lone reply to the three Merthyr Tydfil scored in gaining a shock FA Cup victory.

For the best part of a year Lambden was out of the side, enabling Jersey-born Fred Leamon, a signing from Newport County, to succeed him as Rovers' top scorer, also with thirteen goals, in that first post-war season. Leamon, whose other big sporting interest was in bowls, at which he represented Wales, had a season with Brighton after leaving Eastville, then a final one with Chippenham Town. He afterwards worked as a security man for BBC television, and it was while on duty at St Paul's Cathedral for the Prince of Wales' wedding to Lady Diana Spencer that he suffered the heart attack that resulted in his death, aged 62, a few weeks later.

Another who led the attack during Lambden's absence from the side was Len Hodges, a former Bristol Boys player who joined the local Kingswood club while still at school and then played for Soundwell before joining Rovers. He made a scoring debut against Torquay after losing his best years to the war, but it was at inside-right that he played most of just over 100 games before going to Swansea. After also having a short spell at Reading he, too, wound up at Chippenham, whose player-manager, Jack Preece, had guested for Bristol City during the war after forming an effective full-back partnership for Rovers before it – first with Bill Pickering, then George Tweed. Hodges, a record clerk with BAC on leaving football, was in only his 40th year when he died from meningitis in 1959.

On regaining his place in Rovers' team, Vic Lambden quickly became firmly established, accumulating more than 130 goals in not far off 300 League and Cup games before leaving at the end of his ninth peacetime season. Appropriately enough, the last of the 117 goals he scored in 269 League matches was a winner, at Plymouth on Easter Monday in 1955.

'Baggy' Whitfield was another of the players who were with Rovers in the League both before and after the 1939-45 War. Whitfield, a Derbyshire man, played as an amateur for Sheffield Wednesday in the Yorkshire League after captaining North-East Derbyshire Boys at centre-half. He was only just past his 22nd birthday when he made his Rovers debut at wing-half late in 1938, yet he had already been with Worksop Town and made more than 200 League appearances for Bury. After just ten more for Rovers before the war – during which he served in the Army, played in several representative matches, and guested for Bristol City, Chesterfield, Fulham and Millwall – he turned out sixteen more times for the Eastville club in the Third South on the return of peace. Whitfield then moved to Torquay United early in 1947 and finally wound up back near Bristol with Bath City.

Wilf Smith, a full-back or centre-half who hailed from Pucklechurch, just outside Bristol, also totalled 26 League games for Rovers – seventeen before the war, nine after it. Signed from Clevedon Town, he made the first sixteen of those pre-war appearances in succession before losing his place to Alex Millar. On his return from wartime service in Italy, he had to be content with

a place in the Rovers Reserves side that won the Western League championship in 1945-46. Then, after beginning the following season as first choice
for the right-back position, he found his chances of staying there swiftly nul-
lified by Harry Bamford, a player who became one of the most gifted and
revered in the whole of Bristol Rovers' history in making some 500 appearances over the next dozen years. More about Bamford in the next chapter.

Only a few days before 1946 was out Smith departed to Newport County
in exchange for winger Ken Wookey. A former Welsh schoolboy international, the Newport-born Wookey was another of the many players who had
their League careers interrupted by the war, in which he served in the RAF.
He arrived at Eastville not long after having the demoralising experience at
Newcastle of being in the Newport team that leaked a record thirteen goals
– six of them to the mercurial Len Shackleton on his debut after being bar-
racked out of Bradford. Wookey was a Rovers regular for just over 50 games
until he was dropped after a 1-6 home defeat by Ipswich Town on the opening day of the 1948-49 season and soon afterwards departed to Swansea
Town. It was with Ipswich that he last played in the League, following a short
stay at Hereford.

CHAPTER 4

Gentleman Harry Bamford, a True Sportsman

Bristol Rovers were fortunate indeed to have so many talented local players available to them after the Second World War to augment the powerful Warren-McArthur nucleus remaining from the last few months of the 1930s. The benefits were not readily apparent, especially when a second application for re-election to the League was so narrowly avoided in the second post-war season, but the seeds were being sown that would blossom into the club's most successful years under the management of Bert Tann – and thus make the controversial No Buy, No Sell policy viable.

Foremost among that burgeoning talent on the Eastville doorstep was Henry Charles Bamford. Yet he might well have been lost to Rovers before Army service took him to Burma, for after leaving St Silas School in Bristol, and captaining Bristol Boys, he graduated from assisting the Georges Brewery side to having trials with Bristol City in their Colts team, and then, in April 1939, was signed as an amateur by Ipswich Town. While out in the Far East he also experienced a diversion from soccer in playing as a second-row rugby forward for the Gloucestershire Regiment. It was the trekking he had to do through the mud of Burma after a monsoon that led to his affectionately being known as 'Mucker' in the Rovers' dressing room.

Bamford was back to soccer, playing for St Silas Old Boys shortly after his return home, when he was spotted by Rovers scout Wally Jenkins. This time, his Ipswich registration having lapsed, there was no mistake about getting him onto the books. A few days later, towards the end of 1945 in the season before the Football League swung back into peacetime action, he made his Rovers debut against Crystal Palace at Selhurst Park. Centre-half was his position that afternoon, as a late deputy when Ray Warren could not obtain leave, but within a few months he had also been used at right-half, both inside-forward positions, and centre-forward. As a forward at St Silas School he had scored thirteen goals in one match.

The competence with which he could kick with both feet dated back to his early days at the school. Gilbert Baldwin, the sports master while Bamford was there, recalled that he first saw this 'dour-looking boy of six or seven kicking a tennis ball. I advised him that if he wanted to play for the school he should also use the other foot. I noticed him diligently practising with the other joey, as the St Philip's Marsh people would say. That was so typical of Harry'.

The first time Bamford led Rovers' attack, in a Division Three South (South) cup-tie against Torquay at Eastville on the first Saturday of February in 1946, he scored one of the goals by which they were leading 2-1 when the referee ruled the pitch unfit for further play with just under twenty minutes to go. A week later, again at centre-forward, he scored a goal that did count in an even more complicatedly labelled Division Three South (North and South) cup-tie at home to Port Vale. Rovers won 4-2, but their visitors played from the sixth minute under the handicap of having one of their full-backs in goal following an injury that put Arthur Jepson, who also played cricket for Nottinghamshire, in hospital. Rovers lost the return game with Vale the next Saturday. After that Bamford was moved back to right-half.

Only after being switched about did Bamford settle down at right-back, where for more than 500 matches he was a constant and unfailing choice through the first dozen post-war seasons, an admirable successor to such previous outstanding occupiers of that position as former captains Harold Armitage and Bill Pickering. Even so, as a ball-player at heart, he could not shake off entirely his attacking instincts. While on an FA tour of Australia, during which he was the only member of the party to take part in all the matches, he sometimes reverted to playing in the forward line and scored three goals. He also found time on that tour to help pack the kit and prepare it for the laundry. 'I couldn't have done the job without him,' said the trainer. 'What a player, and what a wonderful man.'

The adventurous aspect of Bamford's game caused him occasionally to worry his fellow defenders by indulging in a spot of close ball control too near Rovers' goal for their comfort (he became known as 'the ball-juggling full-back with a poker-face expression'). In one match with Exeter he went so far as to dribble the ball into his own net rather than lose possession!

Such a slight drawback to his otherwise impeccable style could not in the least detract from the genuine regard and respect in which he was held by his fellow professionals. One of them, Harry Liley, a goalkeeper who changed alongside him as deputy for the more experienced Jack Weare, said he could not have wished for a finer colleague, adding: 'He would not say boo to a goose. He was capable of inspiring real affection.' That summed up the shy Bamford perfectly, a true gentleman and sportsman.

Liley, who was born at Trowbridge but played his schools football in Wales as centre-forward and captain of Newport Boys, turned his height of over six feet to good advantage on switching to keep goal – only to find Weare standing in his way to a regular first-team place when he joined Rovers in the autumn of 1946. After fewer than 30 Third South games in the first four post-war seasons, he was given the greater scope he deserved in making more than 200 appearances for Bath City in the Southern League, 130 of them in succession. The benefit he was granted shortly before leaving

Twerton Park to complete his career with Chippenham Town was well earned.

Weare, who also had a Newport connection in having been born there, was taken on trial by Rovers on 22 September 1945, the day after his 33rd birthday, after having played in the First Division for Wolves, in the Second for West Ham, and then in wartime football for St Mirren. It was immediately apparent that he still had much to offer, and, after establishing himself in the last, transitional, season before the game got back to normal, he took over in 1946 from where Joe Nicholls – a former Grenadier Guards boxing champion and an England soccer trialist during nine years with Tottenham Hotspur – had been forced to leave off in 1939.

For most of the first two post-war seasons in which he and Weare were such integral parts of Rovers' defence, Harry Bamford's partner at full-back was Barry Watkins, a Welshman from Bedlinog, near Merthyr Tydfil. Watkins worked in the Engines Division of the Bristol Aeroplane Company and therefore remained a part-time professional throughout his nine seasons with Rovers after joining them as an amateur in September 1945. He and Ray Warren were the club's only ever-presents in 1946-47, though Lance Carr missed just one match, despite being into his 37th year by the time he reached the end of his only season at Eastville.

Carr, a South African, had, like Nicholls, been a boxer in his youth; like Weare, he had played in the First Division (with Liverpool); and, as in the case of both Liley and Weare, he had an association with Newport. In the second of his two spells with the County he was in the team that in 1939 gained a place in the Second Division – a place that was promptly to be lost after the war had made them wait seven years for it. Carr also had something in common with Watkins. The war took him to work with the BAC at Filton, leading him to guesting for Aldershot, Swindon and Bristol City, then to his short, but effective, stay with Rovers.

Watkins, whose father-in-law, Albert Osborne, played for both Bristol clubs before the 1914-18 War, and whose son-in-law, Richard Crabtree, was a goalkeeper with Rovers in the early 1970s, had a spell as a Wolves amateur before making the Eastville club the only one for which he played in the League. He did so in more than 100 matches, but only intermittently, and as an adaptable squad member who could also be depended upon as a forward, after losing his place alongside Bamford.

The player to whom Watkins had to give way at left-back was the stylish and consistent Geoff Fox, who, as with Harry Bamford, was not only born in Bristol but also tried his luck with Bristol City and Ipswich Town before becoming a Rover. It was as an Ipswich player that Fox entered League football in the first season after the war. He then moved to Eastville on a free transfer (what a bargain that was!), originally as a wing-half, but then converted to full-back because of the club's shortage of adequate players in that position.

Over the next eight seasons Fox played in some 300 League and Cup games – the first of them against Bristol City in front of a then record crowd of over 34,000 inside Eastville's locked gates on the last Saturday of August 1947. It was not, however, a happy debut. City won with two second-half goals and Fox had to return to the Reserves before getting back into the first team towards the end of that season. From then until 1954 he was an automatic choice, making over 100 of his appearances in succession. In four out of six consecutive seasons he was never out of the side, and he was absent only eight times in the two others.

An old friend of mine, the respected sports journalist David Foot, who was with the *Bristol Evening World* before becoming a freelance when that newspaper closed down, once said there were 'a dozen anecdotes from Eastville folklore – all centred on Geoff, who was the guv'nor with the authority, the worldly ways, the social aplomb'. He recalled that Fox was also an accomplished cricketer who played for Gloucestershire Club and Ground, occasionally for that county's second team, and for Suffolk in the Minor Counties competition. It was the summer game, with a soccer link, that came to Geoff's mind when David last spoke to him in looking for a memory to relate. This was the way of it: 'Foxy looked back to the time when he clobbered a long hop straight out of the Downend club's ground and the ball hit an old man, standing near his back door, on the head. He collapsed in a heap. Geoff dropped his bat and led the charge over the wall and into the garden. He was anxiously leaning over the old man, who opened his eyes and said: "Hey, I know you – you're usually wearing a blue and white quartered shirt." He was a Rovers fan, and all was forgiven.'

Fox first came to Bristol City's attention while he was still at school, but it was to Ipswich that he went as an amateur in 1942 after impressing in a works team. When that registration was allowed to lapse, the Ashton Gate club took him onto their books as an amateur during the 1944-45 season, only for Ipswich to step in again by signing him as a professional. Two seasons later he was again released, having played in almost a dozen League games, and that was when he was snapped up by Rovers, becoming one of the many talented home-grown players who enabled Bert Tann to make such a big success of the No Buy, No Sell policy.

For more than 250 matches the Bamford-Fox full-back partnership flourished, both combining resourceful defence with a readiness to ply accurate passes in support of the attack. With first Jack Weare, then Bert Hoyle, behind them in goal, memories were evoked of the club's formidable last lines of defence formed for four successive seasons in the 1920s by Jesse Whatley, Harold Armitage and Jimmy Haydon.

Fox's reign in Bristol Rovers' first team eventually ended in the 1954-55 season, but he went on to play in nearly 50 more League games for Swindon Town. The Wiltshire club were without a manager when he joined them, so they asked him to be player-manager for a few months until Bert Head, a former Torquay United defender, was brought in from Bury to fill the vacancy. Fox was still with Swindon, and still in his early 30s, when he decided to give up professional football despite feeling that he had four good seasons left in him.

Fox reached that decision, which he admitted was 'a very difficult one to make', because he had just been promoted to South-West area manager of a national paint brush manufacturing firm based in Worcestershire, but football had not seen the last of him. He put something back into the game as the Pucklechurch club's player-coach in the Bristol & District League, and later became a director of Bath City. Golf also continued to be a big part of his life. He was playing on the tenth tee of a club in Wales, on New Year's Day in 1994, when he died of a heart attack. He would have been 69 a fortnight later.

Harry Bamford's life was also cut tragically short. On 28 October 1958, just a few weeks before his wife Violet gave birth to their second daughter, he died, without regaining consciousness, from laceration of the brain. It was caused by a fracture of the skull when his motor scooter collided with a lorry – whose driver was exonerated from blame by the coroner – at a road junction in Bristol. Bamford, who had already announced his intention to retire at the end of the season, would have been nowhere near that junction but for his passion for coaching young players. Having gone home for lunch after training during the morning with the other Rovers players, he could have relaxed in the afternoon. Instead, he insisted on going to Clifton College on his scooter to coach schoolboys.

On the first day of the following month the crowd stood bare-headed and in complete silence for one minute in tribute to Bamford before Rovers' home match with Bristol City. Referee Mervyn Griffiths, of Newport, and his two linesmen led out the two teams. Behind them came the Lord Mayor of Bristol, Alderman F G W Chamberlain, Vic Newman, chairman of the Gloucestershire FA, who had been in charge of the Bristol Boys team in which Bamford had played before the war, and the directors and other officials of the two clubs.

'A great Bristolian has passed from our midst,' said John Hare, a Rovers director. 'He graced this particular playing pitch with so rare a distinction, and it is here, where he so loved to play his game, that all of us now assembled pay tribute in a simple manner, but nonetheless affectionately, to him. We remember Harry Bamford for the steadfast example he always set, and for the inspiration that his memory will for ever be.'

Bert Tann said: 'I cannot find words adequate enough to express the tribute due to Harry Bamford. It is true to say that my personal debt to him is
immeasurable. He was part of all that was best in Bristol Rovers, and the
club grew in stature with him.' Alan Hardaker, the Football League secretary,
declared that 'the services given by Bamford to your club have been an
example to all professional footballers'. Walter Winterbottom, the England
team manager, stated: 'It is indeed tragedy when an accident takes away from
football one who has given so much to the game, and one who is so willing
to put back into it all the joy and pleasure he found in it as a player.'

The usual match-day programme was scrapped in favour of a black-
edged leaflet on which was printed Bamford's photograph. Spectators also
observed a minute's silence at Twerton Park, where Bath City played
Trowbridge Town in the FA Cup that afternoon. In the *Bristol Evening Post*,
John Coe wrote: 'He stamped his personality on soccer because he had a
large measure of natural skill, allied to true sportsmanship.'

At the memorial service for Bamford at St Mary Redcliffe Church, Bert
Tann said that 'a part of Bristol Rovers died with him'. His was indeed a
remarkable record of unruffled consistency as the club's unassailable right-
back right through to his 39th year. As another tribute to him, the Harry
Bamford Memorial Trophy was donated as an annual award 'to a player who
has upheld the tradition of sportsmanship created by Harry Bamford'. The
first winner was Geoff Bradford, another big name of the Bert Tann years.
He received it from Bamford's widow at a match in aid of the Bamford Fund
that was played between Arsenal (who waived their rail and hotel expenses)
and a combined Bristol XI on the evening of Friday, 8 May 1959. The crowd
of 28,347 set a record for a non-competitive game at Eastville.

The team fielded by Arsenal, who began their close-season tour of Italy
four days later, included internationals Dave Bowen, Mel Charles, Danny
Clapton, Jack Henderson and Tommy Docherty. Charles – whose elder
brother John was the 'Gentle Giant' who had cost the then world record fee
of £65,000 when transferred from Leeds to Juventus two years earlier – had
himself only recently become the costliest player in British soccer in moving
from Swansea for £42,750, plus two Arsenal reserves, Peter Davies and
David Dodson, in part exchange. That had been after the March deadline for
unrestricted transfers, so he had still to make his League debut for the
Gunners when he paid that visit to Bristol.

The combined side comprised six Rovers players (Geoff Bradford, Peter
Hooper, Ray Mabbutt, Norman Sykes, Dai Ward and John Watling) and five
from City (John Atyeo, Tommy Burden, Tony Cook, Wally Hinshelwood and
Alan Williams). The result, not that it mattered, was a 5-4 win for the Bristol
XI. For those old enough, the game revived memories of the City-Rovers
side that met Aston Villa, who won 3-0, at Ashton Gate in 1914 in aid of the

testimonial fund for Ted Locke, who had died after nearly 21 years as City's honorary secretary. On that occasion City supplied six players (Harris, Jearns, Morton, Moss, Neesam and Wedlock), and Rovers five (Bennett, Crompton, Mainds, Stansfield and Shervey). Ellis Crompton, a wing-half or inside-forward from Ramsbottom in Lancashire, had the double distinction of scoring on his Southern League debut for Rovers in 1913, and of getting their first goal after their election to the Football League seven years later.

The Bamford Fund was launched by Rovers in aid of his dependants because Harry's death did not occur in the course of his recognised footballing duties and therefore did not qualify for any benefit under insurance schemes sponsored by his club, the Football League, or the Professional Footballers' Association. His life savings had been committed to the purchase of a house into which he and his family were to move. He had not married young. Indeed, he had lost his reputation as a confirmed bachelor, who used to spend his close seasons fruit picking in the Vale of Evesham, on unexpectedly deciding to tie the knot. That change to becoming a family man had also compelled him to curb his main interest outside football as a pigeon fancier. There had been nowhere to keep pigeons in the flat to which he and his bride had moved at the start of their married life.

Bristol Rovers started the Bamford Fund with a donation of £1,000, and by the time of the game with Arsenal, which realised receipts of more than £3,500, it had already gone past its target in exceeding £6,000.

In front of Bamford for the resumption of League football in 1946, Rovers were also fortunate to acquire a player as capable and loyal as Jackie Pitt to fill the right-half position alongside Warren and McArthur in the team's middle line. The prematurely balding Pitt was born at Willenhall, in Staffordshire, and was taken on as an amateur by West Bromwich Albion shortly before the war, but RAF service then brought him to the West Country, where he guested for Bath City and Aberavon before joining Rovers. Brough Fletcher signed him on the last day of July in 1946 without having seen him play, on the strong recommendation of chief scout Fred Hyde. It was one of the best pieces of business Fletcher ever did.

Although three months past his 26th birthday by the time he made his Rovers debut against Reading at the end of that August, Pitt held a regular place for eleven seasons, captain in three of them as they twice went close to the First Division, and his total of 467 League appearances (more than 500 in all) was second only to Bamford's 486 for the club when his contract as a player finally ended in June 1958. Both have since been overtaken by Stuart Taylor, a giant of a central defender (the tallest ever fielded by Rovers at 6ft 5in) who had a League aggregate of 546 games from 1966 to 1980. Taylor, yet another of the club's Bristol-born players, emulated Pitt in being an ever-present in four seasons, and in rising to the captaincy. He also set up

Rovers' post-war record for consecutive League appearances – 207 from 1968 to 1973 – and was a pillar of strength in the winning of promotion back to the Second Division in 1974.

Jackie Pitt, who was 84 when he died in his adopted city in August 2004, altogether served on the Eastville staff for more than 40 years. He said it was 'a big wrench' when he finally hung up his boots after making his League farewell in a 3-1 home win against Ipswich and then seeing out his contract in the Football Combination side, but he had his wish of 'always wanting to stay with the club' granted first by being given charge of the Colts team, then by his appointment as groundsman. He held that final job into the late 1980s, culminating in a thoroughly deserved testimonial in 1988 with a game against Wimbledon, that year's shock winners of the FA Cup at the expense of Liverpool's hot favourites. No wonder Pitt said he had been 'heart and soul for the Rovers ever since I first played for them'. His 70th birthday coincided with the day, 20 May 1990, on which Rovers also played at Wembley, though the occasion was marred for them by those other Rovers from Tranmere, winners by the odd goal of three in the final of the Leyland Daf Cup competition.

Another player, so far mentioned only in passing, who was to be a key member of the Bristol Rovers team in the peak seasons of Bert Tann's management was also introduced to League football in the first post-war season of 1946-47. But he was given only a minor role at that time, his first-team games restricted to single figures, despite having shown signs of his ability during the preceding transitional season. This was George Petherbridge, small in stature (5ft 4½in, 9st 10lb and size 5 boots), but big in achievement. Only Syd Homer (5ft 2¾in) and Joe Haverty (5ft 3½in), also wingers, have been shorter among Rovers players than this son of a former Portsmouth player. Petherbridge was born at Devonport, but taken to live in Bristol from the age of three. At sixteen he was invited for a trial by Arsenal, but hard as he tried to impress ('it was fantastic, but a bit frightening') the Gunners made the mistake of deciding not to sign him.

It was a disappointment, however, that turned out for the best. 'Had I gone to Arsenal,' he said some years afterwards, 'I would probably never have joined my local team, Bristol Rovers, and I don't think I would have been so happy at any other club. I have been grateful for a constant ball service from one of the finest wing-halves in the game, Jackie Pitt, and also from Harry Bamford.' Bert Tann believed Bamford and Pitt most unfortunate not to be capped, though age counted against both of them, as well as the fact that players from such an 'unfashionable' club as Rovers were considered to be – especially when they were in the Third Division – so very rarely came into the reckoning of England selectors. Bamford at least got onto an FA tour – as also did Petherbridge – to South Africa in 1956 (he did the hat-trick in one match with the Orange Free State, at Bloemfontein, and played in three of the 'tests').

Petherbridge received the call to Rovers' colours after building on experience gained in local football, especially with Knowle Athletic, as a member of Army sides during the war. 'January 1945 was the beginning of my association with Rovers,' he recalled, 'following a message from the club's secretary Sid Hawkins, who was later with Bristol City. I lived within five minutes of the ground, and had spent many happy afternoons on the Eastville terraces. My hero in those days had been outside-right George McNestry, a clever player. A chance to follow him? I did not need asking twice.'

Not until the 1962-63 season in the post-war period were Rovers without Petherbridge on their playing staff. For League games alone he even edged above Ray Warren with 452 appearances, and there would have been quite a few more but for his injuries. A model of consistency, he went on for another decade after becoming, at 23, the youngest to be awarded a benefit game by Rovers. He was the only player to score for the same League club in each of the first sixteen postwar seasons, and he finally bowed out with 85 League goals to his name – four of them, a record for a Rovers winger, in a 5-0 defeat of Torquay United.

Two of the others were the most crucial, in the 4-0 victory at Ipswich that saved Rovers from having to seek re-election at the end of the 1947-48 season. He was not originally chosen for that game, which he had intended attending as a spectator, but he was on the spot, stationed near Ipswich in the Army, when he received a telegram that morning telling him to report to play. He was urgently needed to replace 'Josser' Watling, who had fallen down some steps.

From Eastville, wee George moved into the Western League, first with Salisbury City, then Falmouth Town, before taking over his last footballing post as manager of Glastonbury in 1964. After that he ran a public house at Sherston, was on the sports staff at Millfield School, and became head groundsman at Wells Cathedral School until his retirement at Easter in 1992.

CHAPTER 5

Dogged by the Greyhound Link

In the early hours of the morning of Tuesday, 3 January 1950 a note pushed under the door of his home in Fishponds Road, Bristol, told 54-year-old Brough Fletcher that he had been sacked as Bristol Rovers' manager.

'I had no hint of what was in the wind,' he said. 'I left a board meeting at nine o'clock last night when a director said he wished to raise a matter under any other business, but there had been no serious disagreement. This is a very cruel blow. Heaven knows, I have carried on in adverse circumstances, and I have always done my best for the club. To think that the club has £6,000 in the bank and affairs are on an even keel. The news is a tragedy.'

Three months later, the findings of an FA Commission inquiring into Bristol Rovers' affairs left Fletcher with a feeling of great relief. 'People have been saying insulting things about me,' he said, 'but today I can walk about the streets a free man.' He had not been associated with alleged wrong-doing.

The Commission decided:

(a) That Mr Con Stevens, former chairman, and directors of the club be censured and the club fined £250;

(b) That Mr C Ferrari, former secretary, be informed that he must not take part in football or football management until he appears before the Commission;

(c) That it is highly undesirable that the controlling interest in the club should be held by the Bristol Greyhound Racing Company (BGRC);

(d) That a new method of book-keeping be evolved and submitted for approval of the FA at the end of the season; and

(e) That the Bristol Rovers FC be required to pay the expenses of the inquiry.

The inquiry, which disclosed that Con Stevens was managing director of the Bristol Greyhound Racing Association, investigated general petty cash payments, the expenses of directors and amateur and professional players, and 'alleged payments to J Stiff, part-time player and office clerk'.

Changes were also to be made in the boardroom after John Hare, secretary of the greyhound company and a former vice-chairman of the football club, had called for the removal of five directors who, however, were complimented by the Football Association for bringing the irregularities to their attention. Those directors were the newly appointed chairman, Eric Lloyd, vice-chairman Harry Hoare, James Richard Bissicks, George Stanley Humphries and Ernest John Smith. The other members of the board at that time were Con Stevens and Lew Champney, the catering manager.

The FA instructed the club to institute a new form of book-keeping by the end of the season, and within six months to report again on the share-holdings of their directors. Three new directors were elected early the fol-lowing year – Philip Hort, a chartered accountant, Dr David Simpson, an ophthalmic surgeon, and Eric Scudamore, a Weston-super-Mare solicitor. Frank Ward, an inspector appointed under the Companies Act 1948, had recommended that 'at least two well-known Bristol personalities should act on the board in the interests of the football profession'. He had further sug-gested that 'a newly constituted or augmented board should function through two sub-committees – one responsible to the whole board for the oversight of financial, legal and administrative matters, the other for the con-duct of football and related matters'.

In May 1952, Judge F H C Wethered was appointed by the Board of Trade to investigate: 'on the application of six members of the Rovers com-pany and the registered holders of 49 shares, to investigate the membership of the company with a view to determining the true persons who are, or have been, financially interested in, or able to control, it.' Undeterred by that convoluted wording, he ruled that the BGRC could no longer take part in general meetings of the Rovers company, and, therefore, no longer control the composition of its board of directors, nor the football club's policy. He added that 'the present board of the Rovers company is a satisfactory board, and for normal business its members work well together'.

The judge recalled that in August 1945 the greyhound company had lent the football club £1,500, secured by a debenture. Consequently, the officials of that company had then had a financial interest in how the Rovers fared, but that had ceased with the repayment of the loan on 27 May 1947, and the debenture had been discharged the following month. As proprietors of the Eastville stadium, the greyhound company were still able to hold shares in the football company – 'so long as the point of view of the FA is recognised and observed, and their holding at all times is explicitly registered'.

Albert Prince-Cox had brought in £800 a year for Bristol Rovers by nego-tiating the lease of the Eastville ground to the greyhound company, to whom the freehold had been sold for £12,500 in 1940 – a decision which proved unpopular except among the new owners, and at a price not only low even by values of the time but also, ludicrously so, in comparison with what it later fetched.

The FA had for some time frowned on what they called 'the marriage of football and greyhound racing on common ground', and the Football League had also regarded it with growing concern. Betting was the big bugbear. As far back as 1908 an FA consultative committee had passed a resolution that 'the FA, having endeavoured for many years past to prevent betting in con-nection with football consider it desirable to call attention to the fact that betting is prohibited by the rules of the Association upon all football grounds'.

In 1927, the FA Council appointed a committee 'to investigate the matter of greyhound racing on the grounds of clubs that were members of the Association'. As a result of their report, the Council decided that 'it would be too great an interference' to prohibit the use of grounds for greyhound racing, but warned clubs that they would be held responsible for preventing betting on their grounds at football matches. Five years later, the Council expressed the opinion that it was undesirable for clubs affiliated to the FA to be financed or controlled by proprietors of greyhound racing. This was modified soon afterwards when the view was taken at a meeting with Football League representatives that the payment to a football club for rent of a ground for greyhound racing was 'not financing a club within the meaning of the earlier resolution'.

At the League's annual meeting in 1946, the management committee endorsed a resolution, put forward by Bolton Wanderers, that in future no League clubs were to permit greyhound racing on their premises, but Bristol Rovers were excused from this because it was added that 'those grounds where greyhound racing still takes place are outside the law and cannot be touched, for the original agreements between the respective managements were settled before the question was first raised by the FA in 1927'. It was made clear, however, that if greyhound racing ceased at any of those grounds it could not be reintroduced. Norman Banks, then chairman of Bolton Wanderers, whose resolution was carried by 26 votes to seventeen, maintained that, as the clubs had been refused money from the pools, it was not consistent to allow any kind of betting on football grounds.

That was the main point with which the Football Association were primarily concerned, stressing that 'within the larger pattern the undesirable influence of greyhound racing upon football grounds bears but small comparison with the continued warfare waged against direct gambling on football matches'.

So Eastville continued to have its Tote end, from which soccer spectators, along with those on the open banking at the other end, viewed the action on the smallest pitch in the Football League at quite a distance across the greyhound track and the flower beds situated in the centre of curved stretches of grass behind the goals. And they often started their trek home at the final whistle to the accompaniment of the eager yelping of the kennelled dogs that were to provide the evening's entertainment for the greyhound racing fraternity.

Eastville Stadium, originally the headquarters of a rugby club, was Rovers' sixth home. After having left Purdown for Three Acres at Ashley Hill, the club then moved to Durdham Downs. In 1891 a one-season lease was signed to play at Schoolmasters Cricket ground in Downend Lane, Horfield. Rover's next move was to Rudgeway in Upper Eastville on the other side of the neighbouring Fishponds Road. They played their first game there, lost 0-5 to Aston Villa on 3 April 1897, and later that year they bought the sixteen-acre site for the bargain sum of £150. The capacity was increased to around 30,000 by the building of a timbered main stand, housing the club's offices and dressing rooms, along the south side of the pitch in 1924. With the help of £10,000 from the Supporters' Club, another stand was erected on the opposite side in 1958, boosting the record crowd to 38,472 for a fourth-round FA Cup-tie with Preston North End two years afterwards.

Rovers would have been hard pressed to meet their commitments without the financial support of the Supporters' Club, which came into existence two years after the 1939-45 war at the instigation of John Hare, then one of the Rovers' directors. The original committee was headed by John Hampden Alpass (chairman) and Harry Edmonds (secretary), but only two members were still serving by the time, at the end of 1963, the Supporters' Club's profits had soared to £100,000 over thirteen years. One was Eric Godfrey, who took over as chairman and secretary in 1949, the other Bill Creed, who had been the travel organiser since the first day. Godfrey, an insurance inspector, was co-opted onto Rovers' board of directors, became a vice-president, and was rightly hailed as the club's No 1 supporter. Creed, a director of a tyre company, had by then supervised travel of more than 250,000 of the Rovers' fans to matches all over the country by road, rail and air. 'We don't make money from running these trips,' he said. 'The object is to help the club with away support.'

Other office holders with the Supporters' Club in those days included treasurer Harry Stansfield, assistant secretary Joan Bruton, Major Frank Fear, a former secretary of the Long Ashton Golf Club who became pools manager, John Stiff, the lottery manager, and Ray Bywater, who ran the Lucky Chance money-raiser and assisted with the organisation of the outings to matches.

Stansfield's father, also Harry, played in Rovers' first three League matches in the new Third Division of 1920-21, a goalkeeper most unusual for wearing spectacles – though there was another one, James Mitchell, who not only played for Preston in the 1922 FA Cup final but also won half-a-dozen amateur international caps. While with Manchester City, Mitchell even kept goal for England's professionals in their defeat of Northern Ireland at Everton's ground in 1924. Over in Belgium, Anderlecht had a bespectacled forward named Josef ('Jeff') Jurion, also an international, who scored the goal that knocked Real Madrid out of the 1962-63 European Cup's first round. In 1938 there was a World Cup captain (of the Dutch East Indies, now Indonesia) who wore glasses. And the report of Burslem Port Vale's record 0-10 home defeat by Sheffield United in 1892 tells us that the hapless goalkeeper 'lost his spectacles in the mud.'

Money that flowed into the Rovers' coffers from the Supporters' Club ranged from the first gift of equipment for the club's treatment room to the payments for floodlighting, a relaid pitch, and that stand on Eastville's northern side. Until October 1963, cheques for some £400 to £500 a week passed from the Supporters' Club to the Rovers, with the lottery schemes the chief source of revenue. Those payments then stopped, but there was no rift. 'The money is there if the club need it,' said Eric Godfrey. 'We have £8,500 in the bank, and have decided to retain it for the time being. Our next ambition is to give the Rovers a home of their own. When the time comes we want to be able to provide the finance for the new ground.'

By that time the ownership of Eastville had passed to the Bristol Stadium Company, which briefly staged speedway meetings as well as greyhound racing. The Rovers obtained a 21-year lease on very favourable terms, but when it came up for renewal at the end of 1979 they found the rent raised to beyond what they were prepared to pay and took their dispute to the High Court because they had no wish to leave. They and their supporters had invested too much money, including £70,000 on safety improvements, to make that an acceptable option. Fate, however, was to force their hand.

The hearing was arranged for the last day of November 1981, but in the middle of August the previous year the wooden South Stand was destroyed by fire after the opening match of the new season. As if that blow was not devastating enough, an even more fraught one followed. When Rovers met officials of the Stadium Company shortly before the scheduled High Court hearing they expected to reach some form of compromise in the difficult circumstances common to both parties. Instead they received the shattering news of being given notice to quit.

The arrangement then arrived at was only temporary. Rovers had to give up their rights under the Landlord and Tenant Act in return for compensation of £280,000. This allowed them to continue to use Eastville rent free – but only until mid-May in 1982. After that they were compelled to move under the additional burden of having been relegated back to the Third Division. Their attempt to find a new home appeared to have succeeded when, much to the dismay of supporters of both clubs, they negotiated to share Bristol City's Ashton Gate ground, on which they had played their first few home games after the fire. But City were forced out of business by the huge debts incurred from the cost of unsuccessfully trying to prolong their reappearance in the First Division, and the board of their reconstituted company doubled the rent required from Rovers to an unacceptable £80,000 a year.

That left the only viable alternative of going back cap in hand to the Bristol Stadium Company, who drove a hard bargain by getting Rovers to pay £1,000 a year rent to continue playing at Eastville even though, with no new stand arising from the ashes, their offices were now several miles away at their training ground in the village of Hambrook. Against that, however, it was agreed in the High Court that they should receive £280,000 from their landlords in compensation.

The deal was for five years, but Rovers pulled out of it after four, fulfilling their last fixture there (a 1-1 draw with Chesterfield) before a crowd of 3,576 on 26 April 1986. They were losing money on almost every match because attendances had dipped well below the already parsimonious limit of 12,500 (7,500 under cover) imposed by safety considerations. It was a situation made all the more intolerable by the fact that the greyhound racing was prospering – so much so that Eastville became that sport's busiest track in Britain with the addition of a fourth weekly meeting following the football club's departure at the end of the 1985-86 season.

Eventually, however, even greyhound racing was lost to Eastville, a large furniture store having long since arisen on the site, with another shopping development close at hand where the Thirteen Arches of the railway viaduct used to be. Also adjacent is the M32 motorway, on the hard shoulder of which fans used to risk arrest to get a good view of games while Rovers were still playing there.

After thoughts of reviving plans to share Ashton Gate had been swiftly thrust aside by City's demand for an annual rent exceeding £60,000, Rovers found Bath City more amenable to such an arrangement at Twerton Park, just over a dozen miles away. They agreed to pay the Southern League club £20,000 each season, plus a percentage of gate receipts, half the cost of laying a new pitch, and a contribution – along with grants from the Football Grounds Improvement Trust – towards £80,000-worth of improvements needed to bring the ground up to the new standards decreed by the Safety of Sports Grounds Act. The initial settlement was for seven seasons, but Rovers stayed for ten, until 1996, before moving in with Bristol Rugby Club at the Memorial Ground, off Filton Avenue in the city's Horfield district, which had previously been considered as an optional home along with the Gloucestershire County Cricket's Club's premises at Nevil Road, and Gloucester City's new stadium.

With Rovers now the landlords, ambitious plans are afoot that will necessitate them and Bristol Rugby Club looking for a new base, if only temporarily, while the Memorial Stadium, as it is now known, is redeveloped – a major building project. Rovers have a provisional agreement to groundshare at Cheltenham Town's Whaddon Road stadium. This was agreed in the summer of 2007, starting in December. However, delays in signing a planning section 106 legal agreement for the stadium redevelopment has delayed the groundshare for at least six months. Crowd capacity at the Mem remains modest at just under 12,000 compared with the bumper gates enjoyed at the height of the Bert Tann era, but rather more than the Twerton record of 9,464 for a fourth-round FA Cup-tie in which Rovers drew 1-1 with Liverpool in 1992 (a player named Saunders scored for both sides). That was also the result of the Anfield replay, where Carl Saunders and his Liverpool namesake Dean again scored as Rovers went out to the eventual Cup winners after leading at half-time. The Memorial Stadium's best of 11,883 was the result of the visit of Leeds in September 2007, the first League meeting of the two clubs for over 45 years, a club record gap between meetings.

CHAPTER 6

McArthur follows 'Mr Bristol Rovers'

One April morning in 1950 Wally McArthur was called into Bert Tann's office and told: 'You're getting a bit too old for playing, Wally. I think you'd better start off next season as assistant trainer.'

So, in the month after his 38th birthday, this durable Yorkshireman from the Doncaster mining area of Denaby Main continued in his service with the Rovers, which then dated back just over seventeen years, as a member of the backroom staff. And in 1962 he was an automatic successor to the retiring trainer Bert Williams, that other Eastville loyalist whose own connection with the club began even before he followed his father as groundsman in 1919.

From his earliest days Bert was at the ground. He and his family lived in the first house, painted in the club's colours of blue and white, outside what became the Muller Road entrance. In those days there was no Muller Road. Instead there were still green fields. Bert used to climb over a five-barred gate across a lush pasture – and there was the Rovers' ground. Two pitches were adjacent to it – one, parallel to the river, that was used by the Bristol North rugby club; the other, in front of the Stapleton Road entrance to Eastville Stadium, on which the players practised and was used for practice and also rented by the Licensed Victuallers FC.

At that time Rovers leased their ground, which covered 21½ acres, from Lady Smythe – whose estate stretched from Ashton to the Duchess area of Stapleton (it was eventually purchased from her for £2,500 by director George Humphreys). Eastville then boasted just one small wooden stand, with seats numbered from 1 to 501. It was hardly ever full. As he grew older, Bert Williams helped his father, who had been groundsman since 1894 and also had a haulage business, by leading the horse that pulled the grass-cutting machine, and the much bigger one that hauled the heavy roller. During the First World War, when Rovers played only occasional games against teams such as the Trams, Temple Meads Porters, the Remount Depot and other Army sides, Williams Senior was paid ten shillings (50p) for looking in on Saturdays to mark out the pitch, clean up and make the tea.

As a full-time groundsman, Bert's father never earned more than £1 2s 6d (£1.25p) a week. Bert was engaged to succeed him by secretary-manager Alf Homer at £2 10s (£2.50p). The trainer at that time, following the departure of Georgie Pay, a former sprinter, was Jack Chaplin, a Scotsman who had been a full-back in his home city of Dundee, and with Tottenham Hotspur and Manchester City, before injury curtailed his playing career and took him to Leeds City, where he rose from assistant trainer to chief trainer and then assistant manager before that club's sensational expulsion from the League for alleged illegal payments to players. Chaplin, who was afterwards with the Wednesday in Sheffield before being appointed at Eastville, found the job with Rovers so exacting that he asked Bert Williams to give him a hand, and thus it was that the young groundsman gained his first experience of looking after players.

On Saturdays the Rovers' reserve team was attended by George Endicott, who worked for the Imperial Tobacco Company, but the club then had no official assistant trainer. Rovers were therefore reluctant to part with Chaplin when he received a good offer from Huddersfield Town, to whom Herbert Chapman had moved as manager after being cast out at Leeds, but Chaplin insisted that Williams was good enough to take over from him, and again Homer gave his support. The directors agreed, but only temporarily. Bert was entrusted with the training duties for just three months before Ted Jones, who had lost his place in the Bristol City team to Charlie Treasure, was brought in as first-team trainer.

Even so, his eager deputy was kept busy enough because Rovers had a team in the Southern League as well as the Western League. Neither did he let the side down when he played a few times for the Reserves in emergencies. On one occasion, at Swindon, he kept goal (in a 2-0 win) when Bert Densley found he could not bend his neck. Another time, the young Ronnie Dix missed the train for a friendly at High Wycombe, and Williams admitted to being a very nervous deputy for such a talented player. 'I was more relieved than I can say when Ronnie turned up before half-time – and he gave them value for money by scoring a couple of goals.'

Bert was also kept in the assistant role until after Joe Palmer had become the first, and only, manager-trainer in Rovers' history, and also while Harry Lake, who had a strong physical resemblance to Paavo Nurmi, the record-breaking Finnish athlete, was trainer in Albert Prince-Cox's time as manager, but his loyalty was eventually rewarded as he fully deserved being dubbed 'Mr Bristol Rovers'.

Wally McArthur was a somewhat anxious, though grateful, appointee as assistant to Bert Williams at Eastville. 'I set off with a bag full of medical stuff,' he said later, 'though I didn't know the first thing about a trainer's job.' But he rapidly gained in experience as, in addition to his other duties, he stayed with Bert late into the evening on Tuesdays and Thursdays when the amateurs and part-timers trained, and also put in a full morning on Sundays. And by the time he became first-team trainer when Williams retired in 1962 he was fully qualified, having studied the medical side of football, attended several courses taking in massage and medical electricity, spent a week at a Maidenhead instructional school, and been on courses at Lilleshall. As he modestly said, 'it gives me a bit more authority with the players when they realise that you know what you're taking about.'

McArthur's 34 years with Rovers ended in May 1967, nearly twenty years after his award of a second benefit for which this team was fielded in a 0-0 draw against Southend at Eastville on 19 March 1949: Weare; Bamford, Fox; Pitt, Warren, McArthur; Bush, Hodges, Lambden, Haddon, Petherbridge. Harry Haddon played only twice in Rovers' League side, after being with Cardiff, Bangor and Newport, but he scored more than 200 goals for Trowbridge Town and was their manager when they won the Western League championship in 1955-56. He was also the first Welshman to gain a full FA coaching certificate.

McArthur, who had first been signed by Rovers after a trial in a friendly match at Watchet, took his departure from Eastville philosophically. 'I have been made redundant,' he said. 'There has been no dispute. I can't say it has come as a great shock, but it has happened rather suddenly.' In retirement he continued to live near the Rovers' ground, at Fishponds, until his death in September 1980, at the age of 68.

The first player to be given an extended run when McArthur played his last four first-team games in the 1949-50 season – after having chalked up more than 100 since the war, despite being in his mid-30s when League football got under way again – was Frank McCourt. A rather shy, soft-spoken young Irishman, McCourt had turned out just a few times for Rovers during the transitional 1945-46 season while stationed locally in the RAF following wartime service in Italy and Egypt. He reappeared at Eastville after being back in the south of the Emerald Isle with Shamrock Rovers, to whom he returned on loan after playing over 30 games on the left of the half-back line in which Pitt and Warren had become such firm fixtures.

McCourt's subsequent transfer to Manchester City in November 1950 would almost certainly never have come about – and therefore not led to the six Northern Ireland caps he won while with the Maine Road club – had he not persisted after receiving no response to the first letter he wrote asking City for a trial because he wanted to go north for domestic reasons.

In his second letter he mentioned what he had omitted before – that he had already played in the Football League with Bristol Rovers. That did catch attention. City invited him up, signed him after an extended trial, and he made nearly 80 appearances in their senior side before going back south four years later to join Colchester United. There he was joined by another former Rovers player, fellow Irishman Paddy Leonard, but an unrewarding experience they found it. Colchester finished bottom in 1954-55's Third Division South, and both players were soon on their way again. Leonard returned to his home city of Dublin to work as a car salesman; McCourt had a few months with Poole Town, then emigrated to Canada.

Eric Thornton, who for many years reported on Manchester City for the *Manchester Evening News*, remembered McCourt for 'always being ready to help anybody', and for his 'dry humour'. He also recalled, in his book about the club, that 'Clancy', as Frank (Francis to be precise) was known at Maine Road, was 'a terror for buying presents', and that when he slipped in a shop in Germany to buy one during a close-season Continental tour he took so long about it that he reached the railway station only just in time to see the train pulling out with the rest of the City party on board. This was how Thornton recounted what happened next:

'Smartly weighing up the position, as he said afterwards, he leapt into the guard's van, only to be told that it would be uncoupling outside the station. So he leapt out again, chasing the vanishing train, but lost the race while the players were egging him on to have another go. But his Irish luck came to the rescue. A motorist outside the station, obviously noticing his sad look, inquired the cause, and was told that the team was playing a game that night at a ground nearly twenty miles away. He told Clancy to step in, drove him there, and refused any payment. He was sufficiently happy with a free ticket for the match.'

Another McCourt tale told by Thornton was of the Frankenstein mask the Irishman bought while on a tour of America as a member of the international team. To quote again: 'He smuggled it home and took it with him next time City were playing in the south, and staying at a London hotel. He never said a word about it to anybody. Well, this was a Victorian hotel, the kind which always wanted peace and quiet and took a long look down its nose at birds and booze. Clancy nipped quietly upstairs when we returned from the theatre, slipped the mask on, and, when he heard what he thought was one of the boys coming along the dimly-lit corridor, suddenly shot round the corner, groaning and moaning, and waving his arms about. But it wasn't one of the City party. It was a dear old lady who never hurried – until she saw Frankenstein and her hair stood up, and then she fairly flew into her room.'

After McCourt, Bristol Rovers came up with a left-half who monopolised the position for most of some 350 matches until his release to Trowbridge Town, whom he captained, in the summer of 1961 – thirteen years after being taken on as a professional. Peter Sampson hailed from Essex, where he was born in the same village as his cousin Les Stubbs, a forward with Southend and Chelsea. Sampson played for Devizes Town and Wiltshire while stationed there in the Army after service in West Africa. He chose to join Rovers, originally as an amateur, in preference to Fulham on buying himself out of the Forces early in 1948. His League debut, on the opening day of the 1948-49 season, was far from being a portent of what was to come. He had the misfortune to be pitched into the team hammered

1-6 at home by Ipswich Town, and had to wait eighteen months before being given another first-team opportunity.

Even then, Sampson was in the League side for only three games in 1949-50, but what a difference there was to be when he was reinstated at the start of the following season. During that one, and the next two, he did not miss a match, and he played in 164 in succession before having to drop out through injury. For four more seasons after that he remained a first choice. Away from football he was a butcher and milkman, and ran a poultry business with Vic Lambden, whose wife Grace was a cousin of Sampson's wife Vera.

It was to Trowbridge that Lambden also moved from Rovers, and he helped them to the Western League title with almost 40 goals in the first of the six seasons he spent with them, scoring about 150 for the club in all. He later became postman back at his home village of Oldland, where he also ran the football club with some assistance in the coaching from Sampson, who was in the team as a permit player after leaving Trowbridge. Vic also played for Oldland at cricket.

CHAPTER 7

Road Crash ends Hoyle's Career

But for an injury that ended goalkeeper Bert Hoyle's career, Bristol Rovers would almost certainly have emulated Huddersfield Town in going through their promotion-winning season of 1952-53 with an unchanged defence in the 1-2-3 formation of the time.

Rovers' defensive ever-presents for 46 Third Division South matches and four FA Cup-ties were full-backs Bamford and Fox, and half-backs Pitt, Warren and Sampson. Huddersfield, also promoted that season in a prompt return to Division One, had Jack Wheeler in goal, Ron Staniforth and Laurie Kelly at full-back, and Bill McGarry, Don McEvoy and Len Quested in the half-back line for their 42 League games and two Cup-ties, the first of them a third-round defeat of Rovers.

Bert Tann's men were on course to equal such a rarity until the fateful night of Saturday, 7 February 1953 on which Hoyle was seriously injured in a car crash on his way home to Dawlish, where he ran a hotel, after keeping a clean sheet in a drawn game with Bristol City at Ashton Gate.

He was being driven back to Devon by Ken Powell, a reserve centre-half who had briefly broken into the League side a year or so earlier (only because injury had ended Ray Warren's run of 180 appearances). Their car over-turned after mounting the pavement at Redhill in Somerset, on a steep hill along the main Bristol to Exeter road. Hoyle's skull was fractured as he was thrown out onto the grass verge a few yards from where the vehicle came to rest upside down. Powell, who had been among Frank McCourt's team-mates in an RAF team in Egypt, had to be freed from the wreck, but was allowed home after treatment for shock.

Bert Tann would insist that everyone in the team travelled to every match together, and returned home to Eastville together – even from Ashton Gate. But fate took a hand when that strict rule was relaxed with the offer to Hoyle of his lift as far as Exeter. Had he travelled back to Eastville on the team's coach he would have gone home by train, and would therefore not have been suffered the injury that forced him out of the game.

It was another change of plan that led to another road accident involv-ing Rovers. That one had tragic consequences, causing the death of a direc-tor, Lew Champney, and seriously injuring his wife Kate. Rovers played at Brighton on the Saturday before the home game with Newport – in which they clinched promotion to Division Two – but they did not then return to Bristol because they had a game at Norwich the following Wednesday. The Champneys were at Bognor Regis, and originally intended to go up to

Norwich with the players. On second thoughts, however, Lew Champney decided to go back to Bristol to attend a board meeting, and it was on that journey that the fatal accident occurred. Like Bert Hoyle, he was much missed. He invariably had a new joke to tell, and his cheery visits to the dressing room before matches did a lot to help ease the tension.

After recuperating in a deckchair on the beach at Teignmouth, Hoyle was next back at Eastville on the last Saturday of March – a spectator at a 2-1 win against Bournemouth. He was invited to sit in the directors' box but preferred to be near the touchline with trainer Bert Williams. A playing comeback for him with the club was immediately ruled out. 'I should not feel justified in playing him after his serious injury,' said Bert Tann. 'It would always be on my conscience.'

Almost twenty years later, the career of Bobby ('Shadow') Williams, a slim inside-forward who spent a short time with Rovers after enjoying his best years with Bristol City, was also ended by a car accident. He suffered multiple fractures and a collapsed lung in a crash on his way home from playing for Weymouth against Yeovil Town.

Bert Hoyle's consolation for having his career in the Rovers' team so abruptly and painfully ended was to have played in enough League games that season (the first 29, taking him to 105 for the club in all) to qualify for a medal when the title was gained. And more than three years after the accident he turned out for Exmouth Town in a midweek friendly against his former Bristol clubmates. By that time he was licensee of the Ship Inn at Cockwood, near Dawlish Warren, and a physical training instructor at the Royal Western Counties Hospital at Starcross, a village on the west side of the river Exe opposite Exmouth.

Hoyle, an extrovert Yorkshireman from Baildon, and a Commando during the war in which he served in Italy, Yugoslavia and Greece, cost all of £350 from Exeter City in the summer of 1950. Rovers' directors explained that, while they intended to continue to foster local talent, they would be prepared to stray from the No Buy, No Sell policy that had been adopted five years earlier, in order to pay for any player they might want to bring in from outside. Hoyle came into that category when they urgently needed a replacement for Jack Weare, who, nearing his 38th birthday after holding the position for most of the first four post-war seasons, had gone back to Wales to join Barry Town.

Before the war Hoyle had been with Bradford Park Avenue, but he had really come to the fore during it by keeping future internationals Bert Williams and Cyril Sidlow out of the Combined Services side. It was through attracting the attention of Stan Cullis, the Wolves and England centre-half, while playing for an RAF team in Italy, that he went to Molineux after demobilisation. Although one of his old rivals, Sidlow, had by then left Wolves for

Liverpool, he found the other, Williams, barring his path to the Wanderers'
first team, making him readily open to the offer from Exeter that came soon
afterwards. He made his belated entry into League football in the Grecians'
first post-war match in the Third South. Despite by then being in his mid-
twenties, and having to contend with strong competition from Barney
Singleton, another former Wolves player, Hoyle had not far off a century of
senior games to his credit when Bristol Rovers came calling.

At Eastville, Hoyle was a most popular figure. After his premature exit
Rovers fans missed not only his agility and ability, but also the chats he
always found time to have after, and even during matches. And when they
learned of his liking for oranges he was never short of a plentiful supply.
Few goalkeepers commanded their penalty area in the way Herbert Hoyle
did. If he decided the ball coming in was his, he would spare nobody, not
even his fellow defenders, in getting it. 'I suppose,' one of those colleagues
once said, 'at one time or another every member of the defence got a thick
ear or black eye as a result of being flattened by Bert. He used to be just as
forceful in the dressing room, building himself and the rest of the team up
to a tremendous pitch just as we were about to go out onto the field.'

Of the other Rovers players of those early post-war years, there was one
who carved out two careers for himself during the fifteen seasons he fea-
tured in the club's League side from 1947 to 1962. After that he continued
to serve as a coach and scout, and also in the first full-time appointment
made by the Supporters' Club when he became their chief agent, on retiring
as a player at the age of 38. John Daniel Watling, affectionately known as
'Josser', even had a road named after him, Watling Way, in the Shirehampton
area of his native Bristol. Signed by Rovers as an amateur in October 1945,
and as a professional in January 1947, he made his League debut at outside-
left on Valentine's Day in 1948 in a defeat at Ashton Gate that could have
been worse than 2-5 if City's Don Clark had not failed with a penalty. On 10
November 1956 he embarked upon a second footballing life as a left-back in
a 3-2 win at Swansea.

Twice Watling played in an FA Cup quarter-final, but, consistent as he
was, he had the misfortune to miss a Third Division championship medal in
being restricted to a mere five League games in 1952-53. It said much for his
capability and determination that he battled his way back over the next five
seasons to play in almost a third of his final total of games, approaching 350
(four of them as captain). Sport ran in the family. Terry Ratcliffe, the Bristol
welterweight boxer, was one of his cousins.

Other Bristol-born players who helped to give the No Buy, No Sell policy its impetus in those early post-war years included Bryan Bush, Jimmy
Morgan and Bill Roost. All three exceeded 100 games, Roost getting close to
a second century in almost ten years with the club. This rusty-haired hustler

and bustler of defenders into errors switched from the rugby of his school-days to soccer while in the Royal Navy (he played regularly for his ship's team at Freetown, in West Africa, and Devonport). He was signed by Rovers after chief scout Wally Jennings had seen him, as an amateur, score all three of Stonehouse's goals in their 3-9 defeat by Soundwell in 1948. 'If I hadn't scored those three goals,' Roost said in looking back over his career, 'I don't think I would have been noticed. I was never a footballer. I wish I had been. My enthusiasm carried me through. I did the work for somebody else to play the football.'

'Ginger' Roost, who scored within a minute of the kick-off in his first Football Combination game, was also modest about his goal inside the first five minutes of his League debut – a 4-1 home win against Reading on Good Friday in 1949. 'It was an easy goal,' he said. 'All the work that time was done by Barry Watkins.' There were over 50 more goals to follow, one of them in the first minute of an FA Cup replay against Orient, before Roost was trans-ferred to Swindon Town as a part-timer in May 1957. He was a leader of the attack when he first went to Eastville, after having also played for Westbury United and Dursley on leaving the Navy he had joined at seventeen. Although he could not otherwise have been accommodated for most of his 180 or so League and Cup appearances, Bert Tann had to be at his persua-sive best to get him to switch to an inside-forward position.

Before being convinced, Roost even offered to play in the Reserves rather than fill that new role in the first team, but the manager was proved percep-tive when several clubs, notably Liverpool, Luton and West Bromwich Albion, subsequently made unsuccessful approaches for the player's transfer. Roost did not want to leave when Don Welsh, then Liverpool's manager, first tried to do a deal. The Anfield club renewed their inquiries on learning a lit-tle later that there had been a change of mind, but Welsh then decided against going ahead after having another look. He did not think Roost had made the expected improvement in the meantime, a reversal of opinion for-tunate for Rovers, who for several more seasons continued to have the ener-getic services of a man Brough Fletcher said was the most wholehearted player he had ever signed.

Roost's lively approach to the game extended to his readiness to query refereeing decisions, and there was one match at Aldershot in which he was lucky not to be booked for the persistence and strength of his argument. The official, his patience exhausted, had his book out, pencil poised, when 'Josser' Watling ran across and stayed his hand by telling him that Bill was deaf and did not understand what was going on. The referee, having no rea-son to believe he was being mischievously misled, apologised profusely, and for the rest of the game explained all his decisions in elaborate sign language for the benefit of a player whose hearing was far from impaired.

When the time eventually came for Roost to leave Rovers he did so most reluctantly, but his first-team chances had been dwindling over the past two seasons and he asked for a move because he was finding it difficult to live on reserve wages. The move to Swindon, to which he travelled three times a week for training, did not work out, however. In his third match for the Wiltshire club, who had had to seek re-election, he dislocated an elbow and was out of action for two months. He played a few more times after his recovery, but admitted he had lost the enthusiasm that had been his trademark. 'I guess my heart was still with Bristol Rovers,' he said.

He was in and out of the Swindon side the following season, at the end of which he was put on the transfer list and went to Yeovil on a two-month trial. That ended in an FA Cup defeat by Bath City, but he felt he might have been retained if Yeovil had won, or he had scored. His next, and final, move was to Minehead, whose team then largely comprised other players from the Bristol region. After another scoring debut, against Barnstaple Town, he held a place for almost 100 games over three years, despite being by then into his late 30s, until his contract ended in 1963. Even then he could not give up football entirely, though he had an unwelcome reminder that he was getting past it when he was injured in a match between Rovers and City players of the past arranged in aid of City defender Jack Connor's testimonial match in 1970.

While a footballing part-timer, Roost had his best-paid job as a barn builder, but that was during the summer, with daylight hours and fine weather needed. In winter his wages dipped appreciably, so he took to lorry driving, delivering corrugated paper in rolls and boxes to many parts of the country. That, however, soon made him 'thoroughly fed up' because the job entailed long hours and at least two nights a week away from his home in the Whitehall district of Bristol. None of the public houses he was offered the chance to run particularly appealed to him, so he became a foreman in a scaffolding yard.

Bryan Bush, a former Bristol Boys forward, was in the Fleet Air Arm and a Bristol City amateur before joining Rovers from the local Soundwell club in the autumn of 1947. He first played in the League in their last two matches of that season, both against Ipswich Town, and opened his goals account in that vital victory at Portman Road that completed a double on the final day's escape from having to seek re-election.

Bush enjoyed his most successful season with Rovers when they won promotion in 1952-53, scoring a dozen goals in his 35 games, but a serious leg injury curtailed his opportunities in the Second Division and his final first-team appearance, his only one of 1954-55, was unfortunately made on the day Tommy Briggs scored seven of Blackburn's goals in an 3-8 defeat at Ewood Park. Off he went to Trowbridge Town, where he was promptly in a team that won the Western League championship under the player-man-agement of Harry Haddon. He afterwards had a trial with Bath City before seeing out his playing career first with Wells City, then back at Bitton, the vil-lage near Bristol where he had been a butcher. Away from football, he became a salesman.

Jimmy Morgan's family was steeped in soccer. His father, George, kept goal for Gloucestershire; one uncle, Jerry, played at inside-left in two League games for Bristol City and over 100 for Bristol Rovers; another uncle, Tom, was also with City; a third uncle, Jim, was a Wolves reserve; and a cousin, Sid, played for City in goal. Jimmy, a Royal Marine during the war, was taken on by Rovers after declining an offer from Sheffield Wednesday. He was a fre-quent choice for a couple of seasons before having to compete with stronger claims for a place from Roost and the player who is the subject of the next chapter – the player who stands out like a beacon in the story of the Bert Tann years, the club's record scorer with 242 goals in 461 League games, plus a dozen or more in the FA Cup. His name? Geoffrey Reginald William Bradford, of course.

CHAPTER 8

Geoff Bradford's Two Serious Injuries

Geoff Bradford would almost certainly never have become the legendary Bristol Rovers player, the main force behind the Eastville club's prosperity throughout the 1950s, if Blackpool and Blackburn Rovers had not both made the mistake of failing to recognise his potential. He might even have gone to Bristol City, but declined their offer of a trial.

Born on the Clifton side of Bristol on 18 July 1927, but brought up in the Soundwell area, Bradford gained his first experience of senior football during the three years of Army service that took him out of England for the first time to Belfast. After demobilisation, at the age of 21, he joined the Soundwell club for which his brother Don kept goal, but soon afterwards moved to Glastonbury, for whom he played at half-back as well as in the forward line. His scoring feats for the Somerset club soon caught the attention of Blackpool's West Country scout, and he was invited up to Lancashire for a trial that lasted seven weeks.

During that period he played in the third team at inside-forward and scored eighteen goals. In practice games he was sometimes in the same forward line as those two big stars of the time, the Stanleys Matthews and Mortensen. 'They both told me I was bound to be retained,' he recalled, but, fortunately for Bristol Rovers, that view was not shared by the man who mattered, manager Joe Smith. As a former England forward who for many years had been a mainstay of the Bolton attack, Smith might have been expected to appreciate the promise of a player who was to have so many goals in his boots, yet it appears that he did not even take the trouble to have a close look at him. 'He greeted me when I arrived at the ground,' said Bradford, 'but the next time I saw him was seven weeks later when he said "Cheerio lad. Keep in touch". It came as a tremendous bombshell.'

So shattered was he that at first he refused the offer of another trial he received from Blackburn before leaving Blackpool, saying that he wanted to go back to Bristol to think about it. Back home he had two more games with Soundwell, and it was after one of them that he went with some of the other players to a dance at Frenchay Village Hall where he first met Betty, the young lady who was to become his wife. By then he had decided to accept Blackburn's invitation after all, only again to be released despite scoring more than a dozen goals for their Colts. So back he went to Soundwell, where his continued good form brought the third trial offer made by Bristol City, who wanted him to play at centre-half in their Reserves. He refused it partly because he was feeling disillusioned about Football League clubs in general, but also because he did not wish to miss any games in the Gloucestershire Senior Amateur Cup, in which Soundwell were doing well.

Soon afterwards he gave the same reply to Bristol Rovers' chief scout, Wally Jennings, who wanted him to play in a Football Combination game against Aldershot. But he did still get to Eastville in that 1948-49 season. Soundwell defeated Hanham 6-1 in the county final in May, and Bradford scored – from wing-half. After the match Jennings approached him again, this time with the offer of a contract, and he duly accepted terms of £7 a week in the first team, £5 in the Reserves. Brough Fletcher was in what were to be his last months as manager, and Bert Tann had not long been taken on as coach. Bradford had yet to even see a League game, never mind play in one.

At the start of the following season this young man who was to become the highest scorer in the club's history made his debut for the Reserves against Fulham at Eastville. The visitors, though handicapped when their goalkeeper, Irish international Hugh Kelly, dislocated a shoulder, were beaten by only one goal. Peter Sampson was the man to get it, but Bradford was seen in what was to be a very familiar role at the next opportunity, completing the first of his Rovers hat-tricks in a 5-3 win at Reading. His first chance in the League quickly followed, away to Crystal Palace on the last Saturday of September. It was not, however, a propitious time to be stepping up to that level. Rovers had made the appalling start that was to lead to Fletcher's dismissal in the first week of January, having won only two of their previous eight games, and defeat at Selhurst Park by a lone goal deposited them at the foot of the Third Division South table.

One of the Rovers' victories up to that point had been gained, by 2-1 at home to Reading, only in the closing minutes – and then they had had to come from behind after Pitt had hit the crossbar and Watling had missed an open goal. One of the five defeats in those eight games had been by the odd goal of five at home to Bristol City. It was the first match watched by the Duke of Beaufort since becoming the Rovers' president, in front of a then record crowd for the ground of 34,251. George Lowrie, the Welsh international newly signed from Newcastle United, had scored City's winner after Roost and Hodges had pulled back a two-goal deficit.

In the circumstances it was hardly surprising that Geoff Bradford failed to make an immediate impact, but he began to settle in during the improvement that lifted Rovers to a final ninth place following Bert Tann's move up to manager. After opening his League account at Walsall he scored two more goals as Rovers lost only one of their last six games of the season – one the Easter Monday winner against Exeter, the other the first in a 5-1 beating of Norwich. And there would have been another if keeper Ansell had not just managed to punch the ball away as Bradford was about to head it in during a scoreless draw with the Northampton Town team that finished runners-up to promoted Notts County.

From then, right through the 1950s into the early 60s, Geoff Bradford was the big name in the Bristol Rovers team, his story of high achievement all the more remarkable for the fact that he twice had to battle back from an horrific injury that would have forced less resolute and courageous players into premature retirement. The first of those injuries came at Plymouth on 7 November 1953, at a time when he was strongly in line for an England cap. He had been told to stand by for the World Cup party, after having already scored five hat-tricks that season, one of them for an FA side against the RAF at Tottenham. He had just taken his League goals tally to eighteen in Rovers' seventeenth game, giving them a 3-2 lead early in the second half, when he chased a pass from George Petherbridge down the right wing. As he centred the ball he slid down with his right leg stretched out, and Paddy Ratcliffe, Argyle's left-back, came down on that leg while tearing across to make a late challenge.

The leg numbed, the bottom part of it out at an angle from the top half, Bradford managed to crawl over the touchline as trainer Bert Williams went to help him. The woman surgeon at the Plymouth hospital to which he was taken for X-rays wanted to keep him there, but Bert Tann insisted he went straight back to a private nursing home in Bristol, so the leg was strapped up and Bradford returned on the team coach. 'The manager's decision not only saved my career,' he said later. 'If it had not been made I might never have walked properly again.' The orthopaedic specialist who opened him up at the Chesterfield Nursing Home found that the main ligaments on the inside of the knee had been snapped, both cartilages had gone, and the bone had cracked. If the severed ligaments had been left any longer they would have shrunk back and it would have been impossible to join them up again.

Bradford was in the nursing home for two weeks after the operation, then on crutches for six weeks with a full-length plaster on the leg. After the size of the plaster was reduced he began to go to Eastville for exercises on a stationary cycle. He also lifted a bucket of sand with the leg on a special pulley system devised by Bert Williams. To help fill in the time between those exercise sessions, he helped in the club's offices. That was how things went until the final week of the season, at the beginning of which he persuaded the reluctant Tann to let him play in a Thursday evening Football Combination game. A crowd of 13,000 turned up, and they saw Bradford score both goals in a 2-1 win against the reserve side of the Brentford club then managed by Bill Dodgin, a former Rovers player who was to be one of Bert Tann's managerial successors at Eastville.

Next morning, Bradford pestered Tann to put him back into the first team for their final Second Division match of the season that Saturday, 24

April 1954, at home to Stoke City. The manager again agreed, but with such trepidation that he went off to Southampton that day, saying that he 'couldn't bear to watch'. It was the first match he had missed since taking over from Brough Fletcher.

What he missed was something out of the wilder realms of schoolboy fiction. Rovers won 3-2, finishing that first season in the League's second tier in a creditable ninth place, and each of their three goals was scored by Geoff Bradford, the hat-trick expert. It was an afternoon when it was said there was not a dry eye at Eastville. Tumultuous indeed were the cheers that erupted as that match-winning third goal went in. 'If,' the scorer was to say years later, 'I had to pick out one moment as meaning more to me than any other, then it would be that one.'

By what he called a million-to-one chance, Bradford suffered an almost identical injury to the other leg, after having fought his way back to full fitness. This happened in a fourth-round floodlit FA Cup replay at Doncaster on Tuesday, the last day of January in 1956 'on the coldest night I ever experienced'. Rovers had outplayed those other Rovers at Eastville the previous Saturday, but big Eddie McMorran, an Irish international, had broken away on his own to equalise. Bradford took a knock during that game, and was not at all certain to take part in the replay. 'We were going well in the Second Division,' he recalled, 'and, as there was a doubt about my fitness, Bert Tann had thought of keeping me back for the League match the following Saturday. Bill Roost was standing by, but the manager made a late decision to include me.' Peter Hooper, scorer of Rovers' goal in the drawn game at Eastville, was ruled out of the replay by influenza, Watling taking his place on the left wing.

Bristol Rovers played well on the frozen snow-covered Belle Vue pitch, but they failed to take their chances, and were then rarely out of their own half after the interval. With twenty minutes of normal time left and the scoresheet still blank, Bradford challenged for the ball with two Doncaster defenders as 'Paddy' Hale, Ray Warren's successor at centre-half, drove a free-kick upfield. This was how Geoff recalled what happened next: 'As I put my left leg up to control the ball one Doncaster player moved in on one side of me, and one on the other. They blocked my leg between them. It was a pure accident, and not even a foul, so play continued as I went down on the frozen snow. It was just over two years earlier that I had last felt pain like that. In my heart I think I knew then that it was a similar injury, but I dragged myself to the touchline and Bert Williams and the Doncaster trainer helped me to the dressing room. As I lay there I heard the cheers greeting the late goal that brought Doncaster victory.'

The scorer of that goal, three minutes from time, was Bert Tindill, a versatile forward who two years later followed Peter Doherty to Bristol City after the former Irish international had been appointed manager at Ashton Gate in succession to Albert ('Pat') Beasley, an ex-England winger who had been with Arsenal, Huddersfield and Fulham before originally joining City as player-manager.

Bradford was put to bed at the Rovers' hotel after being strapped up by Doncaster's club doctor. Next day, the problem was getting him to the railway station for the return to Bristol, but that was eventually solved by the provision of a wheelchair on which he was taken to the train. 'I arrived there in what you might call in state,' he said, 'but that was where the VIP treatment ended. They wanted to put me in the goods van. I didn't fancy that idea, so they managed to prop me up along one of the carriage seats.'

Back in Bristol, he was taken home before returning to the Chesterfield Nursing Home because he wanted to see his wife first. The operation he underwent the same night lasted three hours. Again, the two main ligaments in the knee had snapped, and both cartilages had gone. The only difference this time was that there was no cracking of the bone.

Two days after the operation, propped up in bed, Bradford thought he had a touch of indigestion. 'Something seemed to be lodged in the left side of my chest. I asked Betty to massage it for me, and rang for the nurse. I asked Betty to give it another good rub. As she did, I could suddenly feel something moving across my chest. I began to get short of breath. By the time help arrived my lung had collapsed. I lost consciousness. A clot of blood had moved up from my leg and gone into the lung. For the next few days I was in an oxygen tent, and nobody was allowed to see me while I was on the danger list. I was given a series of injections to break up the clot, and after a couple of days Betty was able to see me. They said the clot was probably the result of the amount of ether they had had to give me during the operation. I could taste ether for days afterwards. For five or six days the leg injury took second place to the collapsed lung. I was in hospital for just over two weeks, and in plaster for a further six.'

CHAPTER 9

'Pressed' out of England's Team

In the summer after Geoff Bradford's second serious injury, he had been due to go on the FA's tour of South Africa with George Petherbridge – a tour on which three players were seriously injured, one of them, Fulham's Bedford Jezzard, never to play again. Bradford had a few games in the Reserves at the start of the next season before getting back into the League side, but he admitted he was 'never quite the same player I had been before', adding: 'I had lost my quickness in turning and hitting the ball, and that had been my strength.'

There was therefore no real prospect of his adding to the one England cap he had been awarded against Denmark in Copenhagen on 2 October 1955. Indeed, his chances of being called up again by his country had already been blighted because, in his opinion, 'the London football reporters were determined to get the young Johnny Haynes into the England team instead of me.' He added: 'I am sure that in those days what the national press said had a considerable bearing on who was selected for the England team. I'm not disputing for one moment that Haynes was a great player, but I'm convinced that if selection had been purely on merit I would have kept my place after the Denmark game.'

He learned of getting that one England call while watching a film with his wife at the King's cinema in Bristol's Old Market. 'I felt a tap on my shoulder. It was Miss Jones, the cinema manager's secretary. She said there was a message for me in the office. The first thought that entered our minds was that something had happened to the children, but Miss Jones told us there was no need to worry.' Indeed there was not. On finding out that his greatest ambition had been fulfilled, Bradford went back to watch the rest of the film, and he and his wife afterwards read about his selection in the *Evening Post* when they got outside.

The opportunity had been clinched by Bradford's performances on the FA tour of the West Indies the previous summer. In eight games he had scored sixteen goals, including four hat-tricks. For one of those matches, against Trinidad, he had been given the captaincy in the absence of the tourists' appointed skipper, Syd Owen, Luton Town's fair-skinned centre-half. Owen had to be confined to bed for three days after catching sunstroke on being persuaded to strip off for a swim at a country club.

Two of Bradford's particular friends on that tour were defenders Jeff Hall, of Birmingham City, and Grenville Hair, of Leeds United, both of whom died tragically early. Hall was only 29 when he succumbed to polio in a Birmingham hospital in 1959; Hair, 36, collapsed while conducting a training session at Bradford City, where he was manager, in 1968.

When Bradford became the first, and still only, Bristol Rovers player to make his full England debut while with the club, Bill Creed charted a Dakota aircraft to fly 34 fans on a Supporters' Club outing to Copenhagen. The game attracted a record Danish crowd of 53,000. The massed bands of the Coldstream Guards, Black Watch and Gordon Highlanders played before the kick-off and at half-time, and the teams were presented to King Frederick, who attended with Queen Ingrid. It all made for a momentous occasion, and Bradford rose to it by scoring one goal in a 5-1 win, having another controversially disallowed, and making two others for Bolton's Nat Lofthouse. Yet one of the London reporters Bradford complained about opined that 'with plenty of space in which to work he did a few good things, but did not impress as an international inside-forward'. It was at least conceded that 'he took his goal well'.

The original plan was for Bradford to play up front with Lofthouse, and for Don Revie, the other inside-forward who was then with Manchester City, to operate in midfield. In the event, however, Revie, scorer of England's two other goals, was the one to play up front and Bradford was left to do the fetching and carrying.

Despite England's biggest win abroad since the 10-0 pulverising of Portugal in Lisbon in 1947 failing to attract wholehearted praise from the critics, the word was that the same side would be chosen to meet Wales the following month. But then it was suggested in some of the newspapers that it would be a better team if Haynes were playing. Although Bradford was not retained at inside-left in Cardiff, neither was Haynes the man brought in to take over. The vote went to Dennis Wilshaw, of Wolves – and after a Welsh victory it was not he who was left out to accommodate Haynes for his second cap, against Northern Ireland at Wembley. Revie was the one to be excluded, as were Lofthouse and Stanley Matthews, from a game in which Wilshaw obtained two of the three goals England scored without reply.

Haynes, the country's first £100-a-week footballer after the lifting of the maximum wage, was in England's forward line for 54 more matches (22 as captain), right through to the summer of 1962. His international career finally came to an end after he had given disappointing displays in the World Cup in Chile and, more decisively, suffered serious injuries in a car crash at Blackpool. One medical opinion was that he would never play football again, and although he proved that diagnosis wrong it was not until about a year later that he was able to return to action.

Haynes' long stay in the England side was clearly on merit, though it is also true that, as a player with a London club and the inspiration of Fulham's attack, he was the man that most members of the national press, based in the capital, wanted in the team – not Geoff Bradford of unfashionable Bristol Rovers. But it was not only Haynes who kept Bradford out. The Rovers marksman's age (he was only a few months from his 28th birthday when he was capped) also counted against him – as did the fact that, in addition to those already mentioned, there were a good number of other, and younger, players putting forward strong claims.

Among these was John Atyeo, Bradford's corresponding 'big gun' on the Bristol soccer scene over at Ashton Gate. Not long after the Denmark game both were in an FA team, and among the scorers, in a 9-0 shooting down of the RAF at City's ground. 'We had been led to understand,' said Bradford, 'that the same side would be chosen for the B match with Yugoslavia at Maine Road in Manchester, but before I left the ground I was told by Walter Winterbottom, the England manager, that Haynes had been chosen to play against Yugoslavia before the RAF game, and that I would be twelfth man. I had scored two goals against the RAF, and laid on at least three more, but again my performance counted for nothing.'

Atyeo scored the first of the five goals the Yugoslavs conceded. His over-all display was so impressive that he was given his full debut against Spain at the end of that November. That televised match at Wembley made history for being the first senior international in Britain for which the floodlights were switched on – at precisely 3.23pm, with fog threatening an abandon-ment and just seventeen minutes left for play. Atyeo had scored the first of the four goals by which England led at that point (Spain made one reply in the remaining time), and he had better luck than Bradford in being given fur-ther chances.

Even so, Atyeo still had some cause for complaint in being summarily discarded, at the young age of 25. He had never been on the losing England side in scoring five goals in his six full internationals – four of them in the last three, which were World Cup qualifiers. Manager Winterbottom, who did not have the final say in team selection, conceded that 'it might have been a mistake to have dropped Atyeo at a time when we were badly in need of a prolific scorer [he might well have said the same about Bradford], but there was some concern among the selectors over the fact that he was a part-time professional'.

It was not for want of opportunity that Atyeo and Bradford remained what might be termed big fish in the small pool of Bristol's soccer backwa-ter, both deciding to stay loyal to their one League club – professionally speaking, that is, for Atyeo was a Portsmouth amateur in about half-a-dozen Football Combination games and a couple in the First Division before Bristol City's millionaire chairman, Harry Dolman, called round at his Dilton Marsh home in Wiltshire and persuaded him to throw in his lot with the Ashton Gate club.

Dolman later said that when he was about to pull up in his Rolls-Royce outside the Atyeos' house, he spotted a car that he knew to be Bert Tann's, so he drove on and returned after the Rovers manager had gone. Eastville, therefore, might instead have been the stage for the player who over the next fifteen years broke Bristol City's records for Cup and League appearances (644) and goals (349), but for Harry Dolman's agreeing to what Atyeo described as 'probably the best contract ever signed by a player in those days'. The main conditions, as insisted upon by John's father, were that he should never be transferred to another club without his consent, be allowed to continue to live at Dilton Marsh, and always remain a part-time player. He was then studying for the diploma he obtained as a quantity surveyor, but, having subsequently qualified as a teacher, he became head of mathematics and a PE instructor at Warminster Secondary School after leaving City.

Harry Dolman, a farmer's son from Langley Burrell, near Chippenham, made his money as the main force behind the firm with which he rose to become chairman after joining it as a junior draughtsman. He was the inventor of many of its products, which varied from ticket-issuing machines to egg graders. In 1960 he saved City from the threat of extinction by wiping out their debts, and when his reign as the club's chairman – dating back to 1949 – ended in 1974 he continued as their president up to the time of his death, aged 80, in November 1977. His lifetime ambition was fulfilled when, in 1976, City won promotion to the First Division – something that, as we shall be coming to in due course, their Rovers neighbours had gone very close to achieving twenty years before. But he was spared seeing the resulting financial crisis that plunged the club back to the brink of oblivion.

John Atyeo admitted to weighing up the prospect of living in a big city such as London or Liverpool during his time at Ashton Gate, but said that 'Dilton had a kind of hold over me; I've never been one for the bright lights.' Don Welsh, the former Charlton forward who was Liverpool's manager during those years, made an offer of £20,000, including two players valued at about £8,000. Ted Drake, who had left Reading for Chelsea, maintained the interest he had shown while Atyeo had been an amateur, and Les McDowall, of Manchester City, was another manager who kept a close watch on the situation. Letters pleading with City not to sell appeared in the local papers and a boycott was threatened by a group of militant fans if they did. But Atyeo declared that 'the simple truth was that I didn't want to move, I certainly didn't want to leave home'. The spate of rumours faded away after Harry Dolman had been stung into issuing a statement that under no circumstances would City consider parting with him.

Chelsea were also among the top clubs reported to be after Geoff Bradford, and, in firmly turning down a £22,000 bid by Liverpool towards the end of 1952, Bert Tann made it clear that 'we are determined more than ever that none of our lads shall leave. We want them all in our great effort to reach the Second Division.' Bradford recalled another occasion, just before his first serious injury, when the Rovers players were out for a stroll on Plymouth Hoe just before a game at Home Park. 'We spotted a scout from a First Division club known to be interested in Vic Lambden and me. He was signalling to us, trying to get us to separate from the others so that he could have a private word with us, but we all stayed as a group. I never thought of asking for a transfer. In the days of the maximum wage I was earning as much as I could in the Second Division and the increase for stepping up into the First was not all that much.'

But Bradford and Atyeo had their regrets in looking back on their careers. Bradford went as far as to say that it was 'one of the regrets of my life that I never played First Division football', explaining that he was 'made sharply aware of just what I had missed' when he played in an FA Cup-tie against Manchester United in front of a crowd of nearly 56,000 at Old Trafford during the 1963-64 season, his last as a professional player. 'I had appeared on First Division grounds before, but nothing quite matched up to the atmosphere of that afternoon.'

Atyeo, speaking a few years after retiring from League football, observed that 'the fees, wages and other cash inducements are now so great that I doubt that I would have stayed at Bristol City if they had been available in my time. Europe wasn't thought about in those days. The chance of playing in the European Cup and in the other major competitions of today would probably have been a temptation I couldn't have resisted. I've often wondered how things would have turned out if I had been tempted by Portsmouth's offer to turn professional with them. I would have gone to Pompey without a shadow of a doubt if they had not then refused to have part-timers, and also had a strict rule banning their players from driving a car.' That latter imposition certainly makes strange reading these days.

Bradford and Atyeo both departed the Bristol soccer scene with a well-deserved testimonial, part of the New Deal for players having changed the regulations so that clubs could now make that award for exceptional service instead of a second or third benefit. Bradford thus became the first Rovers player to be given a testimonial match, on completion of fifteen years at Eastville in July 1964, but not their first employee. Bert Williams, the then recently retired trainer, had previously been granted one – on a very wet October night when receipts from a crowd of only just over 7,000 for a visit by Sheffield Wednesday had amounted to about £800.

Bradford's match was between a combined Rovers/City team and an International XI got together by Bill Dodgin, the former Rovers player who was then the club's chief scout. 'We tried to get a top First Division team down,' said Bradford, 'but they were all tied up in various competitions or had tour commitments. There was a crowd of 9,000, but by the time I had paid all the match expenses and £25 appearance money to each player in the All-Stars team there was not a great deal left. The Supporters' Club stepped in with a generous donation, and in the end I cleared £1,500. I didn't realise it was to be soccer's parting gift.'

In 1963-64, Bradford, at 36, was in what would have been his third benefit season. His return to the first team for its fourth match – at Shrewsbury – marked his 500th overall appearance. He had the added satisfaction of scoring the last of his 242 League goals in a 4-0 home win against Bristol City that December, but both he and Atyeo were to step off the League stage with a sense of some disappointment. Bradford, whose playing days had been prolonged by a successful switch to full-back, after that second leg injury had cost him the zip that had made him such a feared forward, was given reason to believe that he would be staying on to play in the Reserves and help bring on the youngsters. Harry Dolman told Atyeo that he would like him to become a City director in due course. Neither of those prospects became a reality.

Atyeo found that when the invitation to join the board eventually came it was 'not quite in the form I had expected'. To be considered, he was required to put in 'a substantial amount of money', and that he was neither prepared nor able to do. For Bradford, the let-down came when Bert Tann called him in and said that, with the financial situation as it was, there would not be a place for him the following season after all. 'I was upset about it, but somehow felt it was not the end of my Eastville career. But then came the letter saying my services were no longer required and that I was being given a free transfer.'

So, after temporarily joining the Supporters' Club lottery staff, it was to working as a driver for an oil company based at Avonmouth that Bradford turned. Away from that he kept in shape by playing tennis at the Cleeve Hill club at Downend, on the outskirts of Bristol. He continued to take a close interest in Rovers' affairs as he spent the last years of his life at Stoke Gifford, just a few miles outside the city, but he was only 67 when he died on 30 December 1994. Atyeo passed away even younger, aged 61, in June the previous year.

The funeral service for Bradford was held at Frenchay church. It was something he had wanted so that he could be near his old manager Bert Tann, who had lived in a Cotswold-stone house just off the common in that village on the northern outskirts of Bristol, and was buried in the churchyard. Bradford was cremated at Westerleigh.

Atyeo, who twice won promotion with Bristol City, is up there with Billy Wedlock in the Ashton Gate club's player ratings, but Bradford stands alone as Bristol Rovers' greatest player, scorer of a dozen hat-tricks (ending with all four goals against Rotherham on 14 March 1959) in a League haul that puts him more than 60 ahead of the club's next highest aggregate scorer, Alfie Biggs, of whom more in his proper turn. Yet Bradford admitted he was 'a lazy inside-forward'. Because of that there were times when he used to get 'some stick', as he put it, from some of the other players, but Geoff Fox used to say: 'So long as he keeps putting the ball in the net leave him alone. When he stops scoring then you can get on at him.' Jackie Pitt gave him his nickname of 'Rip'. It was an abbreviation for Rest in Peace – not a reflection of his play on the field, but of his ability to rest and sleep even in the last hour before a game.

'As time went on,' recalled Bradford, 'and the team changed and the game itself began to make more demands, I had to work much harder than I did in those early days. In fact, I did far more work after switching to centre-forward than I ever did as an inside-forward.'

CHAPTER 10

Marathon Ties in Record Cup Run

In Bert Tann's first complete season as manager, 1950-51, Bristol Rovers put themselves firmly in soccer's national spotlight by reaching the quarter-finals of the FA Cup for the first time. And then it was only in a replay that they went out after holding Newcastle United, three times winners of the trophy in the first half of the 1950s, to a scoreless draw in their St James' Park fortress.

But what a struggle Rovers had to get through their opening two rounds against Llanelly (now Llanelli), of the Southern League, and Gillingham, who were in their first season back in the Third Division South after having failed to gain re-election a dozen years before. Both took Tann's men to two replays, and not until extra-time in their third meeting in treacherous snow-sprinkled conditions at Cardiff City's Ninian Park, after five and a half hours' playing time, did Rovers get the better of little Llanelly.

Goalkeeper Annetts was the key figure in the original tie at Eastville, going off to a standing ovation after foiling Rovers with a string of fine saves. George Petherbridge was the only man to beat him, and the 37th-minute lead he gained was wiped out by right-back McInnes from the penalty spot as the home side deepened their frustration with too much close passing. That fault was also evident in the first replay – and one that Llanelly surprisingly shared considering the extremely muddy conditions. Indeed, it was the mud that denied Rovers another interval lead, the ball sticking on the goal-line and enabling Annetts to recover after he had been unable to hold a shot from Bryan Bush. That let-off looked like being costly when, midway through the second half, Wallace, the home inside-right, scored from close range following a corner. Bush, who was partnering Roost on the left wing, equalised five minutes later and two tiring teams could not produce the telling blow in the extra half-hour. Geoff Bradford described it as 'one of the worst Rovers performances I can remember'.

Deserving winners though Rovers were of the second replay after another 120 minutes of gruelling football, it did not turn in their favour until ten minutes from the end of the extra period. And then it was only because of some shrewd quick thinking, and, it has to be said, gamesmanship, by the industrious Bill Roost. The scores were still level, centre-forward Mathie having trickled in an equaliser around the hour mark after Petherbridge had again put Rovers ahead in the opening half. Then Dorset referee Browning awarded an indirect free-kick, seven yards out, against McInnes for obstructing Vic Lambden. Defenders ranged alongside Annetts on the goal-line were left powerless as Roost tapped the ball a few inches to his left and Geoff Bradford – who had had a goal disallowed a quarter of an hour earlier – crashed it through the crowd of players with a typically emphatic right-foot finish.

'At such indirect free-kicks,' Bradford was to recall, 'Bill used to kick up a general rumpus, telling the referee the wall of defenders wasn't far enough away and shouting instructions to all and sundry. I would stand close to him, but looking as if I wasn't taking much notice. Then Bill tapped a quick kick for me to whip the ball into the net while everything was still in a state of confusion as a result of Bill's antics.'

Though in luck when Fleck, the Llanelly inside-left, beat Bert Hoyle with a shot that rebounded off the crossbar, Rovers did most of the pressing during extra-time. After only five minutes of the extra period Roost was himself fleetingly thought to have regained the lead. The referee appeared to award a goal as the ball entered the net, but his attention was then drawn to the flag upraised by a linesman, and after consulting him he gave a free-kick to the Welsh club instead.

Until Bradford made the vital breakthrough, Rovers were repeatedly foiled by a determined defence in which skipper John Stein was outstanding at centre-half. After that, however, it was practically all Bristol as tiredness took its toll of Llanelly. Jackie Pitt put the outcome beyond all doubt with a dropping shot from some 35 yards three minutes from the end to the delight of some 2,500 Rovers fans in the crowd of just over 9,000. No wonder the Llanelly players were tired. They were altogether involved in five replays that season – one of them against Barry, who themselves progressed after taking Llanelly to a second replay in the third qualifying round of the Cup the following season.

Extra-time was needed only in the first replay between Bristol Rovers and Gillingham, but the outcome might well have been decided in the original tie at Eastville. Petherbridge eluded a couple of defenders, drew Larry Gage out of his goal, placed the ball past him – but saw it roll inches the wrong side of an upright. So the final whistle sounded with the score 2-2. Bush cancelled out an early goal by Thomas; Lambden and Carr scored in the second half.

On the journey for the second meeting at the Priestfield Stadium in Kent the following Wednesday, the motor coach on which the Rovers players travelled was in a collision in the Blackwall tunnel. But for the first half-hour it was Gillingham who looked more like the side that had been shaken up. Petherbridge and Bradford both hit the crossbar, and in the 26th minute another snap shot from Bradford was deflected past Gage off amateur Ken Gough. A Bristol University medical student from Southampton, Gough had been brought in, after only three games with the Reserves, as the injured

Roost's deputy to partner Watling, Bush's replacement on the left wing. Nine minutes from the interval, however, Rovers conceded the soft goal that was to make another replay necessary after the extra period. Bert Hoyle had no difficulty in gathering a cross from Charlie Burtenshaw, who partnered his brother Bill on Gillingham's right wing, but then made one of his rare errors by inexplicably and gently throwing the ball out to the feet of outside-left Carr, who recovered from his astonishment quickly enough to pop it back into the unguarded net.

That gift perked up Gillingham to wrest the initiative in the second half, and Rovers were particularly fortunate to survive when the ball twice glanced up against their crossbar during the hectic goalmouth scramble that ensued from a corner forced by Thomas. At least, on another frozen surface, they did adopt the better tactics in swinging the ball about instead of sticking to the short-passing game with which Gillingham persisted.

Roost returned alongside Watling for the second replay, which took place in more icy conditions at Tottenham's ground. Another spell of extra-time was only four minutes away, with the score again 1-1, when Rovers squeezed through the second round with a penalty taken by Ray Warren. Gillingham felt hard done by when, amid snowflakes and patches of fog, their left-back, Ron Lewin, was adjudged to have handled the ball when it shot up and struck him on the arm. Goalkeeper Gage, who trained at White Hart Lane, tried to distract the Rovers captain by going up him and asking in which direction he intended to shoot. 'You'll know when you pick the ball out of the net,' was the growled reply, though Warren, Rovers' spot-kick king (the seven he converted in one season set a club record), was afterwards to admit that he found this penalty the most nerve-wracking of all those with which he was entrusted.

He also agreed that the award was 'a tough decision' against Gillingham, explaining that 'if the ball had missed Lewin it would have gone out of play'. He added: 'There was certainly no danger at the time, but I was in no sympathetic mood when I took the kick.'

Referee Arthur Blythe was persuaded by Gillingham's protesting players to consult a linesman after Warren's successful kick, only to find that his colleague had been waving his flag because Gage was not on his line when the penalty was taken, and that it would therefore have had to be retaken if he had saved.

Controversy about that deciding goal was offset, however, by the fact that Bert Hoyle was staggering dazedly along his goal-line after colliding with Derek Lewis when that player opened the scoring early in the second half. Hoyle collapsed in an instinctive attempt to save, but was able to continue after receiving attention. There was an echo of the Roost initiative as Bradford brought the scores level again by neatly turning the ball in when

Petherbridge caught the Gillingham defenders napping with a swiftly taken indirect free-kick inside the penalty area.

This was the game that produced the most famous incident concerning Bert Hoyle's passion for oranges. There had recently been some publicity about his habit of now and again biting into the orange he kept in the back of his net and sucking the juice. The supporters who had travelled from Bristol were behind one of the goals, and when he was down at that end they started throwing oranges into the back of the netting. Some rolled onto the pitch, and he was out collecting them when Gillingham suddenly broke away. He had never been seen to move as fast as he had to do in dropping the oranges and rushing back into his goal.

At the end of that repeated third encounter, Rovers had been striving for ten and a half hours to get among the big boys in the third round, whereas teams have reached the Cup final in three hours fewer. After that, though, these marathon men had comparatively comfortable passages at home to Aldershot (5-1), away to Luton (2-1) and at home to Hull (3-0) before their momentous visit to Newcastle.

The clash with Aldershot, fellow members of the Southern Section of the Third Division, had to be postponed from the first Saturday of January to the following Wednesday. As at Rochdale, where Chelsea were the visitors, a sudden thaw made the pitch waterlogged. Frost in the ground at Eastville made it difficult for the water to drain away, but conditions improved suffi-ciently for the midweek go-ahead, and Rovers revelled in them by taking the lead through Lambden in eight seconds (the quickest ever goal by a Rovers player), then going four up by half-time. Lambden went on to complete his hat-trick, Petherbridge and Roost also scoring.

At Luton, against a side down in the Second Division depths, Warren was again a commanding figure, despite having been in bed with a heavy cold during the week. Not until the morning of the match was he declared fit to play. He kept a close watch on George Stobbart, the Hatters' most danger-ous forward (one which Newcastle had found surplus to requirements), and marshalled a hard-tackling defence that never allowed the home attack to set-tle. Even when wing-half Charlie Watkins gave Luton the lead in the thir-teenth minute, Rovers refused to be dismayed. For the twelfth time that sea-son they wiped out arrears to gain either a draw or a victory. The lively Lambden equalised before half-time, and Petherbridge, who led Eire inter-national Bud Aherne a rare dance, was once more on the mark in a solo effort for the winner early in the second half.

Rovers were in the last sixteen for the first time since 1913, when they had lost at home to Everton. It was also the first time that they and their City neighbours had been together in that stage of the competition, but the Ashton Gate club fell at the next hurdle, away to Birmingham, whereas

Tann's men cruised past Hull, a mid-table Second Division team, in an Eastville quagmire as the adjacent River Frome rose to an alarming level.

The pitch had also been in a dreadful state when Rovers had gained their first Cup win against a First Division side during that previous best run in the competition in the 1912-13 season. It rained heavily throughout the first-round match (the equivalent of the current third) in which they defeated Notts County, who were heading for relegation from the top flight along with Woolwich Arsenal. There were pools of water all over the ground, and when the ball landed in the middle of the biggest, some 30 yards square at the Thirteen Arches end, the players presented the comical sight of standing in a ring around it for a few moments, all of them reluctant to splash in to retrieve it.

The conditions were so atrocious for Hull's visit in 1951 that when Alf Bond, the one-armed referee from Fulham (he lost his right hand above the wrist in an accident at work when only nineteen) went out to inspect the pitch someone was heard to say: 'If he doesn't sink down as far as his knees the game's on.' On deciding play was possible, just about, the referee took the precaution of carrying two whistles, forethought that paid off when he dropped one of them in the clinging mud. Geoff Bradford recalled that 'the mud was so deep in the second half that at one point Ray Warren had to give me a push to get me going again. If you stood still a couple of seconds you'd sink.'

Raich Carter, Hull's player-manager – who had previously played at the ground for the Probables in the final England schools trial of 1927 in which Tann had been his opposite number with the Possibles, and then for England Boys against Wales Boys under the captaincy of Ronnie Dix – was optimistic enough when the draw was made to predict that it was going to be just a matter of how many goals Hull scored. But that was before he had seen the mud that was Rovers' great ally. The Eastville pitch was invariably heavy in those days; this time, with the River Frome swollen, it excelled itself. After the match Carter readily conceded that 'we were beaten by much the better side', but also observed: 'I've played on worse pitches, but I can't remember when.' Considering that he had had plenty of experience of contending with the mud at Derby County's notorious Baseball Ground, that was some statement.

To quote from one contemporary report: 'It seemed incredible that anybody could play football on such an appalling surface, but Rovers did it. In the first half they swung the ball from man to man, never giving it time to settle in the mud. Almost every pass found a ready taker, and their defence always had at least two men as busy to intercept as corvettes. When Hull found their passes too short they, and not Rovers, looked like the hit-and-run Division Three side. A magnificent Rovers defence – all six men in it

(Hoyle; Bamford, Fox; Pitt, Warren, Sampson) playing in their 36th successive game – had to smother only isolated attacks, which became the more rare as the game rushed to its almost hysterical conclusion.'

John Watling had been given the job of keeping a close watch on Don Revie, normally Hull's most creative player, and he not only made a big success of it but also still found the time and space to score two of the goals. He got the first one in the 29th minute, after goalkeeper Joe Robinson had parried his initial shot, the other a dozen minutes into the second half, when he fastened onto a faulty clearance and drove the ball home off the underside of the crossbar. Lambden hooked in the third goal fifteen minutes from time after good work by Bradford and the tireless Roost, and there would have been at least three more but for wonder saves by Robinson, who had been Blackpool's goalkeeper in the FA Cup final only three years earlier.

Another well-known Hull player, Neil Franklin, the £22,500 former Stoke and England centre-half, was ineligible for this game and preferred to play for the Reserves in the Midland League rather than travel with his new team-mates to Eastville as a spectator. 'I need as much match play as possible to get back into my stride,' he said. His debut for Hull in a draw at home to Blackburn the previous Saturday had been his first League appearance since his return from his ill-starred venture to Bogota that had resulted in his suspension by the FA from October until that January.

CHAPTER 11

Newcastle Visit Causes Cup Chaos

Cup fever really began to take a grip at Eastville after Hull's exit. With Rovers into the quarter-finals for the first time in their history – which then dated back 68 years – Bert Tann was granted his wish of 'sharing a giant gate at Sunderland, Newcastle or Manchester if we don't get a home draw'. St James' Park became the venue for his team's tenth Cup-tie of the season.

Memories were revived of a wartime cup-tie, played there in May 1940, in which Rovers had been beaten only by a last-minute goal scored by Billy Cairns, a centre-forward who was later a prolific scorer with Gateshead and Grimsby Town. Cairns was a durable chap who was in his 42nd year when he finally retired nineteen years after making his League debut. Rovers' team on that former occasion had included Jack Weare and Wally McArthur, and a couple of guests, Bobby Caldwell (Bristol City) and Leslie Talbot (Walsall).

On Monday 12 February 1951, Rovers' players went down to the *Bristol Evening Post* offices for the draw. This caught Geoff Bradford on the hop because, not having expected the club to be involved, he had arranged to marry Betty on the Monday before the date of the sixth round. Bert Tann gave him permission to go ahead and all the team attended the ceremony before going off for the special training at Southend. Bradford joined them after being allowed to stay behind for a one-day honeymoon. The new Mrs Bradford then joined the other players' wives in linking up with the Rovers party on the Friday, and they all stayed at Whitley Bay while up in the North-East.

Only a couple of months earlier George Petherbridge had cut his wedding day even finer – on the very morning of a home match with Rovers' City rivals, in fact. The marriage service began at eleven o'clock on 30 December, at 2.30 he was lining up for the kick-off, and by half-time he had helped Vic Lambden to the first of his two goals in a win that increased Rovers' record unbeaten run to eighteen games. Arnold Rodgers made City's only reply, though player-manager Pat Beasley almost equalised with the last kick.

That victory kept Rovers in third place in the Third Division's Southern section. It was gained in their last League fixture before the Cup clash with Aldershot that was to lead – via the wins over Luton and Hull – to the epic meeting with Newcastle. Three days after knocking out Aldershot, however, they suffered their first defeat in twenty matches in losing to a Fred Kurz goal at Crystal Palace after Petherbridge had hit the home bar and brought goalkeeper Charlie Bumstead to the best save. There was only one further setback for Rovers in the eight other games they played before their trip to Newcastle, Bamford scoring one of his rare goals as Hoyle kept Newport down to two. But a team tired by their Cup exertions played under the handicap of losing Petherbridge with a pulled muscle in his right leg during the second half.

Stan Seymour, the former Newcastle left-winger who was then a United director, declared himself no less pleased than Bert Tann with the pairing of their teams in the Cup's last eight. 'Good side, Bristol Rovers – for a Third Division club,' he said. 'Glad we aren't playing on their mud patch.' Those were words he was forced to swallow when, at the end of the 90 minutes, Newcastle were compelled to play at Eastville after all. He grasped Tann by the hand and told him: 'You are not just a good team. You will be a power in the Second Division.' It was a prediction that did come true, but not just yet. As far as the Eastville pitch was concerned, he made no further comment, but could not disguise being worried about it. In marked contrast, the pitch at St James' Park was beautifully firm. 'It was the first time,' said Bert Hoyle, 'that I've had a dry football to handle since Christmas – and that was twelve games ago.'

Some 10,000 fans travelled up to Tyneside from Bristol in special trains, and they were rewarded with a goalless draw deservedly gained in front of a 63,000 crowd. Rovers were handicapped by Petherbridge limping with the recurrence of that pulled muscle from as early as the third minute, when he was running through with a great chance to score. 'I'm sorry, boss,' he said to his manager afterwards. 'I would never have played if I had thought this was going to happen. I felt a twinge when I shot over early on, and I knew then that the leg which had come through a tough fitness test was not as strong as I had thought.' Even so, he was still able to be of some nuisance value after returning to the fray with the affected leg tightly strapped by trainer Bert Williams.

Rovers' draw was no fluke. There were just two flashes of brilliance from a Newcastle team assembled at the then high cost of almost £60,000 – as against the Rovers' £350 outlay for just one player, Hoyle. Rovers contained seven Bristol-born players (Bamford, Fox, Warren, Bradford, Lambden, Roost and Watling) and three others (Pitt, Sampson and Petherbridge) who had cost nothing more than the signing-on fee and were as good as homegrown products.

One of those flashes almost produced a 24th-minute goal for the hero of Geordieland, 'Wor' Jackie Milburn, who had been declared fit after treating a twisted ankle by paddling in the sea. The other, in the second half, resulted from a superb flick by Milburn that sent Chilean George Robledo and little Ernie Taylor racing through. Down among the flailing feet went the courageous Hoyle, regardless of his bandaged right wrist. He had cracked it on Christmas Day during another scoreless draw (that one with Port Vale, in a game switched to Stoke City's ground because Vale Park was unfit). Three times the ball crashed against the plunging goalkeeper before Pitt scrambled it away. Moments later there was very nearly a goal at the other end, skipper Joe Harvey clearing a Bradford shot from off the goal-line. Late in the second half, Lambden hit a post, but it was mainly a backs-to-the-wall battle for Rovers.

Hoyle's wrist injury was kept secret because, with Liley also injured, their only other available keeper was an inexperienced amateur. Hoyle was under treatment several times daily and up to ten o'clock on three nights each week. But for the perseverance of the club's doctor and trainer, with the aid of plastic bandages and electrical equipment, he could never have kept going.

On arriving back from Newcastle on the Sunday after the shock result that brought them into the full glare of national publicity, Rovers were greeted by more than 10,000 people, plus a band, at Temple Meads railway station. Bristol was agog for the midweek replay, and there were frightening scenes outside the Eastville ground as tens of thousands massed in the clamour for the club's share of tickets. Women fainted and were passed over the heads of the crowd to first-aid posts. Six of them were taken to hospital with fractured ribs. So were three men. Children parted from their parents screamed in terror as the crowd packed closer to the turnstiles at which the tickets were being sold. Two of them suffered a broken arm; three others had crushed ribs. Ambulance men had to battle their way through to reach the injured, and an emergency first-aid post was set up. In the club's offices, volunteer helpers took phones off the hooks so as not to answer frenzied appeals for unprocurable tickets.

A neighbouring cinema was showing a newsreel of the epic drawn game at Newcastle, but for some time those inside could not get out, so packed was the surrounding area, and those outside could not get in. Police, mounted and on foot, were sent to try to bring some semblance of order, but were helplessly jammed in amid the milling throng. Attempts by police in radio cars to marshal the multitude proved equally futile.

The first signs of the crush that was to come appeared as early as five o'clock that morning, fourteen hours before tickets were due to be sold. At first light families were settling down in the club car park on chairs and camp stools – among them a young mother with her seventeen-month-old daughter. By midday the car park resembled a fairground. Hurdy-gurdies, accordions and gramophones played as the vast queues lengthened. Blue-and-white favours sold in their hundreds. Tea urns appeared, and new queues formed for them.

By 3pm the size of the crowd was about 22,000. At 6pm, when the selling of tickets started an hour earlier than planned, it was estimated at 75,000, with more arriving after they finished work. That was incredible enough, especially as it was so obvious the vast majority were bound to be disappointed, yet the final figure was said to be as high as 100,000. The record attendance for the ground at that time was 34,463, for the League game with Bristol City in September 1949; the top gate for the season was 31,578, again for a visit by City, on the Saturday after Christmas.

The first to receive their tickets were unable to get out the way they had come, so they were directed through the ground to the far side – only to have to struggle through a mass of over-optimistic fans who were queuing in the hope of reaching the turnstiles from that far away.

Bert Tann found he could not get back to his office after having gone out for tea. He tried to push a way through, but was pinned against a lorry and forced to his knees. A mounted policeman backed his horse to clear a path, helped the manager to his feet, and saw him to safety. Over all this chaos the singing of the Rovers' 'anthem', *Goodnight Irene*, could be heard repeatedly. Queues stretched round to Muller Road one way, and far down Stapleton Road on the other. Traffic had to be diverted, with the whole area in complete chaos. And after all that there was bitter disappointment for the thousands who, after being buffeted for hours, had to squeeze their way homeward empty-handed.

'Up to now,' said Tann after he had got his breath back, 'I've only said I hoped we'd be in the semi-final. Now I'm confident. On our little ground it won't be a Carlisle-Arsenal replay' (referring to Gunners' 4-1 third round win after being held to a shock draw at Highbury by the Third North club).

But it was not to be. Rovers' fairy-tale Cup progress, which altogether lasted eighteen hours, came to a gallant end after Newcastle had shaken off the shock of falling behind to a fifteenth-minute goal to score three times in thirteen first-half minutes. It was Rovers' first home defeat in fourteen months, watched by a crowd of 30,724 which, though well below what could have been expected, produced then-record receipts just short of £4,000. Those unprecedented scenes beforehand made it clear that Rovers disposed of their full allocation of tickets, but it seemed the same could not be said of Newcastle, many of whose supporters doubtless found it difficult, or were unwilling, to make the long journey for a midweek match.

Rovers' early lead, crowning a storming start after they had been set to face a troublesome sun, was gained by Bradford, who drove the ball home left-footed when it ran loose following a centre from Bush (Bush's recall to fill the right-wing vacancy caused by Petherbridge's injury increased the number of Bristolians in the team to eight). 'There was pandemonium,' recalled Bradford, 'but our elation proved our downfall. We were so excited at being ahead, and suddenly we were 1-3 down. We penned Newcastle back, but couldn't get another goal.'

Rovers supporters were still cheering Bradford's goal when Newcastle hit straight back to equalise through Ernie Taylor, who would be a Cup winner with both Newcastle and Blackpool (in the 'Matthews final' of 1953). Taylor would be denied the treble by Bolton after being an emergency signing by Manchester United following the tragic loss of so many of the Old Trafford club's players in the disaster at Munich airport in 1958. Joe Harvey, the Newcastle captain, delivered the cross from the right for that perfect rapid response, and seven minutes later he repeated it for left-half Charlie Crowe to race into the inside-right position and unleash a terrific right-foot shot through a crowded goalmouth. Bert Hoyle, partly unsighted, could only scrape the ball with his fingertips as it flew past him. After five more minutes the otherwise anonymous Robledo provided the pass that sent Milburn streaking through to leave the Rovers goalkeeper well beaten again.

It said much for Rovers' resolution that they recovered from those three swift blows to launch a succession of attacks which Newcastle had to pull back as many as eight players to repulse. But the ball did not run kindly for them and man-of-the-match Harvey twice intercepted when a goal seemed certain. Although class told in the end, Rovers gave an excellent account of themselves in a rousing Cup battle played in a magnificent sporting manner. The team to which they so gallantly yielded was the same as that which Newcastle would field at Wembley: Fairbrother; Cowell, Corbett; Harvey, Brennan, Crowe; Walker, Taylor, Milburn, Robledo, Mitchell.

The preponderance of local talent in Rovers' team that afternoon was the underlying reason for their prosperity in those early years of the Tann regime. As Geoff Bradford put it, 'the strength of Rovers during the successful years of the 1950s was the marvellous team spirit at Eastville. We were all proud to pull on a Rovers shirt and play for the club. That was what mattered most of all. We were doing something we dearly wanted to do, and we were getting paid for it too. Football was always a game to me first, a career second.'

At the time of Harry Bamford's tragic death, Bert Tann reflected on how Rovers' policy of steering as clear as they could of the transfer market, and concentrating on building a settled team of mainly local-born players, had bred close associations and lifelong friendships. 'We were saying in the office only last week,' he said, 'how closely-knit a football club like ours becomes. Men like Harry Bamford, Jack Pitt, Ray Warren, Geoff Bradford, Peter Sampson, George Petherbridge and John Watling played and trained together for years and years. Our office staff is also not constantly changing, and in the background are long-serving staff members such as Bert Williams and Wally McArthur in the dressing room, John Gummow and Ron Moules in the office, and Harry Smith in charge of the ground. Even "newcomer" Fred Ford (of whom more later) has been with us nearly four years. We have our ups and downs and differences of opinion – always freely expressed – but, like all families, we are fundamentally one, and dedicated to the common cause.'

All through their Cup run Rovers trained at Southend, and it was back there that they went for their first away match in the League after being knocked off the path to Wembley. They were lucky to salvage a point, for Southend should have made sure of victory when they had most of the play in the second half. Leslie Stubbs, later one of Chelsea's first champions, had scored a simple goal to equalise Bradford's opener. Some reaction set in after all the Cup euphoria, for whereas Rovers had remained right in the running for promotion despite the distractions of the knock-out competition, they subsequently fell away to a final position of sixth, fifteen points adrift of the club that did go up, Nottingham Forest. Of their seventeen League games after the Cup exit, Rovers won only four, drew seven, and lost six.

In contrast to that, they were as high as second just over a week before going to Newcastle, three points behind Forest, after a 2-1 win at Walsall on a Thursday evening. Two days later, on the Saturday preceding the quarter-final, they were at home to Norwich City, who were in third place only on goal-average. Rovers lost the chance to make up more ground while Forest were losing at Aldershot because their game was abandoned at half-time with Rovers leading 2-1 through two Lambden goals.

In an attempt to kill rumours, Rovers had sent a van round the city to broadcast the assurance that the match was on, so it was scarcely surprising that they were among the most vociferous protesters when referee Wright controversially decided that play was no longer possible on the waterlogged pitch. 'We cannot understand why it was considered unfit after 45 minutes,' said one Rovers official. 'If the ground was fit at the start it was fit at the interval.' The referee explained that he started the game 'because I understood from local conditions and advice that the pitch would improve'. Although that was hardly likely after it had been churned by the players' boots, much of the play during the first half was of a remarkably good standard considering the conditions.

On Good Friday, another referee, Arthur Blythe (of the Rovers v Gillingham tie), had to be smuggled out of the Newport ground disguised as a St John's ambulance man, and driven to the railway station in a police car, to avoid angry crowds. He had abandoned play with Norwich 1-5 down, and twenty minutes still to go, because 'the conditions were getting worse and in my opinion further play was impossible'. He took that decision, with which Newport and their supporters so vehemently disagreed, almost immediately after Reg Foulkes, the Norwich centre-half and captain, had been knocked out in heading the heavy ball. Blythe himself collapsed from exhaustion on reaching his dressing room. He quickly recovered on being attended by a doctor, but more than an hour elapsed before, even under his disguise, it could be considered safe for him to leave by a side entrance as irate fans continued their noisy demonstration.

It was Bristol Rovers, without a match that day, who just over a month later dashed Norwich's last hopes of going up. The East Anglian club had been fortunate to take a point from their rearranged game with a Newport side reduced to nine fit men for the last quarter of an hour. They now went to Eastville knowing that they needed a win to stay in the promotion race with Forest. Norwich had briefly taken the leadership a few weeks earlier, exploiting Forest's concession of a last-minute winning penalty at Southend. Eight minutes from time Norwich were leading Rovers 3-2, but then they, too, gave away a spot-kick. Vic Lambden was brought down, and Ray Warren hammered the ball home for the equaliser that put Forest out of reach. Not for nearly twenty years did Norwich rise to the Second Division, and in the meantime they had to endure an application for re-election.

The draw protected Rovers' unbeaten home record in the League that had lasted for fourteen months, but they surrendered it in their very next match, in the final week of the season. It had also been in danger back in November when Plymouth Argyle, paying their first visit to Eastville for 21 years the week after winning 7-1 at home to Colchester, had deservedly led with twenty minutes left. Their goal had been scored by Maurice Tadman, whose brother George had played a few games for Rovers in the mid-1930s. In the space of five minutes Petherbridge scored and made two other goals for Bradford and Lambden to gain a 3-1 victory.

Now, three days after their narrow escape from defeat by Norwich, Rovers had their undefeated home run in the League ended by Nottingham Forest. Rovers had already lost by the odd goal of three at the City Ground on Easter Monday, after Warren had failed with a penalty in the first minute. Forest completed the double with two first-half goals despite Warren's tight hold on the free-scoring Wally Ardron, whose 36 that season set a record for the Nottingham club that still stands. Two days later, on the final Saturday, Rovers ended with a 1-1 draw at home to lowly Northampton Town, the club against which Ardron had broken the record held by Irish international 'Boy' Martin since 1937 by taking his tally to 32.

This was the Rovers team that saw out that eventful 1950-51 season: Hoyle; Bamford, Watkins (Fox missed only the last two games); Pitt, Warren, Sampson; Bush, Bradford, Lambden, Roost, Petherbridge. For the first half of the final match, Pitt was tried at inside-right, but he was not a success there and reverted to his usual right-half position after the interval.

CHAPTER 12

Clashes with Cricket

Although again missing promotion in the 1951-52 season, dropping one place in the final table to seventh – fourteen points behind Plymouth's champions – Bristol Rovers covered themselves in more Cup glory against one of the clubs from the top half of the First Division.

Their passage through the first two rounds was comfortable enough, no goals being conceded in disposing of non-League visitors from Kettering and Weymouth. Those successes gave them a plum home draw with Proud Preston, who, however, were without their main attraction, Tom Finney, the England winger (or centre-forward) who was one of the truly great players of his, or any other, era. Finney was out with a groin strain. Once more that quagmire of a pitch also counted very much in Rovers' favour as they again kept their goal intact and scored twice, even though they had spent £8,000 on the pitch since the previous season in an attempt to bring about some improvement.

As much as Finney's absence and the state of the pitch contributed to the outcome, it could also be said that it hinged on referee Chadwick's change of mind after at first pointing to the penalty spot. Rovers were leading by a Bradford goal, but having to contend with increasing Preston pressure, when Ken Horton – usually Finney's partner on the field as well as working with him in the plumbing business – fell heavily under challenge. Rovers' protests persuaded the referee from Leicester to consult a linesman, as a result of which he gave a free-kick just outside the area instead of the penalty, and this presented no problem to the home defence. North End's chairman was adamant that the offence occurred inside the area. What was more, his opposite number, Hampden Alpass, agreed with him – but also thought Rovers should have had a penalty when Bill Roost went to ground.

The disputed denial of a penalty to Preston was the focus of a complaint that the normally reticent Tom Finney – one of soccer's gentlemen – made about being misquoted in the Press. 'Although I did not play in the match,' he wrote in his book *Finney on Football*, 'I was a spectator at Eastville when North End were beaten after having strong claims for a penalty kick rejected. On the day after the game I read in a Sunday newspaper of an alleged interview I had given a reporter in the Bristol Rovers boardroom. During that interview (which, believe me, never happened) I ostensibly said: "Preston North End did not deserve to be given that penalty kick; we did deserve to lose the match." Imagine my position at Preston! People called me all sorts of names, saying that I was guilty of sour grapes simply because I had not been playing in the match, and, no matter how I denied all knowledge of the interview, the old saying about where there's smoke there's fire was applied – and I was in trouble. This was obviously a case of mistaken identity. It must have been, because I had never entered the Bristol Rovers boardroom.

'Something had to be done. I did not expect the newspaper concerned to retract the story, so I consulted my solicitor. I rang the newspaper editor and did get the "concession" of an apology, yet even then I was told that the reporter who had "interviewed" me was still prepared to swear he had quoted me in good faith, and that I had been in the boardroom. On that occasion it was probably a genuine mistake. At other times there can be no excuses for manufactured quotes, and stories which are made up.'

The possibility that Preston could at least force a replay remained until Vic Lambden eased the worries of the majority in the 32,000 crowd by scoring Rovers' second goal in the second half. Ray Warren said that 'local pride and team spirit pulled us through', on a day when other shock results eliminated Manchester United, Blackpool, the previous season's losing finalists, and very nearly holders Newcastle, who were 1-2 down at home to Aston Villa nine minutes from time, but then scored three times. Only half the First Division clubs remained to contest the next round.

For Bristol Rovers that fourth round was a sad anti-climax. They went into it straight from a home League defeat by Plymouth, who were described by Bert Tann as 'the best Division Three side I've seen this season', and lost again, by the same 1-2 score, away to Southend United, then just below mid-table in the Southern Section, but only two places below Rovers in the final table. Again there was a contentious penalty incident. Geoff Bradford called it 'the worst case of a referee refusing to give a penalty I can ever remember,' adding: 'The ball was running loose in Southend's penalty area and I had only to tap it into the net, but the goalkeeper put his arms around me and held me back as the ball was cleared.'

All the goals of that Essex tie came in the second half, from Les Stubbs and Jack French to the one by Bradford. When Harry Warren was asked if this was the Southend club's finest achievement since he had taken over as their manager in 1940, he replied: 'No, I would place it second to the day we persuaded Wilf Copping to come over from Belgium to be trainer to the team.' It was the first time Southend had reached the fifth round since 1926, when they had been beaten by an only goal at home to Nottingham Forest, the club French was soon to join. Although they again failed at Roots Hall, losing to Second Division Sheffield United after leading at half-time, they had the consolation of another healthy addition to their financial coffers.

During their early League games that season, Bristol Rovers tried a couple of players who were to have contrasting fortunes with the club. One was

Barrie Meyer, newly aged eighteen, who the previous autumn had made the first two of what were to be some 150 first-team appearances; the other Len Pickard, not far off 27, a former Barnstaple amateur known at Eastville as 'Professor'. Pickard was given only four League chances before following an even more sterile short stay at Bristol City with two seasons as Bradford Park Avenue's top scorer.

In only his third game for the Yorkshire club Pickard, a Devon Boys captain and a noted sprinter before entering professional football, scored four goals against Accrington Stanley. The opening for him at Park Avenue came because Norman Kirkman, who had only recently been appointed manager there, remembered being impressed when playing against him in a reserve match while a full-back at Southampton. From Bradford, Pickard returned to the West Country with Bath City, afterwards going back to his home county as Barnstaple's player-manager. At Bath he joined two other former Rovers reserve players, Doug Hayward and Dick Chappell.

Hayward, born in the same Shropshire village as Gordon Richards, the champion jockey, guested for Bristol City during the war. He played only once in Rovers' League side, as deputy for Pitt, before moving to Newport County, for whose second team he scored four goals in his first Welsh League match. He also became a player-manager, with Frome Town, after leaving Bath, then became manager at Weston-super-Mare.

Barrie Meyer, in a 2-0 home victory against his home-town team Bournemouth on 7 October 1950, and Len Pickard, in a 3-3 draw with Shrewsbury Town, also at Eastville, on 25 August 1951, both scored on their first-team debut for Rovers. Meyer, a schoolboy and boys' club international forward, was given permission to train at Bournemouth's ground as an amateur, and he had hopes of following two of his uncles who had played for the club in League football.

Later, however, Meyer was with the Sneyd Park team in Bristol amateur soccer when Rovers spotted him. He showed what a fine prospect he was by the manner of the goal with which he celebrated his entry into their senior side, one worthy of a seasoned professional. He beat centre-half Gripton, rounded left-back Barry, drew out goalkeeper Bird, and then neatly slotted the ball into the net. His parents, who had travelled up from Bournemouth, could scarcely contain their delight, even though it was their home club on the receiving end.

But Meyer was in the Rovers team that day only because Bradford was unavailable. Although he gave another fine display in a defeat of Swindon on Eastville's newly laid pitch, when recalled soon after the start of the next season, opportunities for him were rare around that time, with National Service intervening. Not until Rovers' first season in the Second Division was he able to have a decent run in the first team.

Then, however, came the complication of Meyer also having a county cricket career as a wicketkeeper with Gloucestershire. It was this that eventually led to his leaving Eastville. Some of the first cracks in the joining of professional soccer and cricket careers – and also in the 'family' bond of which Rovers were so proud – developed from a dispute into which Meyer and goalkeeper Ron Nicholls (in the Gloucestershire team as a batsman,) were drawn with the football club. Both had to leave because they gave cricket priority, but, as Rovers were at pains to point out, their transfers involved no fees 'in conformance with our declared policy'.

This clash of interests came to the boil early in August 1958. Bert Tann had complained bitterly the previous autumn when Nicholls, his first-choice goalkeeper, had continued his cricket with Gloucestershire for a month after the soccer season had started. The following April, Tann had made something of a rod for his own back by releasing Meyer and Nicholls for cricket duty three weeks before the Rovers' final match. As preparations began for the 1958-59 season, the manager and his directors decided to take a firm stand. In the manager's words:

'We cannot allow this situation to continue. After all, we pay them the bulk of their income, and their first loyalty should be to us. If I allowed them to report to us when they liked it would be most unfair to our other players, who report on time and carry out all the arduous pre-season training and the early-season programme of two matches a week. Why should Nicholls and Meyer be treated any differently? I have never quarrelled with anyone who sought to make two careers, but they can't have all of one and a bit of the other when the other plays the bulk of their wages. They have lost their sense of proportion towards the two games.'

Meyer, who had just been awarded his county cap, was completing an impressive first full season as Gloucestershire's wicketkeeper and had good reason to be contemplating a long and successful cricket career. Nicholls, also looking to the longer term, was equally intent on safeguarding the regular place with the county he had gained the previous year, when he had been capped after scoring 1,000 runs in a season for the first of what were to be fifteen times (he topped 2,000 in 1962). Their decision to put cricket first was theirs alone. Harold Thomas, the Gloucestershire club's secretary, emphasised that no pressure had been brought to bear on either player.

The unrepentant pair were playing against Sussex at Hove on the day, 5 August, when the other Rovers players reported back for training at Weston-super-Mare. Next morning, the new deadline given Nicholls and Meyer having expired, Bert Tann announced that Rovers were prepared to receive offers for both of them. 'We have decided to take a stand,' he said. 'Last year I was not too happy about Nicholls' late arrival at Eastville. He is a goalkeeper, but Meyer, as an inside-forward, has far more need to be match fit.

As a club we will do all we can to meet our players' wishes, but these two have made their choice. They have ignored the football club.'

Within a week Nicholls was transferred to Cardiff City in exchange for John Frowen, a centre-half or full-back. Nicholls reached an agreement not to report for training at Ninian Park until after the end of the county cricket season. Ten days later Meyer was offloaded to Plymouth Argyle, with John Timmins, a young defender who had started out with Wolves, moving in the opposite direction. Nicholls continued to live in the Bristol area, at Filton, and Peter Doherty, then Bristol City's manager, readily agreed to allow him to train at Ashton Gate while his wife Pat was in a nursing home expecting their first baby. She gave birth to a son, Laurie, and Nicholls afterwards made the daily train journey to Cardiff to join his new clubmates in training there.

Nicholls, Sharpness born, first became interested in cricket while a pupil at the Whaddon Secondary School in Cheltenham, and he was only thirteen when he first went to the County Ground in Bristol for coaching under the supervision of George Emmett, the Gloucestershire batsman who captained the county and played once for England against Don Bradman's invincible Australian tourists of 1948. At soccer, Nicholls was in the Gloucestershire youth team in 1953 before being called up for National Service, during which he kept goal for an Army amateur side and Hampshire while stationed at Aldershot. He also played as an amateur for Fulham.

Bert Tann watched Nicholls in several games with the London club's reserve team in the Football Combination, and, although Rovers already had four goalkeepers on their books (Howard Radford, Bob Anderson, Ray Chandler and David Tomkins), Rovers' manager was sufficiently impressed with what he saw to have no doubts about signing him – on amateur forms in July 1954, then as a professional in the November.

Nicholls, whose brother Edward, an inside-forward, was also with Rovers as an amateur, but only in their junior teams, made the first of just over 70 first-team appearances for the Eastville club on the last day of the following year, in a 4-2 home win against promotion-bound Sheffield Wednesday. In his second game the next Saturday he kept a clean sheet in another of the FA Cup shocks the Rovers sprang, this one against Manchester United, leaders of the First Division. More about that shortly.

The 50 or so games in which Nicholls guarded Cardiff's goal also included a prized scalp. The newly promoted Welsh club inflicted one of the few defeats Spurs suffered along their path to their League and Cup double of 1960-61. And in almost 40 League games for Bristol City that followed, Nicholls helped in a double defeat of Bristol Rovers in 1962-63 before winding up with Cheltenham Town. Cricket, however, was always his first love, and it was to concentrate on the summer game that he decided, at the age of 32, to end fifteen years of sharing it with soccer by hanging up his football boots. This he did after the 1965-66 season – much to the disappointment of Bobby Etheridge, another Bristol City and Gloucestershire player, who had not long taken over as Cheltenham's player-manager.

'I shall be sorry to leave football after such a long time,' said Nicholls, 'but it is a decision I have planned for some while. I feel I can still play county cricket for a number of years.' So he did – for ten, in fact. Having made his first-class debut at Gloucester in 1951, in a match Derbyshire drew with their last pair together, he finally stepped down in 1975. He had been called out of retirement with John Mortimore, an all-rounder who played for England, as Gloucestershire ran short of experienced players. The three appearances he made that year, each in Bristol, took him to a total of 534 in the County Championship, the fourth highest in Gloucestershire's history, and to an aggregate of 23,607 runs. He was only 60 when he died at Cheltenham during the summer of 1994. Less than a fortnight earlier he had captained the President's XI during the Cheltenham club's cricket week.

Barrie Meyer also ended his Football League career with Bristol City, whom he joined from Newport County after only a short stay at Plymouth. And he left them in the grand manner, signing off with a hat-trick in a 6-3 defeat of Southend United in April 1963. That gave him a nicely rounded tally of 100 goals in 228 League games – but a one-season reprieve after another clash with cricket was required to make it possible. On learning that he was on City's free transfer list, he went to Ashton Gate to discuss his future as soon as Gloucestershire's home match with Hampshire was rained off in May 1962.

'We couldn't afford to pay his wages from July to September while he was playing cricket,' said Fred Ford, who was then City's manager, 'but I told him that if he wasn't fixed up by the time his cricket finished he could come back here and get himself fit for football again. If he reaches full fitness, recaptures his old form, and we have room for an inside-forward at that time, then he will be signed on again.'

So Meyer had one more season with City before moving out of the League with Glastonbury. After that, the cricket career with Gloucestershire for this Frank Sinatra fan who combined a love of American musicals with modern jazz lasted for four more seasons, making fifteen in all. He ended his first-class playing career with over 5,000 runs and 826 dismissals (707 caught, 119 stumped) to his name, then briefly worked as a salesman before becoming an umpire. For many seasons he was a respected and popular man in a white coat at both county and Test level.

Bristol Rovers were not alone in finding the cricket-soccer issue a real bugbear in 1958. Gloucestershire expressed considerable concern when their players reported back for pre-season practice without three of their four footballers. Soccer training with Bristol City prevented Etheridge, Meyer and

David Smith, an opening bowler who was soon to play for England, from getting to the County Ground until the afternoon; Nicholls was available there each day apart from the only morning each week on which, as a goalkeeper, he was required for football training. Harold Thomas and George Emmett visited Ashton Gate to discuss the problem as it affected Etheridge and Smith, who for a while were City's left-wing pair. The response of manager Peter Doherty was to say that 'we want to maintain our friendly relations with the cricketing fraternity of the city', but the situation concerning those two players was quickly to resolve itself in any case. Soccer became the priority for Etheridge, and Smith was to have only one more season at Ashton Gate before moving to Millwall.

Although Barrie Meyer added only five League games with Rovers in 1951-52 to his couple the previous season, he was again on target in a 4-0 home win against Crystal Palace. That lifted the Eastville club to second in the table, on goal-average behind Plymouth, just two days after visitors from Aldershot had been beaten 5-1. In view of those scoring sprees it was ironic that in their very next game Tann's men were given the slow handclap. Fans were peeved to see Watford, who had had to seek re-election, quicker on the ball and into the tackle in ending Rovers' unbeaten home record that season with September just eight days old.

Before that month was out, however, Rovers were restored to better mood by two impressive away performances. A win at Ashton Gate was snatched away by an Atyeo equaliser so late that thousands who left early missed it, and a week later promotion-bound Plymouth suffered what was to be their only home defeat of the season. The margin against Arygle could have been bigger than 2-1 but for a most untypical miss by Vic Lambden. He broke away in his own half, dribbled round Bill Shortt, a Welsh international goalkeeper, but then shot wide four yards from an unguarded net with no other defender near enough to challenge.

In the next match a similar solo run by Geoff Bradford did produce a goal, one that earned a point at home to Norwich City, who had taken advantage of Rovers' victory down in Devon to dislodge Plymouth from the leadership. It proved the only way to unlock a packed defence when Bradford, having gained possession just inside his own half, cleverly warded off three challenges as he went clear to score with a shot that flew in off an upright. Bradford promptly came to the rescue again with two late goals in five minutes to salvage a draw with Northampton. Rovers were so inconsistent at this stage that they went more than two and a half months without a home win until suddenly cutting loose with a Petherbridge-inspired 5-0 defeat of Brighton in which Harry Bamford was also outstanding.

In the meantime, another newcomer was introduced into their team, though his League debut coincided with another setback at Southend. This was Howard Radford, a Welshman from the village of Penrhiwceibr in Mid-Glamorgan. Radford had first kept goal for the first team in a friendly with the Dutch club Haarlem at Eastville on Whit Monday that year, in one of the matches arranged as part of the Festival of Britain celebrations. He was signed as an amateur after that game, then turned professional after playing once for the Colts and twice for the Reserves in the Football Combination. Radford's elevation to the League side came within two more months. After being beaten twice by Southend's Jack French and twice saved by Geoff Fox's clearances – when other shots caught him out of position (on one of those occasions the spinning ball ran along the goal-line and hit the inside of a post before being hooked clear by the full-back) – he was retained for only one more match. Rovers lost it, at home to Bournemouth, and Radford was returned to the Reserves, where his progress was held up by injury.

Radford did not establish himself until after the car crash that put Bert Hoyle out of the game. Although on the small side for a goalkeeper at 5ft 8in, and having to contend with several rivals, fitness and health problems over the ensuing nine seasons, he made in the region of 250 League and Cup appearances before being himself forced out by the recurrence of a knee injury.

For Rovers' first three seasons in the Second Division Radford was their first choice. He was then dogged by misfortune to such an extent that, hoping a change of club would bring him a change of luck, he put in a transfer request that Bert Tann refused to consider until he had regained full fitness. He had to have operations for his tonsils and a cartilage, then broke a thumb in only his second comeback game, and after that enforced lay-off found himself back in the Colts. It said much for his perseverance that he played in all but five of Rovers' 42 League games in his final season, 1961-62, before injury struck again. After that he became a licensee at several hostelries, in the Bristol area and in Devon, before working as a steward at the Chudleigh Conservative Club, then as a security guard at British Aerospace.

On one occasion when Radford was out injured, with a twisted left knee, he was replaced for one match, at Derby, by 'Harry' Sinclair (his given first name was Harvey). Sinclair was hurriedly signed from Yeovil Town 'within the framework of our No Buy, No Sell policy' when Bert Tann was in the sudden dilemma of having no other goalkeeper ready to hand. Only two days earlier Sinclair had played against Rovers, for Yeovil Reserves in a match against the Eastville club's Colts. He conceded three goals in Rovers' defeat at the Baseball Ground – and three in his only previous League game, for Leicester City in a 4-3 victory over Grimsby. A week earlier Rovers had come away from Filbert Street beaten 2-7.

In the 1951-52 season, Rovers maintained a place in the top half of the table despite winning only three of a dozen matches after defeating their City neighbours in the January return at Eastville. That lean sequence included a revenge victory for Plymouth, who by then were firmly back at the top, and a narrow failure at Norwich on a cold February day when crowds around the country stood bareheaded while a one-minute silence was observed in memory of King George VI. The players wore black armlets, and the hymn *Abide With Me* and the National Anthem were sung.

As before, Rovers got back on track with a five-goal flurry, in a home match with Gillingham that was also distinguished by the fact that Bamford and Fox were in their full-back partnership for the 200th time. Two days later, on Easter Monday at Eastville, Rovers went one better with a 6-0 crushing of Colchester. This was the other game in which Vic Lambden scored four goals (after one, eleven, fourteen and 34 minutes). Victory by such a margin was sweet revenge for the Rovers' narrow defeat at Colchester on the Good Friday, after Bradford had given them an early lead, the winning goal having come from a disputed penalty two minutes from the end.

The extent to which Rovers were then relying for their goals on Lambden and Bradford – who scored the two others in that big win against Colchester – was amply demonstrated by the fact that between them they totalled more than 60 that season. Lambden led the way with 29 in the League and four in the Cup; Bradford scored 26 and three respectively. On the final day both were again on the mark in a home draw with Exeter City, Lambden's goal taking him to 100 for the club in Cup and League, and Bradford's giving him an overall tally of 50.

George Petherbridge was the only other Rovers player to get into double figures that season, helped to his bag of fourteen with the four goals he put into Torquay's net. He was an ever-present along with Geoff Fox, Jackie Pitt and Peter Sampson. Bradford missed only one match, Lambden two. Skipper Warren was absent five times, those being the only games for which Rovers were without him in five consecutive seasons from 1948 to 1953. Injury kept him out for just five more the following season before, having entered his 37th year, he finally had his hold on the centre-half position broken towards the end of the ninth post-war campaign.

The only player not so far mentioned who got into the Rovers' first team in 1951-52 was Andy Micklewright, a Birmingham youth who scored his one League goal for the club in a 5-1 home win against Walsall on the last Monday evening of April. He made only one senior appearance, his eighth in all, during the next season in which Rovers won promotion, and only three for their City neighbours when they also went up in 1954-55. That gave him the distinction of having played for both Bristol clubs in seasons when they were champions of the Third Division South.

Micklewright made up for his lack of opportunities at Eastville by playing almost 40 League games for City and more than 100 for Swindon Town

before having his last few appearances with Exeter City and then going into
the Southern League with Nuneaton Borough.

Geoff Bradford with the solitary
England cap he earned, against
Denmark in 1955

BRISTOL ROVERS F.C. 1949-50.
Back row, left to right. F. McCourt. G. Fox. J. Weare. R. Warren. H. Bamford. J. Pitt.
Front row, left to right. B. Bush. L. Hodges. V. Lambden. T. James. J. Watling.

George Petherbridge, right-winger, made 452 League appearances for Rovers in a one-club League career

George Petherbridge

'Best Wishes, Ray Mabbutt.' Mabbutt inscribed his signature over his chest. This game was at Charlton (April 1961)

Rovers players line up for the camera in 1965-66: From left: Parsons, Stone, Hillard, Jones G, Munro, Oldfield, Davis, Mabbutt, Brown, McCrohan, Frude, Hall, Jones R, Hamilton, Petts, Weller, Jarman, Biggs

Welsh international David 'Dai' Ward played 175 League games for Rovers and scored 90 goals

Right-winger Harold Jarman made
over 450 League appearances for
Rovers, scoring 127 goals

Newcastle score at Eastville in the FA Cup replay (February 1951)

Heads are lowered in memory of Harry Bamford in this match against Bristlol City at Eastville (November 1958)

Barrie Meyer started his football career at Rovers before playing for Plymouth, Newport and Bristol City. He was an accomplished cricketer and a long-serving Test umpire

Rovers' skipper Ray Warren leads out a mascot.
Warren played 450 League games for Rovers and was a one-club man

Bert Tann and his players relive one of Rovers' matches around 1950

WILLIAM ROOST, Bristol Rovers

Inside-forward Bill Roost scored 49 League goals from 177 League appearances for Rovers

BRISTOL ROVERS FOOTBALL CLUB LTD.   1950-51 SEASON.

This Rovers side reached the FA Cup quarter-final in 1951, after eleven pulsating ties, before losing 1-3 to eventual Cup winners Newcastle United in a replay

Tommy Briggs scored seven successive goals in Blackburn's 8-3 win over Rovers in February 1955.

George Petherbridge and Rovers coach Fred Ford arrive at Temple Meads station
following their successful Football Association tour of South Africa in 1956

A perfect action shot of me scoring one of three come back goals with a flying header. It was seconds later when I lay winded on the ground, that the cheering suddenly stopped.

This flying header by Geoff Bradford was one of three on his comeback match against Stoke City, in April 1954

Local boy Ray Graydon was discovered by Bert Tann and later went on to fame with Aston Villa. He followed Ian Holloway as a Bristol-born manager of Rovers after their move from Eastville

Bill Dodgin Snr managed Rovers
from 1969 to 1971

The famous Rovers forward line from the mid-1950s:
Petherbridge, Biggs, Bradford, Ward, Hooper

Harry Bamford, Rovers' right-back, ended his Eastville career with
5 League goals from 486 games

Bill Roost scored twice against Ipswich (August 1949)

BROUGH FLETCHER . .

Brough Fletcher managed Bristol Rovers from 1938 to 1949 before handing over to Bert Tann

Rovers' Third Division (South) championship-winning squad 1952-53.
Players only: Pitt, Bamford, Fox, Lambden, Hoyle, Sampson, Radford, Bush, McIlvenny,
Petherbridge, Warren, Bradford, Roost, Watling

Only three Mabbutts have ever
played in the Football League.
Father Ray (pictured) and
younger son Gary played for
Rovers. Elder son Kevin played
for Bristol City

Rovers goalkeeper Bernard Hall in action before his accidental collision with Middlesbrough's John O'Rourke on New Year's Eve, 1966, which ended his career

The Great Man, Bert Tann, represented in this oil painting.
His full managerial League record with Bristol Rovers was:
801 games, 331 wins, 193 draws, 277 defeats, 855 points.
(Source: *Bristol Rovers: Definitive History 1883-2003*, by Mike Jay and Stephen Byrne)

Rovers' Ian Hamilton (far right) shoots at goal against Wrexham (May 1963)

My colleague John Coe, pronounced 'Coey', who reported on Bristol football for so many years

City and Rovers mascots take up arms to the amusement of the crowd

Jackie Pitt

Right-half Jackie Pitt played 467 League games for Rovers, from which he scored 16 goals

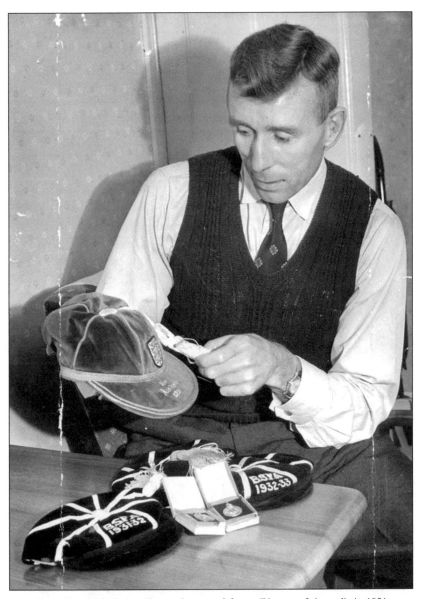

Harry Bamford admires the cap he earned for an FA tour of Australia in 1951

Centre-forward Vic Lambden
scored 117 League goals for Rovers
in 269 appearances

Vic Lambden

This Rovers side reached the FA Cup quarter-finals for the second time
while Bert Tann was manager

Bristol Rovers FC Season 1957–58
Back Row: L. Edwards, P. Sampson, N. Sykes, H. Radford, D. Hale, H. Bamford, B. Doyle.
Front Row: J. Watling, G. Petherbridge, A. Biggs, G. Bradford (Capt.), D. Ward, B. Meyer, P. Hooper, J. Pitt.

The way we were. Rattles, scarves and rosettes have largely disappeared
in favour of replica shirts. Rovers fans in 1959 at Ashton Gate

Prolific Alfie Biggs graced Rovers' forward
line from 1953 to 1967, spending one season
in between at Preston. He scored 178 goals
in 426 League games for Rovers

Robert 'Bobby' Stanley Jones played over 400 games and scored more than 100 goals
for Rovers in two spells

The famous Cup-tie at Newcastle in 1951. Rovers full-back Geoff Fox clears the ball under pressure from United winger Tommy Walker

Peter Hooper was a left-winger with a rocket shot. In 297 League matches between 1954 and 1962 he scored 101 goals

Goalkeeper Esmond Million takes a breather in a match at Millwall.
He played 38 League games for Rovers before his career ended
under a cloud due to a bribery scandal in April 1963

CHAPTER 13

Second Division for the First Time

After losing 0-3 at Millwall on 13 September 1952, Bristol Rovers went through 27 League games without defeat until 21 March 1953, when they conceded two goals without reply at Reading. That impregnable sequence was the springboard from which they launched themselves into the Second Division of the Football League for the first time in their history.

It also included their record League win, 7-0 against Brighton at Eastville on 29 November, six goals coming in a second-half during which there was a snowstorm. That margin of victory has since been equalled twice, against Swansea Town in October 1954, then back in the Third Division against Shrewsbury Town in March 1964.

Another landmark was reached on the first Saturday of January in 1953, when Rovers won 2-0 at home to Walsall. That was their eleventh consecutive League victory, breaking the Third Division record of ten shared by two clubs who were in the Northern Section, Chesterfield (during the 1930s) and Doncaster Rovers (in the first post-war season of 1946-47). It has since been exceeded by Reading's thirteen in 1985-86. The Second Division best of fourteen was set by Manchester United in 1904-05, then equalled by Bristol City in 1905-06 and Preston North End in 1950-51. In 1888-89, Preston were unbeaten in all 22 games of the first League season, winning eighteen and drawing four, and also won all their five FA Cup-ties in completing the double at the first opportunity. In 1893-94, Liverpool carried off the Second Division championship by going through their 28 matches without defeat (22 wins, six draws), but lost to Bolton Wanderers in the third round of the Cup.

At the time of Rovers' undefeated run, the League record was held by Burnley. After losing their first three games of 1920-21, the Turf Moor club went through 30 games (21 wins, nine draws) before they were beaten again on their way to the First Division title – from 6 September to 26 March – when Manchester City stopped their gallop with a 3-0 win at Maine Road. Burnley were knocked out of the Cup's third round by the same score at Hull in the meantime. That was on 19 February, after two dozen League matches and two Cup-ties unbeaten. Twice they gained six victories in a row.

In the old First Division, Preston and Sunderland both had thirteen successive wins in 1891-92, a total Tottenham matched by adding the eleven of their flying start in their double season of 1960-61 to those they gained in their last two games of 1959-60. Since then, Arsenal have chalked up fourteen in a row in the Premiership (the last thirteen of 2001-02 and the first one of 2002-03). And from May 2003 to October 2004 – including the whole of one season in which they won 26 and drew twelve of 38 matches – they exceeded Nottingham Forest's unbeaten run of 42 Division One games from November 1977 to December 1978 by falling only one short of 50 in losing to Manchester United at Old Trafford.

So much for the mass of statistics. Bristol Rovers did not really expect to be indulging in any of them as they embarked upon their 1952-53 season. 'We had no strong thoughts that this was to be our year,' said Geoff Bradford, 'but we had knitted into a useful unit and the Cup run to the sixth round had helped to build a good spirit among the players.' The start was uneventful, and certainly not encouraging. A half-time deficit was turned into a 2-1 home win that Warren clinched with a penalty against Shrewsbury Town, who were to finish the season having to seek re-election with Walsall. Then came defeat by a single goal in a midweek match at Torquay that sank Rovers as low as tenth in the first published table. After that, however, it was very much their year, four successive victories promptly propelling them to the first place that was to be so familiar to them.

The week after Bradford had done all the scoring at home to Torquay on the first day of September – chalking up the first of his dozen first-team hat-tricks for Rovers – they first reached the top, on goal-average from Brighton, with a win at Colchester, also by 3-0. Although they then slipped to second with the defeat by the same margin at Millwall, they went back into the lead on the following Monday evening by completing the double over the Layer Road club. Two days later Millwall regained top spot on goal-average with a scoreless draw at home to Aldershot, but at the end of that week Rovers were first again, despite dropping a point as Bristol City's visit to Eastville produced the same blank result. Millwall were unable to take advantage in losing to a lone goal at Exeter.

Rovers were now launching themselves into their undefeated run, yet goal-average was still the deciding factor once more over Brighton, who went in front with a 4-2 home win against Exeter the evening before Rovers dislodged them by winning 3-2 at Watford. This time Tann's team were at the head of the heap to stay. In consecutive weeks their closest challengers were Norwich City, Southend United, Northampton Town, then Norwich again, and the gap widened to four points when Rovers scored their seven goals against Brighton.

That record victory was gained with this team: Hoyle; Bamford, Fox; Pitt, Warren, Sampson; McIlvenny, Roost, Lambden, Bradford, Petherbridge. It was the sixth in the winning run Rovers took to twelve in the League before being held to a 1-1 draw in their return match with Millwall. They embarked upon that successful spell on 18 October with a home win over Leyton Orient. The first of their two goals was the first to be scored for the club by

John McIlvenny, a 22-year-old winger newly signed after a season as a regular member of Cheltenham Town's team. The sequence ended after a 4-0 win at Gillingham on 17 January in which Geoff Fox netted the first of his two League goals, but it had been interrupted the week before by defeat at Huddersfield in the third round of the FA Cup. Rovers had reached that stage in successive seasons for the first time by narrowly knocking out Orient (in a replay) and Peterborough United.

McIlvenny, who had played for his home club Hinckley Athletic, and then Stafford Rangers, before first attempting to break into League football with West Bromwich Albion, made 80 appearances in Rovers' first team. He then left to turn out in almost as many for Reading, but that season in which he gained a championship medal was the only one of his seven at Eastville in which he was a regular choice – and even then he missed almost a dozen games. For the rest of the time he was on the fringe, though still a useful man to call upon when injuries created a vacancy. After leaving the League scene he did what so many ex-footballers did in those days – became the licensee of a public house.

Towards the end of their winning run along their path to promotion, Bristol Rovers were as many as nine points clear of the field. They were still six ahead on the February day when Bert Hoyle was so seriously injured in a car crash on his way home from the goalless draw with Bristol City that was watched by an Ashton Gate crowd of more than 35,000. With the unbeaten League run then 22 games old, and seventeen more to be played, Howard Radford was left as the only professional goalkeeper on Rovers' books, so another break had to be made in the No Buy, No Sell policy to obtain another one as cover. The man they turned to was Durham-born Bob Anderson, whose wife's parents lived near the Eastville ground. The fee of £2,000 handed to Crystal Palace was the first Rovers had paid since signing Hoyle, and chairman Hampden Alpass was quick to emphasise that 'the move represents no fundamental change in the views of the board'.

With Radford stepping into the goalkeeping breach, Rovers moved a further point in front despite again failing to score in a draw at Exeter, thanks to a 3-4 defeat for Northampton at Crystal Palace. And a week later Rovers were back to having a lead of nine, when Bristol City did them a good turn by winning at Northampton. Rovers themselves were rediscovering their scoring touch with two goals apiece for Bradford and Lambden in a 5-2 caning of Coventry at Eastville. In becoming the first to beat Northampton on their own ground that season, City also displaced the Cobblers as the closest challengers. They had zoomed up from mid-table with a run of success that would have had them firmly in line for the title if Rovers had not been setting such a hot pace. City's turn would come, but not just yet. This time they were to slip back to finish fifth.

Rovers also wobbled as the winning post loomed on the horizon, making them thankful to have built up such a big advantage. Draws at home to Northampton and at Orient were followed by a 3-0 win against Ipswich at Eastville. Then came the defeat at Reading that ended the unbeaten run three short of Burnley's record. Bristol City drew 4-4 at home to QPR that afternoon, after being 1-3 down at half-time, to reduce the gap to six points, but Rovers revived with a home win over Bournemouth and a 3-1 Good Friday success at Swindon to go eight points clear with eight games to go. City, meanwhile, played the third of four successive draws.

Now, however, came a particularly bad patch. Defeat at Southend, on a day when Manchester United introduced a sixteen-year-old named Duncan Edwards to League football against Cardiff, was the first of four setbacks in six matches from which only two points were taken – in draws at Newport and Norwich. On Easter Monday, despite having gone into special training, Rovers lost their unbeaten home record as Swindon gained 2-1 revenge, and in their very next outing at Eastville five days later they conceded three goals to Watford without reply. Two more days of toning-up at Bognor failed to have the desired effect before next facing Brighton at Hove. Another defeat by the odd goal of three cut their lead to just two points, from Northampton but with a game in hand, under the handicap of Rovers losing their scorer, Paddy Leonard, at Brighton through injury. With the side so settled, there were few other first-team chances for Leonard, a former Bath City player, before he rejoined Frank McCourt at Colchester.

Rovers won only one of their four remaining games after that reverse against Brighton, but the day they won it was also the day they became assured of the title. Bradford was not certain to play until shortly before the kick-off because of an ankle injury suffered at Norwich, and he attended the East Anglian club's ground for treatment before returning to Eastville with the rest of the squad on the morning of the match with Newport County that was to prove so decisive. Even then, with Barrie Meyer standing by to deputise, Bradford needed a pain-killing injection before being declared fit. And how thankful Rovers were that he was, for he responded with another of his hat-tricks in a 3-1 win, his three goals (all headers) taking him to a club record 34 for the season, one of them in the Cup.

Northampton, winners at Colchester, were then still in second place, but they had only one more match to play, as against the Rovers' two, and were a couple of points behind with an inferior goal-average. The sole remaining club with the remotest chance of preventing Rovers reaching the Second Division for the first time were third-placed Millwall. After the final whistle had blown at Eastville Tann's men and their fans had to wait for the outcome of the Lions' home game with Brighton, which had started a quarter of an hour later, to be absolutely sure of the championship. It was just before five o'clock when that result came through – a 1-1 draw, for which Millwall were indebted to full-back Alex Jardine's successful penalty-kick. Even if Millwall had won they would have been required to do some exceptional scoring in their two remaining matches to prevail on goal-average – and then only if Rovers had failed to take another point (which so nearly happened).

So, promotion assured, thousands swarmed across the sunlit Eastville ground to acclaim their heroes. They repeatedly bade goodnight to Irene, blissfully regardless of the various theories about how this sentimental ditty became Rovers' theme song, and demanded speeches from chairman Hampden Alpass, manager Tann and skipper Warren. Bert Hoyle, who by now had made a good recovery but had been advised not to play in League football again, sportingly took that timely opportunity to carry a collecting box round the ground to help swell the benefit fund for Geoff Fox and Bryan Bush.

Rovers went scoreless through their last two games, picking up a point at Aldershot but losing by an only goal to Crystal Palace at Selhurst Park, where 'Gentleman Bob' Anderson, who had displaced Radford after the Easter Monday defeat by Swindon, was made captain for the day against his old club.

These were the final leading positions in 1952-53's Third South table:

	P	W	D	L	F	A	Pts
BRISTOL ROVERS	46	26	12	8	92	46	64
Millwall	46	24	14	8	82	44	62
Northampton	46	26	10	10	109	70	62
Norwich	46	25	10	11	99	55	60
Bristol City	46	22	15	9	95	61	59

Anderson kept his place for Rovers' entry into the Second Division, but soon lost it through injury. On being unable re-establish himself because of Radford's good form, he was transferred to Bristol City. This led to his having a stronger claim than Andrew Micklewright's of playing in championship winning seasons in the same division with two clubs in the same city. In 1954-55 he helped the Ashton Gate club to follow Rovers into the Second Division, but, like Hoyle and later Radford, he was to have his career prematurely ended by injury. He had begun it on a bleak note by conceding seven goals to Arsenal in his only League appearance for Middlesbrough on Good Friday in 1948, and he bowed out in another painful manner, this time literally, not long after he had completed a century of League games for Bristol's other club.

A prolapsed disc paralysed Anderson for several minutes during successive matches, and, although he resumed playing on both occasions after only a short delay, he was in and out of plaster jackets for almost three months. He was then put on a special course of weight-lifting exercises in an attempt to strengthen his back, but found a comeback beyond him. He was not retained by City at the end of 1960-61, but for a while maintained some connection with them as joint promoter and chief agent for the Supporters' Club, in addition to doing some coaching with a boys' club.

     All that had to be abandoned, however, when Anderson's condition deteriorated, necessitating an operation for the removal of the disc, with bone grafted from his hip onto his spinal cord. 'When I look back,' he said years afterwards, 'I realise what a lucky bloke I was not to be going around in a wheelchair. I might have been paralysed for life. Even now I have to go around with six of my vertebrae wired up. I'm just thankful to be in the position I'm in now.' He became an area manager with a dry-cleaning firm in Bristol before suffering a stroke in 1986, eight years before his death.

CHAPTER 14

Enter Biggs and Hooper

There was a rare midweek start to the season when Bristol Rovers began life in Division Two, and also an unusual result as they drew 4-4 at Fulham on the evening of Thursday, 20 August 1953. Bradford completed another of his hat-tricks and Geoff Fox scored his second League goal. Bobby Robson, a future England manager, was twice on target for Fulham, whose other scorers were Arthur Stevens and Johnny Haynes.

Mention of Stevens, a winger who was a familiar figure on the Fulham scene for a dozen seasons, recalls the time, five and a half years earlier, when he was said to have won an overcoat in a side bet with comedian Tommy Trinder – a director who was also chairman of the London club. It concerned Stevens scoring three goals in a 5-2 FA Cup defeat of Bristol Rovers in the fourth round at sodden Craven Cottage. According to the word that went round later, Stevens did not get the coat.

That match, watched by a crowd of just over 26,000 – which included 1,200 Rovers fans who travelled in a fleet of motor coaches – was finely balanced at half-time. Rovers were only 2-3 down after conceding two goals in the first eighteen minutes, but Stevens polished them off by completing the first of his career's three hat-tricks in the 55th and 86th minutes.

Stevens had again been Rovers' bogy man in the Cup when they were paired with Fulham in the sixth round in 1958. A few weeks earlier Fulham had spent £15,000 on Maurice Cook, the Watford centre-forward, but he was ineligible to play for them in the Cup that season. Stevens, then 37, was therefore recalled to deputise, and he scored twice in Fulham's 3-1 home win. After that he was out of the side once more until the semi-final, in which he scored in a 2-2 draw with Manchester United at Villa Park, and also in the 3-5 replay defeat at Highbury.

In reaching that quarter-final against Fulham, Bristol Rovers claimed another prized First Division scalp by beating Burnley 3-2 in a replay at Turf Moor, despite having to field a makeshift forward line led by Norman Sykes, who scored their first goal, and then winning a seven-goal thriller with Bristol City at Ashton Gate. City were convinced that Geoff Bradford's deciding goal was offside, but this was how he saw it: 'We were under pressure when Dai Ward broke away with me on his right. Mike Thresher (City's left-back) was covering me, but as Dai went on he had to leave me and go to Dai. I had kept behind Dai all the time, and the linesman was right with me. Dai slipped the ball to me and I hit it past Bob Anderson as he came out to meet me. I know I wasn't offside.'

Bradford had only one more hat-trick in him at that stage of his career, but they were very much in fashion for him in his first Second Division season. By the end of October he had no fewer than five to his name, adding three for Rovers to that one at Fulham, and notching another in the 4-0 victory for an FA team against the RAF at Tottenham. He did all the scoring in a victory at Brentford (a few weeks before Tommy Lawton left that struggling club to return to the First Division with Arsenal), made a three-goal switch to centre-forward in the absence of the injured Lambden in a 5-1 away win over Notts County, and earned a 3-3 draw at Luton a few days before again sparkling (but this time not scoring) as the FA defeated the Army 3-1 at Newcastle.

With twenty goals by then to his name and the season only just over two months old, Bradford was at the height of his career, firmly in line for elevation to an England place. That was when, three days after that representative game on Tyneside, he suffered the first of those two serious injuries at Plymouth. As already recalled, not until the final day of the season did he reappear in Rovers' first team – with another hat-trick.

To fill the yawning gap caused by the loss of his talisman, Bert Tann first called upon Michael Lyons, a 21-year-old Bristolian who had been given a free transfer by Bristol City. Lyons was not alone in failing to score for Rovers in a home defeat by Swansea, for whom Melvyn Charles, younger brother of John, snatched the only goal five minutes from time. Lyons was omitted after a draw at Rotherham – gained with a goal by Meyer – had left Rovers in the lowest position, fourteenth, they were to occupy all season. As had also been the case with City, there were only two League chances for Lyons at one of his other clubs, Swindon, but he found a niche at full-back, in just over 100 games, while with Bournemouth. And another niche afterwards cropped up for him back at Eastville after all. For fifteen years he was trainer of Rovers Reserves before Bath City made him their trainer-coach.

Lyons was followed as Rovers' centre-forward by a robust character from Clevedon who was always known as 'Paddy' Hale – with absolute disregard for his given first name of Denzil. He was to be converted into Ray Warren's strong and reliable successor at centre-half for most of the 120 League games he played across half-a-dozen seasons before leaving for Bath City and then going back to Clevedon Town. But for now he was a more than adequate stop-gap as an attacker. In nineteen games that season he scored a dozen goals, the first of them on his League debut on the last Saturday of November – some twenty months since his first run-out with the Reserves. It came in a 3-0 home win against Leicester City, the Second Division leaders and coming champions. Most of his other goals were particularly valuable – among them winners against Fulham, Derby County, Lincoln City and Nottingham Forest, and draw-earners against West Ham, Notts County and

Leeds United. But there were to be no more. Hale was kept too busy defending after that.

For the home game with Leeds in late February, in which Hale scored in a 1-1 draw from inside-forward, the attack was led by Peter Wilshire. A nineteen-year-old former Fairfield Grammar School boy, Wilshire had joined Rovers as an apprentice two years previously, but had only recently turned professional. Just over a week after what was to be his only League appearance, Wilshire was also at centre-forward for the Western League in a flood-lit match with an FA XI at Ashton Gate that marked the league's 60th anniversary.

Unfortunately, the weather did not co-operate for the occasion. Snow set in, and the white ball with which play started soon had to be replaced when two players standing nearby could not see where it lay. The normal brown ball then used was also difficult to spot after being passed along the ground, and twenty minutes into the second half Bristol referee Stan Vickery had no option but to abandon play in a blinding snowstorm with the FA team – which included Geoff Fox and Peter Sampson from Rovers – leading 4-0 through Bedford Jezzard, of Fulham, who scored twice; and City's John Atyeo and Jack Boxley.

Wilshire, a prolific scorer for the Rovers' junior side, was subsequently with Bristol City and Bath City before scouting for the Ashton Gate club. He had to make a special appeal to the FA to obtain a free transfer to Bath after City had listed him at £1,500, even though he had cost them nothing more than the signing-on fee and had been unable to progress beyond their Reserves.

After Hale, two other players who were to exert a big influence on Bristol Rovers' fortunes during what still stands as the most consistently successful period of their history were introduced during that first season in the Second Division. They were Alfred George Biggs, a product of the Connaught Road School in Bristol, who was to become the club's most prolific scorer behind Geoff Bradford (and to take from him the club's record for the number of goals in one season) and Peter Hooper – a left-winger possessed of good close control and a cannonball shot. Hooper arrived with the diverting distinction of having played for Kenya against Uganda while serving out there with the Army.

Biggs, who was born in the Knowle district of Bristol, was given his first senior chance, at the age of eighteen, along with two seventeen-year-old half-backs, Ian Muir and Norman Sykes. The occasion was a friendly home game with Manchester United arranged for the day of the Cup's fourth round after both clubs had been knocked out of the competition. Despite having had special beach training and brine baths at Weston-super-Mare, Rovers had been beaten at home in the third round by a Blackburn goal scored by Eddie

Quigley, once the costliest player in the game, who only a few weeks earlier Quigley had netted both goals by which Blackburn also won at Eastville in the League. Manchester United, who tried out a nineteen-year-old Irishman, Noel McFarlane, on their right wing for the friendly, had lost 3-5 at Burnley.

On the first Saturday of February, after that match with United – won by the Reds with a first-half goal from Eddie Lewis – Alfie Biggs made his League debut in a 2-1 win at Lincoln. Vic Lambden made his comeback in that match after having been out of the side since being injured against the same opponents at Eastville back in September.

Ian Muir was also introduced to League action that season, for one game, a 1-4 defeat at Hull in April, whereas Biggs kept his place for the remaining fixtures – but Norman Sykes had to wait nearly two more years for his big chance. Biggs took another season to become properly established, then in two spells with the club reached some 450 appearances and scored not far off 200 goals, with respective League figures of 424 and 178.

The tall and willowy Muir, who came from a footballing family – his grandfather played for Third Lanark, and his father John was a wing-half with Rovers between the wars – came on a free transfer from Motherwell, his home club, as an intended replacement for Ray Warren. He was mainly confined to the Reserves, which he captained, before bringing in a £200 fee from Oldham Athletic in the summer of 1957. In his one season as a regular choice, and club captain, at Boundary Park the disappointment of seeing the Latics finish just below halfway in the Third Division North, and thus consigned to the new Division Four, was offset to some extent by his picking up a Lancashire Cup winners' medal. After that he was tempted away by a bigger pay packet outside the League at Rhyl, where he spent five years before returning to Bristol to work in a shoe factory and help for a time in the running of Rovers' 'A' team.

Peter Hooper, to whom 'Josser' Watling had to give way on Rovers' left wing, was a Devonian from Bert Hoyle's part of the world at Teignmouth. Bert Tann delegated the former goalkeeper to check him out after receiving a strong recommendation in a letter received from the commanding officer of Hooper's Army unit in Hong Kong. Hoyle's verdict ('he will play for England one day') led to this crowd-pleasing winger being snapped up after only one trial. Hooper was not to win that forecast cap, but he played for the Football League against the League of Ireland, at Leeds in 1957, and in the course of just over 300 games – 163 of them in succession from October 1957 to August 1961 – became one of the select six players to score a century of goals for Rovers in the League (101 to be exact). He was the club's leading scorer with twenty in the 1960-61 season.

In a Boxing Day match with Bury in 1956 Hooper completed a hat-trick inside half-an-hour, and the power he packed into his shooting made him an

automatic taker of free-kicks and penalties. One of his spot-kicks was converted in the opening minutes of a 5-0 Cup defeat of Mansfield. Another
cannoned back off an upright with such force that it enabled Leicester City
to break away and score one of the goals with which they took home both
points.

Owing to an unusually large injury list, Rovers called up 26 players in their
first Second Division season, eight more than when they won promotion,
and eleven of them did not reach double figures. Among those was left-back
Frank Allcock, a Nottingham man who had been with Forest and Aston Villa
before joining Rovers from Cheltenham Town, but without seeing League
action. It looked like being the same story for him again when, with Geoff
Fox so firmly installed alongside Harry Bamford, he had to wait a year for
his first senior chance with Rovers. It came in the Gloucestershire Cup final
of 1953 against Bristol City, and he had to wait another year for his League
debut in a Good Friday home victory over Oldham Athletic in 1954.

But Fox's hold was broken soon after the start of the next season, and
Allcock stepped in to become the regular successor in more than 60 games.
And there might well have been considerably more than that but for the seri-
ous knee injury he suffered soon after taking part in the sensational 4-0 FA
Cup defeat of Manchester United in January 1956. Sustained treatment failed
to have the desired effect, and he was forced into retirement that November.

CHAPTER 15

Butchered by Seven-Goal Briggs

Geoff Bradford got away to a flying start in the 1954-55 season, carrying on from where he had left off at the end of the previous one by notching two more hat-tricks in scoring in every one of Bristol Rovers' first six games. Ten of the club's dozen goals in that period were credited to him.

The hat-tricks came in the space of three days in early September – in a 4-1 home win against Derby County on the Saturday, and in a 3-0 defeat of Liverpool, also at Eastville, on the Monday evening. Geoff Fox was unfit for the match with Derby, so Leslie Edwards, a former Bristol City amateur, was brought into the side for the first time since he had been a brief deputy for Jackie Pitt in 1951. The Guildford-born Edwards, who had captained the Surrey Youth team and also boxed with some success while in the RAF, was unable to secure a regular place until after Frank Allcock's career-ending injury. Even then, at 32, it was only for the 1956-57 season, the last he spent with the club before leaving for Trowbridge Town. Later, while working as a carpenter, he was with the Somerset club Nailsea United.

Talk of an England cap for Bradford was at its height after the international selectors had seen him send Liverpool packing, and it certainly seemed a little closer when he was named as a reserve for the Football League's match with the League of Ireland in Dublin. Fate, however, favoured the other reserve, Johnny Wheeler, of Bolton Wanderers, who was brought in at right-half when Wolves' Bill Slater dropped out with a pulled thigh muscle – suffered against Bolton. Wheeler impressed in a 6-0 victory, while Bradford's hopes of an England call receded when he failed to score as Rovers conceded five goals in both their next two games, at West Ham and Liverpool.

There were six new caps in the England team announced to meet Northern Ireland in Belfast, and a seventh when Brian Pilkington, Burnley's diminutive left-winger, was summoned from his RAF camp to replace Tom Finney, who was stricken with fibrositis. Sure enough, Geoff Bradford was not among them – but Wheeler was. And, ironically, on the day England won with goals scored by Johnny Haynes and Don Revie – two of the men who were keeping Bradford out – Bristol Rovers and their ace marksman were back to their best with the club's record-equalling 7-0 thrashing of Swansea Town. Two of the seven were own-goals, and one of them cost Bradford another hat-trick as Dave Thomas, a former inside-forward turned full-back, deflected his shot into the net.

All of Liverpool's goals in their 5-3 revenge win at Anfield were scored by John Evans, who had been a surprise signing by Don Welsh the previous

Christmas. He was signed from the manager's old club Charlton Athletic, along with full-back Frank Lock. Peter Hooper scored a couple for Rovers, Harry Bamford reviving basic instincts by dribbling through for the other. Evans was the first to bag four in a match for Liverpool in more than 50 years, since Andy McGuigan netted five against Stoke in 1902. It was also the biggest individual scoring feat at Rovers' expense since the cold Easter Monday of 1936, when, with rain turning to sleet, Joe Payne had acquired his Ten-Goal tag in Luton's 12-0 avalanche.

Payne – such a late deputy for Scottish international Billy Boyd that his name was not in the match programme – was playing in his first game at centre-forward after being a reserve half-back with only three League games behind him. He was credited with his goals after 23, 40, 43, 49, 55, 57, 65, 76, 84 and 86 minutes, but there was a definite doubt about one of those in the second half, according to Wally McArthur, who had the job of marking him before being switched to left-half after the interval. As McArthur saw it: 'Our goalkeeper, Jack Ellis, saved from Payne and was then charged into the net with the ball by another player. There was no doubt in my mind that the ball was not over the line from Payne's header, but the referee decided to give the goal to him.'

So it was in those rather debatable circumstances that Payne took the record away from Robert ('Bunny') Bell, a part-timer who only four months earlier, on Boxing Day in 1935, had scored nine goals for Tranmere Rovers in a 13-4 Third North win that amply avenged a 1-4 defeat suffered at Oldham the day before – and he could have been the first to ten had he not failed with a penalty.

'At the time,' recalled Bell, 'it was just a joke that I missed a penalty while I scored nine other goals, but when Payne got his big haul it suddenly came to mean much more – a couple of inches away from keeping a record. It was one of those daft days when every time I aimed the ball at goal it went in, except for that one from the penalty spot which I pulled just wide. I still don't know how I did it.' Soon afterwards Bell became a full-time professional with Everton, only to be followed there by a youngster from Burnley named Tommy Lawton. 'That just about finished me at Goodison,' he said. 'I certainly wasn't in his class, nine goals or no nine goals.'

Unpleasant as were the memories stirred for Bristol Rovers by John Evans, another individual broadside – to surpass that of the Liverpool forward – was in the offing. On February's first Saturday of that 1954-55 season, Tommy Briggs, a butcher by trade away from football, set up a record for the Second Division by putting seven successive goals past Howard Radford in Blackburn's 8-3 home rout of Bristol Rovers. Yes, thanks to the 6ft 3in, 11st Briggs, it did end in a rout, yet three times the visitors took the lead, and they were 3-2 ahead at the interval. The game was only six minutes old when Bill Roost opened the scoring in the Bristol club's first attack. He was obliged to George Petherbridge for providing the centre, and also to Bill Eckersley. The England full-back allowed the winger to get away by stopping to help back to his feet a linesman he had accidentally bowled over.

Severe pressure inevitably led to an equaliser, headed by Irish international Eddie Crossan midway through the first half, but within a minute Vic Lambden put his side back in front. Briggs then first made his presence felt by unleashing an unstoppable low drive just after the half-hour, only for Lambden to score again shortly before half-time. It took Briggs only three minutes into the second half to bring the scores level again, applying the finishing touch at the far post when Crossan floated a free-kick over the hapless Radford, after winger Frank Mooney had been brought down just outside the penalty area.

Even then Bristol Rovers were still in the hunt, and although. Blackburn went in front for the first time after 62 minutes – Briggs completing his hat-trick, getting an outstretched foot to a centre pulled back by Bobby Langton, a pre-war winger of post-war England class – that was how the score stood until only twelve minutes from time. At that point, however, the game galloped away from Tann's men as their defence fell apart and Blackburn's score was doubled by the bustling Briggs.

Though not noted for dainty footwork, the big, former England 'B' centre-forward, left four defenders floundering before hitting home another blistering low drive in the 78th minute. Six minutes later he again smashed the ball into the net when a pass from Eddie Quigley found him unmarked, and after hitting a post he volleyed a centre from Mooney into the roof of the net to round off another hat-trick. His seventh goal in the closing minutes came from a penalty, but he took it only reluctantly, though coolly and efficiently enough, because Langton, the player who had been hauled down, was the team's spot specialist. One report said that Briggs, a modest and shy man, had 'almost to be dragged' to take the kick.

Only one other player had previously scored seven goals in a League game since the war – Eric Gemmell, a part-timer who had been signed on a free transfer from Manchester City, in Oldham's 11-2 Third North defeat of Chester in January 1952. Neville ('Tim') Coleman would be the next, his seven of Stoke's eight setting a record for a winger against Lincoln City in February 1957.

Briggs was presented with the match ball, autographed and inscribed 'Well done, Tommy,' by Blackburn chairman Tom Blackshaw after his Bristol bombardment. The strange thing was that this glutton for goals, shared between Grimsby, Coventry and Birmingham before Blackburn, had not been among the scorers in the Lancashire club's record 9-0 victory against Middlesbrough only three months before.

Some explanation for Bristol Rovers' crushing defeat could be derived from the fact that they were without three of their key players, Bamford, Sampson and Bradford. Allcock moved over to right-back, with Fox as his partner, Sampson's place was taken by 'Chick' Cairney, a Scot from Blantyre (also the birthplace of David Livingstone, the 19th century explorer), and Bush was with Roost at inside-forward on either side of Lambden. Eastville had been the venue for Cairney's entry into League football with Leyton Orient just over four years earlier, but they had given him only three other opportunities before his departure to Barry Town. Rovers were to allow him very few more after he had spent a couple of seasons with the Welsh club in the Southern League. He later played for Headington United and Worcester City.

The chastening trip to Blackburn came straight after Rovers' elimination from the FA Cup's fourth round by Chelsea, and at the end of a depressing run from which only two victories had been gained in eleven games. Earlier, a 4-0 home win against Ipswich had lifted them to third place in the table, the highest position they occupied all season. Those isolated successes came on successive Saturdays, both at Eastville – one in the League, by a Bradford goal against Doncaster on New Year's Day, the other the toppling of First Division Portsmouth out of the Cup.

Pompey, twice champions in the late 1940s, were beaten by Bradford and Roost goals to one by Johnny Gordon, all in the second half, in front of a crowd of 35,921. That figure lasted as an Eastville record only until 35,972 were packed in for Chelsea's fourth-round visit three weeks later. Hopes of another big scalp were quickly snuffed out, however, as the London club forged a 3-0 lead by half-time. Although Chelsea were unable to add to it, all Rovers could manage in reply was a Pitt penalty.

It was in the next round that Chelsea were victims of the upset Eastville had been denied, beaten by one goal away to Notts County, to whom Rovers had twice lost in the League over Christmas. But Chelsea were soon to have ideal compensation. This was the season in which the First Division championship went to Stamford Bridge for the first time. For Notts County, the seeming formality of a quarter-final meeting with York City, especially as they were again at home, was transformed into the story-book progress of a Third Division club into the last four for only the third time. York followed Millwall and Port Vale to that stage with a goal thirteen minutes from the end which even the scorer, Arthur Bottom, thought was offside. It was only after a replay that York then went out to Newcastle United, winners of the trophy that year for the third time in five seasons.

Fluctuations in form prevented Bristol Rovers from sustaining another promotion challenge that season. Having followed their record-equalling win over Swansea with a narrow home victory in their first meeting with Luton since Joe Payne's day out nearly twenty years before, they stumbled to a 2-6 defeat at Rotherham, but promptly bounced back with a 5-1 triumph against Leeds. Later, they won the return with Rotherham, then lost at Leeds next time out. After that they were beaten just once in eight games, only to finish with three consecutive defeats. That left them in the ninth position they had occupied at the end of their first Second Division season.

One of those concluding setbacks was suffered at Luton, whose 2-0 win took them back to the top of the table on goal-average in a battle for promotion that was Division Two's closest on record, resulting in the first triple tie on points. Luton completed their programme with 54 points, following up their win over Rovers with one at Doncaster on the final Saturday. But Birmingham (third) and Rotherham (fifth), both on 52, still had one more game to play. On the Monday evening Rotherham dislodged Leeds, who had ended with 53 points, from second place by achieving a victory that makes very peculiar reading these days. Left-winger Ian Wilson scored four goals in a 6-1 trouncing of Liverpool. And on the Wednesday, Birmingham crushed Doncaster 5-1 at Belle Vue to snatch the title from Luton, promoted to the top flight for the first time as runners-up. Third and thwarted Rotherham were pipped for promotion by 0.191 of a goal. They learned their sad fate after playing in a benefit match at Darlington.

The last of the nineteen wins Bristol Rovers set against sixteen defeats in the League that season was gained at home to Nottingham Forest, by 2-1 on 16 April 1955. It was a match in which another player who was to have a big impact on the club's fortunes over the next few seasons was introduced into the first team. David Ward, a twenty-year-old Welshman, naturally known as Dai, did not make a scoring debut (Biggs and Meyer netted the goals to which Hughie McLaren replied), and he was not retained for the remaining three matches.

Soon afterwards, however, Ward was to show that Rovers had acquired a natural marksman – one who was to do what no other player has achieved for the club, scoring in each of eight consecutive games. In one match with Doncaster Rovers he did the hat-trick in four minutes. Against Bristol City in a Gloucestershire Cup final he scored only seven seconds after the kick-off. And in 175 League games he totalled 90 goals, reaching his century with those he scored in other competitive games for the club. In two seasons he was their leading scorer.

Although it was to turn sour in the long run, Bert Tann could therefore count it one of his lucky days when he opened the letter in which the Barry-born Ward, who had been on Cardiff City's books as an amateur, wrote to ask for a trial. It proved an expensive lapse by the Welsh club to let him go, for they had to pay out £11,000, and also part with Johnny Watkins, a Bristolian valued at £4,000 who had been with Bristol City, in part exchange when Ward moved to Ninian Park on 21 February 1961. John Atyeo recalled that City's release of Watkins was the 'one big shock' when the Ashton Gate club's retained list was announced at the end of the 1958-59 season. 'On the day he received his letter Johnny sat next to me in the dressing room with tears in his eyes,' said Atyeo. 'He was a good friend of mine, and I remember telling him perhaps it could turn out for the best. Within four months he was tearing us apart playing for Cardiff, and he did well for them when they went into the First Division.'

By the time Dai Ward moved to Cardiff he had become the first to play for Wales while with Bristol Rovers since Jack Lewis, who was chosen against England in 1906. The call for Ward came for the match with England at Villa Park on Wednesday, 26 November 1958. Twice Wales went into the lead, on the second occasion only twenty minutes from time, and they looked set to spring one of the biggest surprises in the post-war home international championship until Peter Broadbent, the skilful Wolves inside-forward who was deputising for Johnny Haynes, forced a draw with his second goal in the 74th minute.

Ward played a prominent part in the regaining of the lead first obtained by Arsenal's Derek Tapscott, exchanging passes for Ivor Allchurch, then of Newcastle, to beat Colin McDonald in the England goal with a precise lob. But he had the misfortune to spend much of the match in the unfamiliar position of left-half (in direct opposition to Broadbent) because of an injury to Dave Bowen, the Welsh captain. Bowen moved to the left wing for the last hour, his bruised shoulder heavily strapped.

For all his goals, however, Ward had a volatile temperament that made him a difficult player to deal with at times. Near the end of the 1956-57 season – in which he was Rovers' top scorer despite missing a third of their games with cartilage trouble for which he needed an operation – he was put on the transfer list after giving a much-criticised disinterested display in a home defeat by Blackburn.

Bert Tann described it as 'a source of bewilderment to many people', adding: 'It is most regrettable that this course of action has had to be taken, but it has always been the club's view, and the view of those most closely connected with the club, that the club is greater than the individual. The club take the view that, should there be a repetition of last Saturday's exhibition, the effect on other members of the team could be very serious indeed. The effect on many members of the paying public has been deplorable.'

Only a few weeks later, however, a contrite Ward was reinstated after going to Tann's office to express his regrets and give firm assurances about his future conduct. 'I am grateful to the club for giving me another chance following my display in the Blackburn game,' he said. 'It will never happen again.' Tann declared himself 'very happy' about the outcome, but it was a peacemaking not destined to last. Several times Ward indicated through the Press that he was unhappy at Eastville, and matters came to a head when he refused to re-sign and started a job selling ice cream in the 1960 close season. 'It's only supposed to be for the summer,' he explained, 'but it will keep me going if my football pay stops.'

Ward's wife Hazel, who was born in Bristol, had been a keen Rovers fan since a teenager, but said that 'any move from Eastville is bound to be a good one'. The exasperated Tann felt he had 'exhausted all means possible of persuading this man to continue with Bristol Rovers as a contented member of staff', so that was how the transfer to Cardiff came about. It was a significant break in the 'family spirit' of which Rovers had been so proud.

With Cardiff, Ward soon made up for the disappointment of having missed a second Welsh cap through injury before leaving Rovers. He earned another international chance as the Welsh club's leading scorer during the 1961-62 season. That was also against England, at Ninian Park, and again the result was a draw, with wingers Bryan Douglas and Graham Williams getting the goals. But Ward's international career ended with that match, as also, at the end of that season, did his stay with Cardiff, after 35 appearances and eighteen goals. Despite his efforts, Cardiff were relegated from the First Division (as Bristol Rovers dropped from the Second), and during the summer he moved into the Third with Watford.

From there, just over a year later, having scored 31 more goals in 59 games, Ward went for £8,000 to Brentford, newly promoted as champions of the Fourth, and his eleven goals for them in 47 appearances included a couple in their record 9-0 victory over Wrexham before he went out of the League with first Worcester City, then Bath City. In 1993 he travelled from his Cambridge home to attend Watford's centenary dinner, but less than three years later, in January 1996, he died at the age of 61.

Other players capped by Wales while with Bristol Rovers have included Wayne Jones and, since Bert Tann's time, Neil Slatter and Marcus Browning. After appearing for his country at youth and Under-23 level, Jones, a clever midfielder with good close control, was awarded his one full cap in a European Championship group qualifying match against Finland in front of a crowd of little more than 5,000 in Helsinki in May 1971. Wales won with a goal from John Toshack, who was later to be the national team manager, but they failed to get through to the knock-out stages in finishing third behind Romania and Czechoslovakia.

Jones was also selected for a Welsh FA tour of Australia and New Zealand, but was forced to give up playing only a fortnight after his 24th birthday. That was because of a knee injury suffered during a home game with Brentford, in which he scored in a 3-1 victory, at the beginning of November in 1972. The trouble was later diagnosed as a rare bone condition.

Nothing daunted, Jones qualified as a physiotherapist and later obtained a full FA coaching badge. In those capacities he returned to Eastville as assistant to David Williams. A stylish midfielder, Williams in 1983 became the youngest manager then in the League, at 28, with his appointment as Rovers' player-manager. He held the post for two seasons before giving it up to become assistant manager to the long-serving Dave Stringer at Norwich City while continuing as a player.

For Wayne Jones, the path out of Eastville for the second time, following Williams's departure, first led abroad to the United Arab Emirates, where he briefly worked with another former Rovers colleague, Colin Dobson. A winger who had helped Huddersfield Town back to the First Division in 1970, Dobson had started out nine years earlier in a Sheffield Wednesday team that also included Don Megson, who was to be a Bristol Rovers manager of the early post-Tann era.

Dobson, who joined Rovers as player-coach on a free transfer after recovering from a broken leg while on loan to Brighton, subsequently assisted another ex-Rover, John Rudge, at Port Vale. He then went out East and guided the Rayyan club to the UAR League title. Back in England, Wayne Jones resumed his physio work with Notts County, by whom he was also employed as assistant manager, Huddersfield., Gillingham and currently with Hereford United, who returned to the Football League in 2006.

CHAPTER 16

Ford adds to Charlton Connection

Eastville's Charlton connection, first doubled when Bob Wright was Bert Tann's part-time assistant in the 1951-52 season, was again doubled when Fred Ford joined Bristol Rovers as chief coach and assistant manager in 1955. Both had been among Tann's clubmates at the Valley before the Second World War.

Robert Cooper Allen Wright, a Glaswegian, had his playing career curtailed by the war, most of which he spent abroad, after guesting for Middlesbrough; Dartford-born Frederick George Luther Ford, like Tann, had to give up playing prematurely because of injury. Wright became Charlton's assistant manager following his return from the war, in which he was a captain in the Royal Armoured Brigade, then preceded 'Pat' Beasley as Bristol City's manager before resigning with the complaint that he was not given a free hand. It was while he was afterwards licensee of the White Hart in Bristol's Lower Maudlin Street that he devoted some of his time towards helping out at Eastville.

Ford also had something in common with Tann in having been with the Erith & Belverdere club, but as a player, not as a coach. He was there before becoming an Arsenal amateur and then joining Charlton Athletic as a constructive, industrious defender. After the war, during which he suffered the wound that caused the amputation of his trigger finger while on the Normandy beaches, he guested a few times for Tottenham early in the 1945-46 transitional season. He was then with Millwall until his transfer to Carlisle United in the summer of 1947.

When his troublesome leg injury forced him to give up playing, Ford was appointed assistant trainer at Brunton Park for a couple of seasons. He was then upgraded to trainer-coach in succession to Jimmy Wallbanks, who returned to Millwall. Ford's harmonious working relationship with manager Bill Shankly was instrumental in Carlisle's achieving a final third place in the Northern Section of Division Three in 1950-51.

As Shankly wrote in his autobiography, they had a novel way of giving the players clues as to whether they were going to be in the first team. 'Rationing was still on,' he recalled, 'and there was a farmer who used to bring us a few dozen eggs and a big lump of butter at the weekend. Freddie Ford's job was to count out the eggs and cut the butter into chunks. He even had a little pair of scales. Having a reserve team, we had more players than we had butter and eggs, and consequently only twelve or thirteen of them had a share.' They were the ones who were going to be in the first-team squad.

Ford benefited greatly from his association with Shankly, who at Carlisle set the tone for his vigorous, indefatigable style of management that was to make him one of the most respected and hero-worshipped figures in the game. He endeared himself to Carlisle fans by speaking to them over the public address system at each home match, keeping them up to date with the club's affairs. It was inevitable, however, that such a dynamic personality would soon be coveted by others, especially as the scope for development at that Cumbrian outpost was strictly limited, and the offer that led him to part company with his close friend Ford came only weeks after the 1950-51 season in which Carlisle, though nine points behind promoted Rotherham, enjoyed some overdue prosperity.

Shankly, who in the 1930s had played with typical verve and tenacity at wing-half for Carlisle before being capped by Scotland and gaining an FA Cup winner's medal with Preston North End, was tempted away by Grimsby Town – but only at their second attempt. Carlisle warded them off with an increase in his salary when the first approach was made that spring. Frank Womack, holder of Birmingham's appearances record with almost 500 League games, was left in temporary charge at Blundell Park in the absence through ill health of Charles Spencer, an England international who had been one of the first 'stopper' centre-halves with Newcastle United. But when the post became vacant with Spencer's resignation during the summer of 1951 Shankly accepted it and twice took the Mariners close to promotion from the Third North. Workington and Huddersfield (where the fledgling Denis Law came under his wing) were the other stepping stones to his transformation of Liverpool into one of the most powerful clubs in Europe.

When Fred Ford left Carlisle for Eastville four years after Shankly's departure, Rovers acquired a coach whose efficiency was soon acknowledged at international level. He was appointed trainer to England's 'B' and Under-23 teams, and to the FA party that included Rovers' George Petherbridge on a tour of South Africa. While at Carlisle he had been chief coach to the Cumberland FA, and after his move to the South-West he held a similar post with the Gloucestershire Association. John Gummow, Rovers' secretary, was quick to appreciate the dedication of Bert Tann's new right-hand man. 'Fred is one of the greatest possible enthusiasts there is for football,' he declared. 'You can say he lives for the game.' John Atyeo, who also had a close view of Ford's methods when Fred was later Bristol City's manager, said: 'I always felt there was not a better coach in the country. He had the knack of getting the best out of players, whether in training or in a match. The team spirit was always excellent under Fred, who was steady, unspectacular and dependable.'

Those qualities made Ford a key influence on the renaissance that was to take Bristol Rovers to the brink of promotion to the First Division in his first season with them, and then keep them in the top half of the Second for the next four, so it is not difficult to appreciate the huge sense of loss that was felt when he transferred his allegiance across to the other side of the city on 14 June 1960. Betrayal, indeed, was not too strong a word for it in the eyes of some of the Eastville faithful, especially as it was to their big local rivals that he departed. What a blow for the much-vaunted 'family' feeling, though it would have been an even bigger one if Bert Tann had not declared himself 'perfectly happy with the Rovers' when envious eyes had been cast in his direction from Ashton Gate before the appointment of the man Ford was selected from nearly 60 applicants to replace.

That man was Peter Doherty, generally accepted as the greatest inside-forward ever to come out of Ireland, winner of a League championship with Manchester City and an FA Cup winner's medal with Derby County. He had been a big success as player-manager of Doncaster, and as the manager who guided Northern Ireland to the World Cup quarter-finals in 1958 but he had resigned from the Yorkshire club after his team selection had been bitterly criticised by a director, Hubert Bates, who had refused a demand for his own resignation only through the deciding vote of chairman Alfred Butler.

Doherty had got off to a reasonable start with Bristol City, who had first sought him as player-manager while he was with Huddersfield Town before going to Doncaster. He had then run into problems over some transfer deals, and results had fallen away alarmingly. Whereas at the time of Ford's departure Rovers had just occupied a comfortable ninth place in the table, well satisfied with having finished above their neighbours in each of their five seasons together in the Second Division, City had ended three points adrift at the bottom and fallen back to the Third with Hull City three months after Doherty's dismissal.

The month before his appointment at Ashton Gate, Fred Ford, then in his mid-40s, was on tour as the England Under-23 trainer in East Germany, Poland and Israel. Now as a manager, however, he had to relinquish his international 'sideline', and he was also required to give up his outside job as the Gloucestershire FA's chief coach. Jackie Pitt, who succeeded him with Rovers, was not a fully qualified coach, so could not also follow him in the county post. Consequently, Gloucestershire were without someone to fill it until the autumn of 1963, when it was decided to split the county in two for the control of coaching, a new idea that several members of the coaching committee had been urging for some time.

For the north of the county the post was given to Tommy Casey, a former Northern Ireland wing-half whose clubs had included Bristol City, but who was then player-manager of Gloucester City. For the south, it went to Bobby Campbell, a versatile former Chelsea and Scotland player who had joined Bristol Rovers as chief coach eighteen months before, following a season as manager of Dumbarton. Campbell, a coaching examiner with the

Scottish FA, was to remain at Eastville for just over seventeen years, the last two of them as manager. Though in his mid-50s when he followed Don Megson in that role, he took it on with the vigour of a much younger man and achieved a fair degree of success until a poor start to the 1979-80 season led to his dismissal. He afterwards was one of Casey's successors at Gloucester, then was employed by Bristol City Council to arrange football matches for the unemployed in the community.

Fred Ford also began well when he set about trying to revive Bristol City. As John Atyeo said, he was not the spectacular sort, but after two top-six finishes had been interspersed with a couple just below halfway, he did what he had been engaged to do. At the end of his fifth season in charge, City were back in Division Two – in the second promotion position behind Carlisle United. Mind you, it was a desperately close thing. Although only one point behind Ford's former club, City pushed Mansfield Town into third place only on goal average, 92-55 to 95-61, after both had won 24 of their 46 matches, drawn eleven and lost eleven.

Leaving Rovers behind in the Third Division (they had been relegated three years before), City, who had cornered much of the Bristol Boys talent, were not all that far off another rise a year later. All that counted for nothing when they began to falter the season after that. The 1967 campaign was into only its second month when Fred Ford became the 643rd manager to leave a League club since the war. He was dismissed for the unusual reason that, as the directors put it, 'he refused to spend money on new players.' A few years earlier he had come under fire from City supporters for not signing new players before the transfer deadline. Shortly before his sacking, he could have borrowed a five-figure sum from chairman Harry Dolman, free of interest, but he spurned it saying: 'We have been paying our own way, and I am reluctant to rely on Mr Dolman's generosity any more.'

Ford did not take long to find another job, as coach with Swindon Town, but he had been in it for not much more than six months when he became a manager again – back with Bristol Rovers. This was as a result of Rovers' decision to move Bert Tann 'upstairs' as their first general manager, and to appoint a team manager in his place. As had happened twenty years earlier, when tipped off about Tann after asking the Football Association for a recommendation when seeking a chief coach, they contacted the same source for advice and Ford's name was at the top of the list supplied. 'The FA recommended a number of people to us,' said Tann, 'but added that they considered Fred was by far the most suitable choice.'

So, on Saturday, 23 March 1968 Bert Tann was in charge of the senior side for the last time in a home game before handing over. 'A change was inevitable,' he stated, 'and no-one is happier than I am that Fred has got the job. We worked together before and were considered a good partnership. I am sure we can be a good partnership again. I said we were looking for a capable, confident, ambitious man. Fred fulfils all these requirements.'

Rovers were only three points clear of the relegation zone in the Third Division when Ford accepted the post, with a difficult run-in. 'My aim is to improve the individual and collective skills of the players, most of whom I already know,' he said. 'Then we will go from there.' He successfully negotiated that first hurdle, Rovers ending six points clear as Grimsby, Colchester and Scunthorpe went down with Peterborough United, who, although finishing just inside the top half, were demoted for irregularities in their books.

But it did not work out well after that. In 1968-69 Rovers were sixteenth, on 43 points, only three ahead of Northampton Town, the best placed of the four that went down. On the eve of the new season Ford left to accept the vacant post of manager at Swindon Town. This was a serious blow to Rovers, whose youth policy was beginning to bear fruit.

Back he went the same month to Swindon, a managerial vacancy having conveniently opened up there with the departure of Danny Williams to Sheffield Wednesday. Williams, formerly a player (in more than 600 games) and manager with Rotherham, had just seen the Wiltshire club to a giant-killing League Cup final victory over Arsenal and to promotion from Division Three. Fred Ford made a reasonable stab at following suit, taking Town to fifth place in the Second Division and an FA Cup quarter-final in which they went out to another First Division force, Leeds United. After only one more season, however, he was squeezed out following the arrival of Dave Mackay. The Scottish icon arrived fresh – adding to earlier triumphs at Hearts and Tottenham – from his inspirational captaincy of a Derby County side transformed under the management of the controversial Brian Clough.

Ford quickly bounced back again, as coach and assistant manager at Torquay, then finally became Oxford United's chief scout and youth organiser from 1974 up to his death in October 1981, aged 65. A minute's silence was observed in his memory on Bristol City's visit to Oxford that month.

CHAPTER 17

Dodgin Gamble after Ten-Year Gap

Bristol Rovers kept their managerial appointment 'in the family' by choosing Bill Dodgin, another with a Charlton connection, as their successor to Fred Ford in the autumn of 1969, but it was also something of a gamble.

Dodgin, a doughty wing-half with Rovers in 1936-37, had returned to Eastville as chief scout in 1961, but more than ten years had elapsed since he had been the manager of a League club. The maximum wage had been abandoned in the meantime, and he acknowledged that the game was very much changed in admitting that 'the old-fashioned, all-purpose manager is a thing of the past; there is too much to be done outside the playing side of the game'.

Even so, he also said that his interest had always been in the dressing room with the players, especially in bringing on the youngsters he had signed when chief scout, and that was where a team manager now had to live. He continued: 'They say I'm the oldest team manager in the League [he had celebrated his 60th birthday the previous April], but although I may be old in years I sometimes feel fitter and younger than some of the less senior managers in the game. I have refused two managerial jobs since coming back to Eastville because Bristol Rovers seemed the right set-up for me. My greatest thrill is finding and coaching young players, and my work at Eastville has given me plenty of scope for it. I never thought I would ever be a manager again, and I wouldn't have accepted the job with any other club.'

Dodgin was a man of many other clubs, beginning as a player with several in his native North-East (he was born at Gateshead) before first entering the Football League with Huddersfield Town on the opening day of the 1930-31 season. From there he went via the captaincy of Lincoln City to Charlton Athletic, whom he helped to the Third South title in 1934-35. He then made just a few more first-team appearances when a second successive promotion lifted Charlton into the First Division for the first time. It was from the Valley that he spent his one season with Bristol Rovers, after which he played for Clapton Orient before completing his playing career at Southampton.

He was at centre-half for the Saints when Alf Ramsey, then serving in the Duke of Cornwall's Light Infantry, began playing for the club in 1945. 'Alf considered his best position to be centre-half,' he recalled, 'and whenever he came to play for us I used to move to full-back. But once I had become manager there, and Alf had signed for us, I switched him to full-back. He was a bit reluctant, but I told him he would play for England as a full-back. He had two good feet, was very accurate, and had great anticipation. Two years later he gained the first of his 32 England caps.'

But it was because of Ramsey that Dodgin fell out with Southampton. When Tottenham made a £20,000 offer for Ramsey in 1949, Dodgin wanted to accept it, but the directors disagreed. What happened next is best told in Dodgin's own words: 'During the summer of that year I went to Rio [to attend the World Cup finals]. While I was there Spurs came in with another bid for Alf. They offered £6,000 and Ernie Jones, a winger who later played for Bristol City, and the board accepted it. I was annoyed that they should have sold him so cheaply while I was away, and when Fulham made me an offer a month after I returned to England I decided to accept.'

Dodgin thus became Fulham's first manager as a First Division club, promotion having been clinched as Division Two champions the month before his appointment. Twice he had looked likely to reach that exalted sphere with Southampton. In successive seasons under his management they had finished third in Division Two – on the second occasion after being eight points clear at the top with only seven games to go before losing their top scorer Charlie Wayman through injury.

Dodgin's younger brother Norman, previously with Newcastle and Reading, made his debut in Northampton Town's reserve team at Fulham while Bill was the London club's manager. And Bill's son, also Bill, played for both Southampton (as an amateur) and Fulham under his management before turning out for Young England and captaining the Under-23 side during his eight years with Arsenal. Bill Junior went into management when a broken leg virtually ended his playing career after his return to Fulham. He was in charge at Craven Cottage when Bill Senior's appointment at Eastville provided the unique case of a father and son both managing a League club in the same division at the same time.

Furthermore, in following his father, though not directly, as manager of Fulham, young Bill emulated Joe Bradshaw. In the 1920s Bradshaw had filled the post held by his father, Harry, with the same club twenty years earlier. Bristol City were among the other clubs managed by Joe Bradshaw, who had also played for Fulham while his father was manager there.

Rovers won narrowly at Eastville the first time they met Fulham when the Dodgins were in opposition, but they were beaten in the return game, and also lost their two meetings in the League during the following 1970-71 season, in which Fulham won promotion as runners-up to Preston. Those setbacks were offset, however, by a 2-1 victory Rovers gained at Craven Cottage in the first round of the FA Cup in November 1970, with a couple of goals from Carl Gilbert, though they fell at the next hurdle, a home replay with Aldershot. One fair-haired forward was exchanged for another when, a year almost to the day before that Cup win at Fulham, Gilbert joined Rovers from

Gillingham. He was exchanged for Ken Ronaldson, a Scot who had landed up at Eastville as one of no fewer than seventeen players given a free transfer by Aberdeen.

Ronaldson, remembered best while with Rovers for a goal scored inside the first 30 seconds of a home match with Southport, showed his skills in almost 80 League games before that transfer swap, but injury forced his retirement after only half-a-dozen more for Gillingham. It was against Rovers that he made his final appearance for the Kent club. On the same day Robin Stubbs, whose £10,000 transfer from Torquay was one of the last negotiated while Fred Ford was manager at Eastville, became the first player to score four goals for Rovers in an away match – at Gillingham on the second Saturday of October in 1970.

Stubbs, whose career was also ended by injury, had gone one better with five goals in an 8-3 defeat of Newport, soon after joining Torquay from Birmingham City. After nearly 100 games and over 30 goals for Rovers, he went back to Torquay in exchange for John Rudge, a utility player who later successfully managed Port Vale. In his two spells with the Devon club, Stubbs scored about 130 goals at an average of almost one every two games.

Rudge also rejoined Torquay, as coach, after having been in Rovers' promotion-winning team of 1973-74 and then spending a couple of years with Bournemouth. But it was with Port Vale that he significantly made his mark. In his nineteen years there, initially as coach and then as caretaker before being appointed manager, he guided them to two play-off finals – winning promotion in the first, ironically, at the expense of Bristol Rovers. Rudge's Vale also won an automatic promotion to Division One and a win at Wembley over Stockport in the Autoglass Trophy competition. He also had his disappointments, including a play-off defeat by West Bromwich after finishing third. His controversial dismissal in January 1999, culminating in a court battle to win compensation after he had declined an offer to become the club's Director of Football, was a most unfortunate end to such a long period of loyalty. He subsequently joined Stoke City in an advisory capacity.

Carl Gilbert had made a scoring League debut for Gillingham against Mansfield after buying himself out of the Army. He also netted the goal that defeated Rovers at the Priestfield Stadium in Bill Dodgin's first season as manager, but a few weeks later was in the side that lost 0-7 to Rovers Reserves at Eastville. Neither that heavy defeat, nor his sending-off in a reserve match with Bristol City that quickly followed, deterred Dodgin from deciding to put him in attack alongside Stubbs, and that faith was promptly repaid with another debut goal that saved a point in a Boxing Day home match with Reading.

There were to be only fourteen more in fewer than 50 games, but the last of them earned another point, against Bradford City, on Gilbert's final appearance before bringing in £17,000 from his transfer to Rotherham. His most eventful game for the Yorkshire club resulted in a 2-7 defeat by Bournemouth. He scored both their goals, then conceded three as an emergency goalkeeper.

It was under the management of Bill Dodgin Senior that Johnny Haynes entered League football, against Southampton, on Boxing Day in 1952, but by then Dodgin had been unable to prevent Fulham from dropping back into the Second Division. He was asked to resign when, in September 1953, they were the only club in the League without a win in the season they had started with the 4-4 home draw with Bristol Rovers. His contract had another year to run, but, although he felt that the Cottagers had a promising team, and bad luck had contributed to their plight, he readily agreed to go 'because I do not want to stand in anybody's way'. In any case, as one door closed, another quickly opened for him at nearby Brentford, where former England centre-forward Tommy Lawton had recently resigned prior to making a belated First Division comeback as a player with Arsenal.

Dodgin, whose brother Norman had joined him in management by becoming Exeter City's player-manager only a few weeks earlier, found himself with another club at the bottom of the Second Division table when he took over at Griffin Park. On the Saturday in which he was briefly between jobs, Brentford were deposited there by a defeat at Hull, while Fulham rose a couple of places with a victory – at the eleventh attempt – at home to Nottingham Forest. For his first match at the helm of his new club, Dodgin could have wished for something better than a visit from leaders Everton, the only unbeaten team in the four divisions – an away banker if there ever was one. Naturally, the fickleness of football decreed otherwise. Brentford promptly handed over last place with a win, only their second of the season, fittingly gained with a goal scored by a player named Dare.

Of their next six matches Brentford lost only one, but there was to be no happy ending. Dodgin was again powerless to ward off relegation, and after three seasons with no real sign of getting back he was on his way again – this time to Italy as manager of Sampdoria. Two years later he was in the Southern League with Yiewsley, from where he rejoined Bristol Rovers.

Back at Eastville, he fielded some attractive attacking sides that finished in the top six in each of his three seasons as manager, going close to promotion just behind the top two in 1969-70. Rovers also twice reached the fifth round of the League Cup, on the first occasion doing what Rovers had failed to do in 1951 – knock out First Division Newcastle. Bobby Jones, another local discovery who played in more than 400 games for the club, scored their goals in the 2-1 defeat of United at Eastville. And it was by only one goal, in a replay, that Rovers eventually went out to Aston Villa, losing finalists against a Tottenham side that had beaten Bristol City over the two legs of their semi-final. When Rovers again got to the quarter-finals in the following 1971-72 season, their run was ended by Stoke, who went on to gain their first big prize by defeating Chelsea in the final.

After Bill Dodgin stepped down in July 1972 – to be succeeded by Don Megson, a member of that successful side against Newcastle as player-coach – he went back to being chief scout until his retirement in 1983. Megson, whose son Gary followed him into League football, was the fourth former Sheffield Wednesday player to manage Rovers (after Andrew Wilson, Brough Fletcher and David McLean). In eighteen years at Hillsborough he was an adaptable defender in nearly 450 League and Cup games, many of them as captain.

He led his men on a unique losers' lap of honour when Wednesday were beaten by Everton in the 1966 FA Cup final after gaining a two-goal lead – a bitter setback of the kind his son, Gary, was also to experience in three times being a losing semi-finalist with Wednesday. Apart from one appearance in a Football League XI, honours eluded Don Megson until he joined Bristol Rovers and guided them to a Watney Cup win in 1972 and back to the Second Division two years later.

CHAPTER 18

Cup Defeat of the Coming Champions

From linking the Eastville stewardship of Fred Ford and Bill Dodgin, back now to the 1955-56 season in which Bristol Rovers fell just two matches short of rising into the First Division's elite of the Football League.

The final table for that season shows that Rovers finished as low as sixth, on goal-average the last of four clubs on 48 points. They were four points adrift of runners-up Leeds, who were three behind Sheffield Wednesday's champions. But as late as mid-April, only a fortnight from the winning post, they were in the second promotion position. They had halved Wednesday's lead to three points since Easter by gaining three successive victories – at Plymouth and Middlesbrough, and home to Notts County – without conceding a goal, while the Yorkshire club faltered with a draw at West Ham and a home defeat by Fulham.

Indeed, during the first few weeks of the season Rovers were themselves the pacesetters. They dropped only one point in their first four matches, in a 1-1 draw at Port Vale on a gloriously sunny opening day. The next two games were both won 4-2 at home, against Stoke and Doncaster, as the temperatures continued to soar into the 80sF. They then went to the top of the table for the first time by completing the double over Stoke, by 2-1 with Bradford goals, on a late August evening when Fulham and Lincoln, the previous leading pair, both lost their unbeaten record.

Next time out, however, it was Rovers' turn to be on the wrong end of a 2-4 result, away to the Wednesday. The closeness of the struggle between the leading teams was underlined by the fact that this defeat sent them down to fifth, on seven points with Fulham, Port Vale and the Owls of Sheffield, all one point behind Lincoln's 7-1 winners against Leicester. That was a day for high scoring – especially at Cardiff, where the hungry Wolves equalled a 47-year-old record for a First Division away win by thrashing their Welsh hosts 9-1. Only Sheffield United (with ten in Division Two at Port Vale in 1892) had surpassed that total away from home in the League. The record Wolves matched was set in 1908 at Newcastle by Sunderland, who on the afternoon of the Ninian Nine let in seven goals at Blackpool.

The setback in Sheffield was the only one Bristol Rovers suffered in their first nine matches, and they were again at the head of the pack, following a 2-0 win at Liverpool with a 4-1 victory over Nottingham Forest back at Eastville. Alfie Biggs and Geoff Bradford equally shared six goals in those games, and on the following Saturday Bradford collected another couple in a win at Hull that restored Rovers to first place after they had dropped back to third in having no fixture, while Stoke and Fulham gained midweek victories. Rovers now had both a point and a game in hand over those nearest challengers, who both gave ground in losing at West Ham and Blackburn, respectively, on the afternoon of the Bristol club's success on Humberside. Blackburn were the next visitors to Eastville, and Rovers further strengthened their hand by beating them with Peter Sampson's first League goal in four seasons – and only the third of the four he was to score in all.

But only four points covered the top ten teams – among them Port Vale, whose 4-1 victory at Fulham enabled Swansea, 5-1 winners at Notts County, to slip into third place behind Stoke, with Vale tucked in close behind after having let in only four goals in a dozen hours' play. In an unprecedented soccer boom for Bristol, City were also inside that top ten (just), and they would have their turn at the leadership before drifting back to a final place in mid-table. For one heady week late in November, after eighteen games apiece, the Bristol pair were the top two, only one point apart.

During the last week of September, following the defeat of Blackburn that kept Rovers at the head of the heap, Fulham's Johnny Haynes, still a month short of 22, was man of the match with two goals and two assists in England's 5-1 defeat of Denmark at Under-23 level under the Portsmouth club's floodlights. Consequently, there were moans that 'the greatest inside-forward in the game' would be missing when the full England party flew off for the Copenhagen encounter that was to have the same outcome. Rovers were rightly proud to have Geoff Bradford as a member of that party, but in his absence they came unstuck at Lincoln on the first day of October, conceding two goals without reply after a scoreless first half.

Defeat for Stoke at Leicester, and a draw for Swansea at home to Leeds, meant that Rovers remained a point ahead, still with their game in hand over both Potters and Swans as well as Fulham, who climbed back to second place with a win at Rotherham. It was the start, however, of a run of four games from which Rovers gleaned just one point and slipped to seventh. They were unable to follow Fulham's example, losing by a lone goal at Rotherham a week later, and surrendered the leadership to the London club, for whom Bedford Jezzard swamped bottom-of-the-table Hull with five goals. That onslaught made Jezzard the season's leading scorer in the country and took him to a record Fulham individual aggregate of 143 goals – two more than Jim Hammond had reached in the League from 1928-39. Hammond, who for ten seasons was also a county cricketer with Sussex, altogether scored 150 goals for Fulham in nearly 350 games; Jezzard totalled 154 in just over 300 before an ankle injury ended his career at the age of 28.

Geoff Bradford, overlooked for England's forthcoming match with Wales in Cardiff, was back on target at his next opportunity, but it was not enough to avert the loss of Rovers' unbeaten home record to a Swansea side that ousted Fulham (beaten at Forest) from the leadership with goals from Melvyn Charles and Ivor Allchurch. The one point Rovers picked up from this bad patch was taken from their City neighbours in front of an Ashton Gate crowd of nearly 40,000. John Atyeo, as usual, had been the man mainly behind a successful sequence of one defeat in seven games that had lifted City above Rovers to fourth place in the table, but Jimmy Rogers scored the goal that Barrie Meyer cancelled out to prevent a fourth consecutive Rovers defeat.

It was after this that Dai Ward began to make his presence felt. Brought back into the team for the regular place he was to hold for most of five seasons, he sparked a revival with the first goal in a 4-1 home win against Leeds. United's victory in the return game on the penultimate Saturday of the season was to wreck Rovers' hopes of promotion and lead to their own accompaniment of Sheffield Wednesday up into the First Division.

Two goals from Bradford and one from Meyer completed the Eastville discomfort of a Leeds side in which John Charles, elder brother of Mel, was switched from centre-half to centre-forward for the first time for a year. 'It's been on the cards for some time,' said Raich Carter, then the Leeds manager, 'and now we think we can do it because we have such a good centre-half.' The player he was referring to was Jack Charlton, ten years later to be at the heart of England's first, and still only, World Cup-winning team. On that late October afternoon in 1955, however, Charlton was unable to subdue a revitalised Rovers attack, and Charles failed to supply the punch United were seeking. Harold Brook made Leeds' only reply.

That win raised Rovers to fourth, one of four clubs on eighteen points behind Sheffield Wednesday, who led with 22, and one worse off than Bristol City, whose 6-4 victory at Blackburn (three more for Atyeo) moved them up to second. A trip to Fulham, who were third, was next on Rovers' list, and they sprang one of the surprises of the day by beating them 5-3 with a Meyer hat-trick and other goals from Ward and Bradford. Meanwhile, despite England's 1-2 defeat by Wales, Bradford was again overlooked when the national selectors had a rethink – one account went as far as to call it a 'spring-clean' – for the match in which Northern Ireland lost 0-3 at Wembley.

Neither could room be found for Bradford in the Football League side that won 4-2 against the Scottish League at Hillsborough, nor in the England team that enjoyed a 5-1 romp against Yugoslavia in a 'B' international at Maine Road. He was not even in an FA XI that drew with the Army at Newcastle, or among the seventeen players called up for special training before the game with Spain at Wembley. Younger men, including Atyeo and Haynes – the inside-forwards either side of Bolton's Lofthouse in the 4-1 victory over the Spaniards – were ahead of him in the queue, and so were

Jezzard and Wilshaw (Wolves), who were on stand-by when Haynes had to go into hospital for treatment of an ear abscess.

There was to be no second chance for Bradford with England, regardless of the fact that around this time he was on song in another of his scoring sequences. He continued it with one goal in a 4-2 home win against Bury, two more in a 3-4 defeat at Barnsley, and another couple, taking him to twenty for the season, as Rovers rounded off November with a 7-2 trouncing of Middlesbrough at Eastville. It was after this game, in which Ward and Hooper also scored twice, with the other goal from Petherbridge, that the two Bristol clubs sat proudly at the top of the table. City hung onto the lead by one point, despite losing 2-3 at Doncaster Rovers after being two up at half-time.

One week later City were back to form with a 5-1 trimming of Lincoln (another Atyeo hat-trick), but Rovers came a cropper, and an unexpectedly heavy one at that, in going under by 2-5 away to Notts County, a club in the bottom six. Notts were also to contribute to City's loss of the leadership, beating them at Ashton Gate three weeks later on a day when Rovers went through their fourth consecutive match without a win, suffering a narrow defeat at Doncaster that sent them down to eighth, the lowest position they were to occupy all season.

That was on Christmas Eve, and in their two other games over the holiday Rovers defeated Leicester at Eastville but lost to them at Filbert Street. One win in six games was an unlikely prelude to the purple patch with which Rovers saw out the old year by beating the new leaders, Sheffield Wednesday, and began the new one with the epic FA Cup victory over Manchester United. Wednesday led at half-time with a goal from Albert Quixall, another of the players ahead of Bradford in the England reckoning, but Rovers rallied with two Biggs goals, and others from Bradford and Meyer. The Owls could muster only one more, through Roy Shiner, one of the few players from the Isle of Wight to make good in League football. Rovers' win over the Busby Babes, joint Cup favourites with Sunderland, was even more emphatic, for United had no response to the same Rovers scorers.

United, just two years short of the Munich air disaster that took such a tragic toll of life, turned up as coming champions, four points clear at the head of the First Division, and at full strength apart from the considerable absence of Duncan Edwards with a boil on a leg. Their team of other glittering stars finished with their lead extended to eleven points for the first of two successive League titles, but at Eastville it was one of those occasions when everything went right for Rovers. Every member of their team did the club proud, three of them in particular.

'Paddy' Hale made a wonderful job of marking the dangerous Tommy Taylor, George Petherbridge gave United's captain, the experienced England full-back Roger Byrne, a torrid time, and Alfie Biggs was again at the top of his form in scoring two more goals. Bradford rounded things off from the penalty spot. 'Byrne had seen me take a penalty before,' he recalled, 'and he went up to tell Ray Wood, United's goalkeeper, which side of the goal I was going to place the ball. Ray said: "I know where he's going to put it. It's a question of whether I can get there in time." He couldn't.'

That triumph stands as one of the greatest in Rovers' long history, the peak one of the Tann era, but in the first season after that era had ended they went even better by beating the Red Devils in their own Old Trafford stronghold. In 1972, in the third round of the League Cup, Rovers held a team with a forward line of Morgan, Kidd, Charlton, Best and Storey-Moore to a 1-1 draw, then won the replay 2-1. John Rudge, who had also scored at Eastville, and Bruce Bannister got the goals that caused the upset, the lone reply coming from Sammy McIlroy, substitute for Kidd. United, however, were then a team in temporary decline. They finished that season uncomfortably close to the relegation from the First Division they were unable to avoid a year later.

Even so, to win against such glamorous opponents was a real turn-up for the form book, making it all the more of a let-down when Rovers were devoured 0-4 by Wolves in the next round. In 1956, too, there was something of a downside, for much of the national limelight was diverted from Rovers after their FA Cup defeat of United by Bedford Town's recovery to draw their third-round tie with Arsenal at Highbury after being two goals down with only thirteen minutes remaining. Bedford, the only non-League club left in the competition, and with just one full-time professional in their line-up, were only four minutes from the biggest Cup upset since Walsall's famous victory over Arsenal in 1933, before losing the replay in extra-time.

For Bristol Rovers the 1956 Cup glory was also swiftly to dissipate. The next round led them to the double depression of the replay at Doncaster in which they lost Geoff Bradford to his second serious injury and went out to a late only goal.

Floodlights having saved England's recent game with Spain from being abandoned because of the deteriorating conditions, with twenty minutes still to play, the FA had agreed to lights being used from the third round of the Cup, so that replay became the first competitive match to be played under lights at Doncaster's Belle Vue ground. It very nearly also became the first to be televised from there. When the FA gave permission for the second half to be screened, the Doncaster club flatly refused a BBC approach, only to reconsider when compensation for loss of gate money was offered. But the amount of the compensation was then not thought sufficient, and after a day of frenzied negotiations the BBC reluctantly announced that they had been unable to come to terms 'in time for the necessary technical arrangements to be made'.

Doncaster's team that freezing night included the latest 'Boy Wonder', Alick Jeffrey, who the year before, almost to the day, had made his Cup debut on his sixteenth birthday, 29 January 1955, in a fourth-round clash with Aston Villa. It went to a fourth replay in which Jeffrey's two goals helped the Yorkshire club to victory at West Bromwich on 15 February. Five days after the completion of that marathon of eight and a half hours, a Doncaster side deprived of Jeffrey lost in the next round at Birmingham City. While he was at Milford Haven, doing the hat-trick for England in a youth international against Wales, his place at St Andrew's was taken by another Cup newcomer, eighteen-year-old Reece Nicholson.

The soccer world was then at Jeffrey's feet, but less than nine months after Doncaster's defeat of Bristol Rovers he was in the same plight as Geoff Bradford, battling to recover from serious injury. I was among those in the 26,000 crowd at the first Under-23 international match to be staged at Ashton Gate that mid-October night who heard the sickening crack when Jeffrey suffered a double fracture of his right leg in colliding with centre-half Richard Tylinski only eight minutes into England's scoreless game against France. Colin Booth, of Wolves, substituted.

Nearly three years later Jeffrey broke his other leg, also in two places, in attempting a comeback with Skegness, whose manager, George Raynor, had coached Sweden to a World Cup final, but in the 1963-64 season Jeffrey returned from a spell in Australia with the Sydney club Prague to prove medical opinion wrong by reappearing in Doncaster's League side.

And, at 24 and despite having some weight to shed, what a huge success he made of it. Jeffrey ended the second season of his second career as the joint leading scorer in England, on 39 League and Cup goals with Torquay's future Rover Robin Stubbs. In the season after that he helped Doncaster to the Fourth Division championship with 22 more, and although they were immediately relegated they soon bounced back as twelve-goal Jeffrey finally bowed out as their main marksman once more. For a player who had been written off as a hopeless medical case, it was indeed remarkable that he altogether scored nearly 100 goals in some 200 games after a seven-year absence from League football.

After so much of which to be rightfully proud, it was, as his defence counsel put it, 'a tremendous disgrace' when Jeffrey, while a licensee in Doncaster, was later in court with his son and daughter, charged with unlawfully wounding his daughter's husband in an act of revenge for abusing and humiliating her in front of a jeering crowd in his public house. Jeffrey, who died at the age of 61 towards the end of 2000, incurred a six-month jail sentence, suspended for two years. His son, also Alick, was sent to prison for six months; the estranged wife was fined £75.

CHAPTER 19

The First Division Near-Miss

The heavy reliance Bristol Rovers placed on Geoff Bradford for goals was as evident as Doncaster's on Alick Jeffrey when Bristol had to manage without him after the FA Cup replay at Belle Vue on the last day of January 1956.

Tann's men went into the first of those two meetings with Doncaster as holders of third place in the Second Division, behind the Wednesday and Bristol City. They did so on the back of another Bradford hat-trick that, combined with a Hooper goal, turned a 0-2 half-time deficit into a 4-2 victory against Hull City. Without their injured sharpshooter, Rovers failed to win five of their next seven matches, though the struggle for promotion was still so tight that they remained one of the ten clubs still in the running, falling no lower than fifth.

That man Tommy Briggs was again on the mark against them in their first match after the Cup exit, but this time with only one goal as Rovers conceded just two in another defeat at Blackburn. The other scorer, on his home debut in the League, was Donal O'Leary, a nineteen-year-old left-winger who had been a left-back as a junior with Cork.

Rovers too had a scoring newcomer in their next match, at home to Lincoln City. Ray Seatherton, a Devonian from Tiverton, was signed by Bert Tann in face of strong competition from Bristol City, Plymouth Arygle and West Bromwich Albion after averaging two goals a game in netting nearly 50 for Minehead. What a find he appeared to be when he scored on his debut for Rovers Reserves. He earned his first League chance with a hat-trick in the first half-hour of another second-team match, and followed up his opening goal in a 3-0 defeat of Lincoln with another that earned a home draw with Barnsley a week later. But those were to be his only appearances in Rovers' League side. He had to undergo a knee operation and soon afterwards was on his way back to Minehead, then to Taunton Town.

A few years later a similar injury curtailed the Rovers career of another promising discovery from non-League football. Len Drake was signed after impressing against Rovers for his home club, Dorchester Town, in a friendly game, but he failed to get into double figures for first-team appearances before having to drop out with an arthritic knee. This did not prevent him, however, from turning out at a lower level, and he both played for and managed the Dorchester and Weymouth clubs. Laurie Sheffield was another promising forward, a former Swansea Boys captain and Welsh schools international. He joined Rovers straight from school, but failed to progress beyond the Colts and Reserves before leaving for Barry Town.

There was also disappointment concerning Cornishman Brian Tallamy – not because he failed to make the grade as a centre-forward with Rovers, but because he was not allowed the opportunity to do so. He bought himself out of the Royal Navy with the intention of joining the Eastville playing staff, only for the FA to refuse his registration both as an amateur or a professional. One of their rules stipulated that a player could not become a professional until twelve months after the date of a discharge obtained by purchase. Neither could he play as an amateur during that period without the FA's permission. And that permission was not forthcoming because the powers-that-be considered the wage Rovers planned to pay him too much for a groundstaff worker, even though it was below that of a reserve-team player. So Rovers found employment as an electrician for Tallamy, who had been spotted playing for Bodmin Town, but he was not to get beyond the two games he had played for the Colts while still in the Navy.

Tallamy opted instead to join Devizes Town, only to have Welton Rovers protest to the FA that he was ineligible after he had helped to defeat them in the last qualifying round of the FA Amateur Cup. Paradoxically, although Tallamy was ruled ineligible, the protest was dismissed, and the result allowed to stand. The FA also returned Welton's appeal fee and fined Devizes one guinea. As if all that was not confusing enough, Tallamy was allowed to carry on playing for Devizes. Looking at it from the perspective of Welton Rovers, one of his county's clubs, the Somerset FA secretary, C A Webb, felt compelled to call it 'the silliest decision in football I can remember'. He added: 'I can't make head or tail of it. It contradicts itself.' I have sought clarification from the FA, but without success.

In the first round proper of that season's Amateur Cup, Tallamy headed Devizes in front from a corner in the eighth minute of their home tie with Finchley. Though subsequently handicapped by the loss through injury of their right-winger, the Wiltshire League side continued to play well, but they were unable to build on that lead and were taken to a replay in which they were well beaten. At least they had the consolation of having earned exemption from the qualifying rounds of the following season's competition.

Tony Edge, a youngster from the Wirral, signed by Bristol Rovers from Devizes shortly before Tallamy went there, became another of the stand-ins for Geoff Bradford. But he only just got into double figures for first-team appearances, despite scoring three goals in the first five, before moving into the Southern League with Bath City. From Twerton Park he went back to Devizes, for whom he scored 90 goals in the 1963-64 season. He was afterwards their player-manager for a couple of years.

Although held at home by Barnsley on the day Seatherton maintained a goal-a-game League record (which he retained because he had no more first-team chances), Rovers moved up to third place above their City neighbours, whose defeat by leaders Sheffield Wednesday at Hillsborough sent them down to fifth. Leicester were now second, but only on goal-average, instead of Swansea, who lost more ground the following weekend as two Meyer goals gave Rovers both points at the Vetch Field.

So to the month of March, and to the eagerly awaited meeting of the two Bristol clubs at Eastville. But what a let-down it was for Rovers, in front of crowd boosted to 35,324, then the record. They went into the game only two points behind Wednesday, and with a match in hand over both the Owls and Leicester. Yet they came out of it well beaten by two Atyeo goals and another from Jimmy Rogers, a lively forward who might eventually have been signed by Rovers but for that No Buy, No Sell policy. It was said that a deal was suggested by Coventry manager, Billy Frith, who contacted Tann about Rogers shortly before he rejoined City. Rogers had spent a couple of years with the Midlands club, but the £3,000 fee it cost to take him back to Ashton Gate was too big an obstacle as far as Rovers were concerned.

Although Sheffield Wednesday moved four points clear at the top by turning a 0-2 half-time deficit into a 3-2 win at Rotherham, the struggle for the second promotion place, as the 1955-56 season entered its finishing straight in early March, stayed so tight that only five points covered the next ten teams. Bristol Rovers were beaten again, by the odd goal of three at West Ham, but four of their rivals – Leicester, Bristol City, Swansea and Leeds – also failed that day. Liverpool, 5-0 winners at Barnsley, had now climbed into third place, tucked in a point behind Leicester and a point ahead the Bristol pair, Port Vale and Swansea, all on 37.

Around this time there was the distraction of a dispute between the Football League and the Players' Union about extra pay for floodlit and televised games. A threatened ban on such fixtures was withdrawn, but unrest continued to simmer just beneath the surface. Prolonged talks led at the League's next annual meeting to an increase in the weekly wage from £15 to £17 in the playing season, and to £14 in the close season. At the same time bonuses that had been static for 36 years were doubled to £4 for a win and £2 for a draw. Television fees were set at 'about £2 a match'.

In the background, however, still loomed the vexed question of the maximum wage. The Union were seen by many to be on dangerous ground in insisting on the abolition of both it and the transfer system. One critic, Frank Coles of *The Daily Telegraph*, went as far as to say that they formed 'the unshakable rock on which the integrity of League football has been built'. He saw the football legislators of 50 years before as 'wise, far-seeing men' who 'sensed dangers of abuse of every kind if players were to be given freedom to sell their services to the highest bidder anywhere'. In his view, the maximum wage had 'undoubtedly saved professional soccer from the racketeers and stood the test of time'. How soon events were to contradict him, and also those League officials who thought that the pay increases promised 'a new and happier era in English football'.

Bristol Rovers were to be among the biggest sufferers from the coming removal of the restriction on the amount players could be paid, but as the 1955-56 season approached its close there were few clouds on their horizon as they found fresh vigour with which to renew their challenge for First Division glory. After the defeat at West Ham the impetus for their late revival was provided by Dai Ward as he set the Rovers record of scoring in each of the club's next eight matches.

That sequence began with the opening goal in a 2-2 home draw with Fulham, followed by the winner at Bury and two more in a Good Friday victory over Plymouth at Eastville. That hoisted Rovers back to second place, four points behind Wednesday and one ahead of Leicester and Port Vale – each from 36 games. Wednesday and Leicester were without a match that day while Vale improved their prospects with a comfortable win against Bristol City, who were slipping towards a final eleventh place. Liverpool, the other club above which Rovers climbed, lost at Doncaster to a controversial goal by Jeffrey that provoked ugly crowd scenes. Three table knives and a pepper pot, identified as stolen from excursion trains, were among objects thrown into the Doncaster goalmouth after Jeffrey had looked well offside in lobbing the ball over the goalkeeper. One policeman's hat was knocked off, two players were hit by missiles, and fighting broke out on the terraces during a melee that lasted some ten minutes.

There was trouble of a different kind ahead for Bristol Rovers. Again at home next day, they stumbled to a 1-4 defeat by lowly Rotherham, for whom winger Ian Wilson did the hat-trick. Ward's usual goal at least ensured equality until the second half, and although Rovers sank to fourth they were one of four clubs closest to Wednesday on 42 points, if six adrift. While the leaders were only just managing to account for Notts County, a side striving to avoid relegation, Liverpool rose to second place by coming from behind to beat Bristol City. Leicester stayed third by drawing with Middlesbrough after also being a goal down at the interval.

From that unexpected loss at the hands of Rotherham, Rovers bounced back with three wins in a row, promptly regaining the runners-up spot. Another Ward goal completed the double at Plymouth on Easter Monday, while Liverpool lost again to Doncaster – this time without any ructions. Over the next two weekends Wednesday's lead was halved to three points as they drew 3-3 at West Ham and lost 2-3 at home to Fulham. Rovers followed a win at Middlesbrough, thanks again to Ward, with a 2-0 victory gained at Eastville against Notts County through goals by Ward and Meyer.

Everything therefore hung tantalisingly in the balance on the evening of Saturday, 14 April, a day on which the 1-1 draw between Scotland and

England at Hampden Park meant that, with goal-average not counting, the home international championship was shared by all four countries for the first time in the 72 years of the competition. These were the leading positions in the Second Division for clubs still in contention for promotion:

	P	W	D	L	F	A	Pts
Sheffield Wed	40	19	13	8	93	57	51
BRISTOL ROVERS	40	21	6	13	82	66	48
Leeds United	39	20	6	13	72	58	46
Blackburn Rov	39	20	5	14	80	61	45
Liverpool	39	19	6	14	82	60	44
Leicester City	40	19	6	15	88	76	44
Nott'm Forest	38	19	6	13	63	57	44

Bristol Rovers could certainly have wished for easier remaining opponents than Leeds and Liverpool, and both those clubs also had a game in hand. Another daunting factor was that Rovers had to visit Elland Road, where Leeds had lost only once, to Blackburn, in the League all season (though Leeds had been beaten at home in the Cup by Cardiff. By one of football's quirkiest coincidences, Cardiff were to repeat that success at the same ground, in the same round, and by the same 2-1 score, in each of the next two seasons).

It was at Leeds that Dai Ward completed his record scoring sequence, but this time his single strike was not quite enough. The ground's biggest crowd of the season, 49,274, saw another game of three goals, all of them in the first half, go in the home team's favour. Rovers had most of the play, hitting the bar and missing chances, until the balance began to tilt away from them when John Charles moved up from centre-half to swap places with centre-forward Bob Forrest. The Welsh international, a giant in both stature and ability, scored one great goal and inspired winger Jack Overfield's decider, then went back into defence to help ensure there would be no Rovers equaliser.

That win lifted Leeds level with Rovers on points, but ahead of them on goal-average, and on the Monday evening they strengthened their hold on the second promotion place by also winning that vital game in hand, by 2-0 at Rotherham with goals from Albert Nightingale – an inside-forward they had acquired only at the third attempt after being beaten to his transfer by Huddersfield and Blackburn.

So Bristol Rovers went into the final Saturday unhappily aware that their hopes of joining the League's elite had gone, and with supporters complaining that the opportunity had been missed because no experienced centre-forward had been signed to take the place of the injured Bradford. Their goals figures were inferior not only to Leeds United's but also to those of the three other clubs with whom they were to finish four points behind the Yorkshire club.

In any case, unimpressive though Leeds had been away from home, their journey for their final match took them to already doomed Hull City. Leeds made sure of not being caught in emphatic 4-1 style, with two goals apiece from John Charles, his second one from the penalty spot, and Harold Brook. So Raich Carter saw his Leeds team clinch their climb at the ground of the club he had, as player-manager, also guided to promotion. If Leeds had lost, Liverpool could have thwarted them on goal-average after winning 2-1 at Eastville that afternoon. Liverpool would have been just two points behind with one more game to play, but, with that possibility no longer viable, the Merseysiders finished on a flat note by having no response to the two goals they conceded at Lincoln the following Wednesday.

Peter Hooper was the scorer of Rovers' goal against Liverpool, after John Evans had put the visitors ahead as early as the seventh minute. The winner, ten minutes from time, was snatched by Geoff Twentyman, whose son, also Geoff and also a central defender, joined Rovers from Preston 30 years later and became one of their finest free-transfer signings.

With Sheffield Wednesday having recovered from their slip-up against Fulham with a five-goal onslaught in both their last two matches, at Bury and home to Lincoln, this was how the 1955-56 top positions looked:

	P	W	D	L	F	A	Pts
Sheffield Wed	42	21	13	8	101	62	55
Leeds United	42	23	6	13	80	60	52
Liverpool	42	21	6	15	85	63	48
Blackburn Rov	42	21	6	15	84	65	48
Leicester City	42	21	6	15	94	78	48
BRISTOL ROVERS	42	21	6	15	84	70	48
Nott'm Forest	42	19	9	14	68	63	47

CHAPTER 20

Sykes Dents the Family Shield

'It feels great to be back, and my first League game can't come soon enough. I'm perfectly fit now.' So said Geoff Bradford after coming through the public trial match that clubs used to hold in those days, on his return from his second serious leg injury in preparation for the 1956-57 season.

Bradford, who was taking over the captaincy from Ray Warren, did not find the net in the Probables' 9-3 win, but he had several powerful shots saved by Powell, a young local goalkeeper, and made three of the goals. For scoring he was outdone by four-goal Dai Ward, who had done so much to keep promotion hopes alive in Bradford's absence the previous season, and Barrie Meyer, who did the hat-trick for the Possibles.

There was much talk of First Division football being 'just round the corner' for Bristol after both Rovers and City had been so strongly in the running for it, but that corner was to take a lot of turning. Not for twenty years were the top clubs in the land to be seen in League action again in the city – and then only at Ashton Gate, and very quickly with dire financial consequences. Rovers did reach Division One in 1992, but only because that was what Division Two became under Barclays' sponsorship with the formation of the FA Premier League. They stayed there for just the one season in pitching up a poor last of the three teams that went down.

Renewed hopes at Eastville were raised as Bradford began his second comeback in an attack that looked full of firepower with Biggs and Ward on either side of him and Petherbridge and Hooper on the wings. Indeed, after their fourth game Rovers were the pace-setters, if only for three days before other clubs caught up with the advantage they had gained by playing on a Monday. Although they were to finish mid-table, right through to Christmas Rovers were outside the top four only once – and that because of a 3-5 defeat in the all-Bristol battle by a City side languishing near the foot of the table.

Sobering as that unexpected setback was, it paled by comparison with the blow Rovers suffered at Barnsley a few weeks later. Although they won at Oakwell, with goals from Hooper and Ward, this was the match in which the little Welshman suffered the twisted left knee that necessitated a cartilage operation. Ward signalled his return with a hat-trick in a 6-1 demolition of Doncaster on the Saturday before Christmas, but that was also the first match in which Bradford scored for Rovers since early October – a lean spell that was to lead to his being dropped, or euphemistically 'rested', early in the New Year. Bradford was not as 'perfectly fit' as he had thought, and, as already recalled, he was later to admit that he was never the same player after that second injury.

There were, however, two goals for Bradford during his Rovers drought. He scored them at the Olympic Stadium in Amsterdam, as a late deputy for Portsmouth's Jackie Henderson in the Football Combination's 6-0 defeat of a Dutch XI that included nine players who had recently beaten Germany, the World Cup holders. According to one report, there were 'at least ten offside decisions against Bradford in the second half, most of them hair-line', and although he put the ball into the net a third time the effort was disallowed.

Bradford's temporary omission from Rovers' team came in the wake of a second 2-7 defeat in a matter of weeks, this one away to Leicester's champions-elect, and a fourth-round FA Cup exit at home to Preston. North End exacted 4-1 revenge for their Eastville defeat of five years previously. Tom Finney was in Preston's team this time, and he scored two of their goals. Rovers' solitary reply came from a Hooper penalty against a side flying high in the First Division (they were pushed into a final third place by Tottenham only on goal-average behind Manchester United's champions). The following Saturday Preston scored seven goals against Portsmouth.

Rovers and Preston were paired again in the Cup in 1960, when Finney was once more outstanding in a 5-1 replay win at Deepdale, following a 3-3 draw at Eastville in which Geoff Bradford was concussed in the first half and remembered little of the second. He was told afterwards that he had a good chance of scoring the winner, but shot from long range when he had plenty of time to go closer. Another eventful Cup clash between the clubs came in 1981, when Rovers edged a seven-goal thriller at Deepdale after being four up at half-time. The young goalkeeper beaten three times in Preston's second-half recovery was local-born Phil Kite, a former England Boys player who made the first of nearly 100 League appearances for the club a week later.

The other 2-7 setback Rovers suffered in the 1956-57 season was inflicted at Bury on Christmas Day, incongruously sandwiched in the space of five bitterly cold days between the big win against Doncaster and another 6-1 victory in the return with Bury on Boxing Day. As already recalled, Hooper was the hat-trick hero that afternoon, when Rovers, on their notorious pitch, were lucky to escape the worst of weather that turned from icy rain to heavy snow. Torquay's players, travelling home from London after a scoreless draw at Griffin Park, were stuck in snowdrifts on Salisbury Plain and did not complete their journey until five o'clock in the morning – yet they still managed to win when they met Brentford again that afternoon.

Later in 1957, ten days before the following Christmas, another seven-goal broadside – this one by Grimsby Town – toppled Rovers to their heaviest home defeat in twenty years – since that 1-8 shellacking by QPR in the

Cup on 27 November 1937. Their previous biggest at Eastville since the war had been by 1-6 against Ipswich on the opening day of the 1948-49 season. Rovers could not muster even one goal in reply to the Mariners, though Hooper and Biggs missed good chances in the opening five minutes. It was a black day indeed for Bristol football. City crashed 1-5 at Swansea.

Another match in which Rovers let in seven goals, in the 1920s, is worth a mention for the fact that they went three up in the first seventeen minutes, prompting George Humphreys, then their chairman, to the premature remark: 'We've got these points all right, and we can do with them.' Crystal Palace were 7-4 winners.

Geoff Bradford began 1957 by scoring two of the goals in a 4-3 win at Hull that earned Rovers the Cup visit from Preston. That was the club's only success in five matches before his exclusion from the goalless Eastville clash with Bristol City on the second day of February. Alfie Biggs was switched to centre-forward, and the vacancy on the other side of him from Ward was filled by Norman Sykes, who had made his League debut in the Boxing Day beating of Bury.

The strongly built Sykes was the first to follow the long-serving Jackie Pitt at right-half, a position he regularly filled, but he started out as an inside-forward. He first came to Rovers' notice when, on the verge of his teens, he went to Eastville to ask if there might be a future for him on the playing staff while he was on holiday from the Air Balloon Hill School in the St George district of Bristol. The Rovers were then just starting their scheme to encourage juniors, but they told Sykes to go away and return when he had left school. In the interim, he captained Bristol Boys and played for England in a schools international against Scotland at Wembley. He showed then that he had the right temperament for the big occasion, also earning a place in the England Youth team. Rovers had to resort to subterfuge to sign him as a professional after he had played in their reserve side at the age of sixteen.

Word having got around that other clubs were interested in him, Rovers turned to Bert Hoyle for assistance, and their former goalkeeper took Sykes away to stay with relatives of Hoyle's in Bradford for a week. The day before his seventeenth birthday in October 1953, Sykes travelled with Hoyle from Yorkshire to London, to join up with Bert Tann and Geoff Bradford, who were there for the match in which Bradford scored three of an FA team's four goals in the defeat of an RAF side at Tottenham. On the train from Paddington back to Temple Meads in Bristol, the four men checked their watches, and one minute before midnight Tann produced the forms that Sykes signed to become a Rovers professional and collect the £10 signing-on fee, which was all that could then be legally allowed.

While serving his apprenticeship in the Football Combination side, Sykes saved up to go to Switzerland for the World Cup finals of 1954, taking in

Paris on the way. His patient wait for a place in the first team was rewarded at the end of the season before that Boxing Day debut in the League, in the annual Gloucestershire Cup game against Bristol City. Once established, his consistent form soon attracted the attention of Tottenham Hotspur, whose manager, Bill Nicholson, would have offered £20,000 for him if Rovers had given him any encouragement.

In his 80th League match, at Fulham on the last day of January 1959, Sykes became the Eastville club's youngest captain at the age of 22, but only a year later he asked for a transfer after losing both his place and the captaincy, saying 'I have been playing badly and the only hope is to get away to another club'. He did not take long to have second thoughts, however, and withdrew his request, which Tann had not been prepared to grant anyway. 'Everyone in football knows our policy,' said the manager, who was stirred into the denial of a London newspaper report that the Rovers were 'a troubled club'.

That there was some truth in the claim soon afterwards became evident, however, when Sykes was known to be unhappy again, unable to dispel a feeling that he had been 'messed about long enough'. The League's recent abandonment of the maximum wage had left players open to the temptation of greener pastures elsewhere, and Sykes put another deep dent in the 'family' shield that had so proudly safeguarded loyalty at Eastville when he declared that he 'must look to the future and try to earn more money now that more money is open to professionals under the new agreement'.

In the summer of 1961, Sykes rejected Rovers' offer of £25-a-week basic pay and, with the No Buy, No Sell policy having been made redundant, he was put on the transfer list at £25,000. Later that year he refused to sign another monthly contract and collected his cards, saying: 'I am sick and tired of the whole affair. I'm finished with Rovers.' He took a job outside football, but soon afterwards agreed to accept monthly terms again when the price on his head was reduced to £15,000 and there was a chance of joining Chelsea. His trial at Stamford Bridge did not prompt a bid, so early in 1962 he decided to sign for Rovers again after all, following talks with Tann.

Sykes held his first-team place for the rest of that season and most of the next, altogether exceeding 200, but by then he was being so troubled by a persistent knee injury that in November 1963 – two months after becoming a part-timer and one month after his 27th birthday – he announced his decision to retire from football completely. 'I just do not want to end up a cripple,' he said. 'The doctor told me that is what would happen if I continued to play. I have four young children, and I want to be able to live an active life with them and not be hobbling around on crutches. In the last few weeks I have had some discomfort in my right hip, an arthritic condition, which has worried me. I have thought about part-time football or returning to local amateur soccer as a permit player because I love the game so much, but it would not be wise. I am the type of player who can enjoy playing only if I am giving it everything I have got.'

Rovers continued to pay Sykes until his contract expired at the end of the following June, and he also received a second benefit cheque for £750 on having completed ten years as a professional. The first benefit, five years before, had amounted to £600. Hopes, however, of insurance compensation for retiring on medical advice were soon dashed when Cliff Lloyd, secretary of the Professional Footballers' Association, made inquiries for him. 'He told me that my arthritic hip is not classed as an injury, but a disease. They say it is something that was not caused by football, so I am not eligible for compensation. I had hopes of about £500 insurance money, which would have helped to settle some financial affairs.'

Even so, the income he was to have from Eastville for the rest of the season was augmented by the job he held outside football. On becoming a part-time player two months earlier, he had joined a sand company as a trainee salesman at nearby Tytherington. He now left to become a salesman for the Rolls Prestcold electrical appliance firm controlled by millionaire John Bloom, a former director of Queen's Park Rangers. All well and good you might think, yet, incredibly, despite all the health warnings and his apparent attention to them, off he went to Canada without Rovers' permission in May 1964, making himself the subject of a FIFA ban, and played for Toronto City until his contract at Eastville expired.

Sykes made an impressive debut for the Canadian club in an 8-3 defeat of Hamilton Steelers, who had sold John Kurila to Bristol City the previous season, but spoiled it by being sent off three minutes from time for abusive language to his own players. 'I couldn't tolerate his language any longer,' said referee Hugh McLean, 'so I thumbed him out of the game.' Tony Book, then a Bath City full-back, was also in the Toronto team and had his name taken for the same offence. 'We were all shouting where the ball should be passed,' Book explained, although they had quite a problem in making themselves understood because half their team-mates spoke very little English.

Two other players with a Bath City connection did almost all the scoring in that match with the Steelers. Charlie ('Cannonball') Fleming, a Scottish international while with East Fife and later of Sunderland before becoming Bath's player-manager, led the way with four goals; Ted Purdon, a South African whose many clubs included not only Sunderland but also Bristol Rovers, netted three. After being taken on trial from Bath in 1960, Purdon played in Rovers' first-ever League Cup-tie, won 2-1 at home to Fulham (they reached the third round before losing at future finalists Rotherham). Purdon's League appearances for the Eastville club were limited to fewer than half-a-dozen, the last of them in a 2-5 home defeat by Plymouth.

Plymouth was to be the next stop for Norman Sykes, it being no mere coincidence that Argyle's newly appointed manager, Malcolm Allison, was Toronto City's coach while Sykes was out there. As might have been expected, in the more demanding sphere of the Football League, it was a move fated to fail. The hip problem did not take long to dog his days in Devon, and he played only three games in the Second Division before being dropped after a heavy defeat at Bolton. Was he then convinced that it was folly to keep on trying to defy medical advice? Oh no! Incredibly, he still had nearly 70 League appearances to make, over 50 of them with Stockport and fifteen with Doncaster. Even Eastville had not seen the last of him. Sykes played there again in a Doncaster team beaten 2-4 in February 1967. Not until after he had gone out of the League with Altrincham did he finally bow out. Remarkably, Sykes bucked the trend of former professional footballers by opening a tee-total nightclub in Manchester in 1975.

CHAPTER 21

The Mabbutt Family

Besides Norman Sykes, the rich array of young talent that followed Alfie Biggs and Peter Hooper off the Eastville production line included Ray Mabbutt and Doug Hillard. They helped sustain Bristol Rovers as a Second Division force for most of the 1950s.

Raymond William Mabbutt played in every position except centre-half in the course of making more than 400 first-team appearances over the dozen seasons from 1957 to 1969, but he settled down at wing-half after first dropping back from his original place on the right wing when Londoner Tommy Baker was injured during a reserve game. Although Mabbutt made a great success of the switch, he was moved back to the wing for the next few matches before Bert Tann, in his own words, 'was pushed for choice one week and decided to give him another chance at wing-half. He has been playing there with considerable success ever since.'

Baker was on Rovers' books for six years before being given what was to be his only senior chance in a 2-5 defeat at Wrexham, and he also had the bad luck to need a cartilage operation before 'Pat' Beasley, the former Bristol City manager, took him to Dover.

Ray Mabbutt hailed from Aylesbury, but enjoyed his first footballing success on the right wing in the Yorkshire Amateurs team that won the West Riding title by beating Lancashire in the final at Burnley's ground. That was while he was on National Service in the Army, stationed at Durham and Catterick. He also assisted Spennymoor United around that time, and was chosen for the Northern Command side that included Stan Anderson – a wing-half who went on to play for England and captain all three of the major North-East clubs, Sunderland, Newcastle and Middlesbrough – and Eddie Colman, the Manchester United half-back who would surely have been capped but for being among those who died in the plane disaster at Munich.

Before his call-up into the Army, Mabbutt played in the Berks & Bucks youth team and for Aylesbury United. He was with the Aylesbury club when he first came to the notice of Bristol Rovers, who signed him shortly after his demobilisation. Five other players made the first team in the Colts team in which he made his professional debut against Bristol City Colts in a Western League Cup-tie – goalkeeper Ron Nicholls, full-back Cecil Steeds, half-backs Graham Ricketts and Joe Davis, and Ray Seatherton. In common with Seatherton, however, Steeds, a Bristolian who crossed over from City, was afflicted by a knee injury and also played only twice with the seniors –

in an FA Cup defeat at Blackburn three years before deputising in the 2-7 trouncing at Leicester for Les Edwards, the former boxer who was Frank Allcock's successor at left-back when into his 30s.

Ricketts also had restricted opportunities with Rovers after graduating from local league football, in which he represented the Suburban League against the Downs League, and playing for England Youth. He fared better on moving to Stockport, Doncaster (where he was again a clubmate of Norman Sykes) and Peterborough. He was only seventeen when he made his League debut as another of Pitt's deputies. In a short spell at centre-forward in one of Geoff Bradford's absences he almost snatched a dramatic victory in a home match with Leeds as Rovers dramatically recovered to draw after being four goals down at half-time.

Davis, a cousin of Bobby Jones, the sharp and speedy forward who features prominently in a later chapter, played more than 200 times for Rovers, one of them as the first substitute to be used by the club in a 3-0 home win against Walsall in October 1965. He entered League football as centre-half successor to David Pyle, a former Trowbridge Town player who took over from 'Paddy' Hale for nearly 150 games before having just a few more with Bristol City. Davis later formed a successful full-back partnership with Doug Hillard. Captain of the side during the 1960s, in which he was also one of the winners of the club's Player of the Year award, this influential player with the famous name from the world of billiards and snooker rendered further fine service on his return to Eastville as youth coach and scout. His playing career had been ended by injury soon after his transfer in 1967 to Swansea.

It was as a scorer that Ray Mabbutt enjoyed one of his most memorable afternoons – scoring a hat-trick in a 5-4 win at Northampton – but he is remembered chiefly for his creative and defensive qualities as a dependable and wholehearted holder of the right-half position vacated by Norman Sykes. He wound up his senior career with Newport County, taking his aggregate of games beyond 500, before including Frome Town – whom he captained and coached – among the non-League clubs he assisted. In one friendly match for Frome he turned out against Bristol Rovers aged 41.

Mabbutt's two sons followed him into League football – Gary with Bristol Rovers and Tottenham, Kevin with Bristol City and Crystal Palace. 'I was determined to turn them into top-class players as soon as they began to toddle,' he revealed many years later. 'Their first toy was a fluffy ball. Gradually I worked out basic exercises which had to be done every day. By eight or nine they were doing twenty different exercises every day – limbering up, passing, controlling and taking the pace off the ball, and ten-yard sprints. They never grumbled or wanted to back out, and I never drove them. Our top game was one-a-side soccer. We'd play that for two or three hours at a time.'

But Gary had to surmount a seemingly unassailable obstacle to save all that effort going to waste. His story is one of football's most remarkable, an inspirational one for any youngster with the ambition to make good in sport who finds himself with a similarly serious health problem. Signed by Rovers as an apprentice on his sixteenth birthday, 23 August 1977, he was told two years later that diabetes had ruined his chance of making a career out of football, yet he went on to play more than 100 games for Rovers, over 600 for Spurs, and sixteen for England, in a career that lasted 21 years before his retirement from top-class soccer at the age of 37.

He began as a striker, as the front men had by then become known, but for both his League clubs and his country he demonstrated exceptional versatility in also being thoroughly reliable in defence and midfield. His stamina and consistency were all the more amazing for the fact that he had to inject himself with insulin before, during and after each match. He needed four such injections every day to avoid falling into a coma, and he regularly conducted his own blood tests – as many as six of them on match days to make sure he did not collapse on the field. It was only to be expected that he admitted to feeling depressed sometimes, but he gained encouragement from thinking that 'perhaps I have been chosen to prove to others what can be done'. He certainly succeeded in that.

In Norway on one of England's pre-season tours, his room-mate Gary Lineker thought he was drunk when he had little control over what he was saying or doing because he had become too low on insulin. He had his most alarming experience in that respect when he took an afternoon nap before Tottenham's home League Cup-tie against Barnsley in 1986 after having his lunch and giving himself an injection. The next thing he remembered was waking up in hospital with two glucose drips in each arm. He had fallen into a deep diabetic coma and had been found lying face down at his home after failing to turn up for the match, bleeding from cuts where he had been trying to give himself a blood test. Yet, so quickly can a recovery be made from that kind of trauma, on the very next Saturday, just three days later, he helped Spurs to only their second victory against Liverpool at Anfield in more than 70 years.

Gary Mabbutt's indomitable spirit was also to the fore when he fought back to fitness after suffering four fractures of the cheekbone and three of an eye socket during a match with Wimbledon. Members of an FA Commission decided not to charge John Fashanu, whose elbow caused that horrific damage, because they were not convinced there was 'sufficient intent' – even though referee Keith Hackett had since said that he felt there was 'a measure of intent' and he would have cautioned the Wimbledon striker for dangerous play if he had seen the incident clearly at the time. Incredibly, Mabbutt was back in action for Spurs' Reserves within 80 days, complete with a 'Phantom' mask that he continued to wear for a while in his first-team comeback to protect his repaired eye socket.

On another occasion, at Derby, he had to have sixteen stitches in a nasty head wound, but was playing again only a couple of weeks later. He also battled back to fitness after breaking his left leg in a match at Blackburn, though on that occasion more than a year elapsed before he reappeared in the Premiership as a substitute who helped Spurs to recover from a goal down to beat Aston Villa. It was at the end of that season, 1997-98, that his magnificent service to Spurs finally came to an end when he was given a free transfer.

Perseverance to the degree shown by Mabbutt was truly exceptional, as was the strength of character and forbearance that led him to decide not to take legal action against Fashanu, whose own career was ended by injury while with Aston Villa less than two years later – at a time when Fashanu was involved in alleged match-fixing charges of which he was eventually cleared.

While with Rovers, for whom he made his League debut as a substitute at Burnley on 16 December 1978, when still an apprentice, Gary Mabbutt was selected as a striker for the England Youth team, which he captained against Denmark in 1980. He was also in the national Under-21 side for three matches before his £105,000 transfer to Tottenham during the 1982 close season, by which time Rovers had dropped back into the Third Division for the second time since the heyday of the Tann era. 'He has given us marvellous service,' said Bobby Gould, Rovers' manager at that time. 'We didn't want to lose him, but the lad wanted First Division football and we could not stand in his way as his contract had expired.' Peter Shreeve, Spurs' assistant manager, described the fee as 'very good value in a depressed transfer market'. Quite an understatement.

The first dividend on that outlay came after only 60 seconds, the time he took to score the winning goal, when Mabbutt first played for Tottenham in a challenge match with Glasgow Rangers, the Scottish League Cup winners, at Ibrox. He had been a Spurs player for only three months when he won the first of his full England caps, and in 1984 he picked up a UEFA Cup-winner's medal as a member of the side that defeated Anderlecht on penalties after drawing both legs of the final. He was also in the Tottenham team that in 1987 lost to Coventry City in one of the best FA Cup finals since the Second World War, but gained some kind of a distinction by becoming only the third player in the long history of the competition to score for both sides in the final (the others were Bert Turner, of Charlton, in 1946, and Tommy Hutchison, of Manchester City, in 1981).

Compensation for that defeat came in 1991, when Gary Mabbutt skippered Spurs to victory over Nottingham Forest at Wembley, again showing his incredible endurance in lasting the pace right through extra-time. His award of the MBE in the 1994 New Year's Honours brought thoroughly deserved recognition of his magnificent achievements, as the title of his autobiography so aptly put it, *Against All Odds*.

Kevin Mabbutt, three years older than Gary, also rose to England Under-21 rank, gaining a place in the squad during Bristol City's four seasons back in the First Division towards the end of the 1970s. 'Gary is still "my little brother", except that he's now bigger than me physically,' he said while they were still in opposite Bristol camps. 'And whereas he used to learn things from me, he's now showing me a couple of things.' At that time Ray Mabbutt, then in his mid-40s, was still playing in midfield for Keynsham Town in the Western League. When his sons were in opposition in matches between the Bristol clubs he confessed to being 'full of torn loyalties' even though he had been a Rovers player. 'Whatever happens,' he added, 'development of my two boys is the biggest source of satisfaction in my life. I rate myself a lucky father.'

Doug Hillard, one of Ray Mabbutt's team-mates in the majority of his near-350 games for Bristol Rovers, was signed as a forward at the end of May in 1957 after catching their attention by scoring eight goals in one match for his first local side, Maywood, and then netting the winner for the Bristol Mental Hospital club in that year's Gloucestershire Intermediate Cup final against Bristol City's 'A' team, but Bert Tann converted him into a full-back because Rovers were well off for inside-forwards at the time. It was just another of the adroit decisions the manager made.

Hillard almost made his League debut a year before he actually did. He was chosen to play against Barnsley at Eastville, but the injured Watling, whose place he was taking, made an unexpectedly rapid recovery. It was as deputy for another unfit player, Brian Doyle – Harry Bamford's first successor at right-back – that he was eventually given his first chance shortly before Christmas in 1958. That drawn home match was against Sheffield United, the club against which Doyle had made his debut in the corresponding game of the previous season.

With Doyle, a Mancunian who had previously played for Stoke and Exeter, soon afterwards forced to retire because of nasal trouble for which, while playing, he had to have an operation every year to enable him to breathe, Hillard went on to make 313 League appearances as first choice for the best part of a decade, plus five more as a substitute. And there would have been still more but for an injury that kept him out for most of the 1961-62 season. Restored to the attack in an emergency arising from Rovers' plunge to the foot of the Second Division with defeats in their first five matches, he broke a leg as they lost again on a midweek visit to Scunthorpe, the club against which he had scored the first of what were to be a dozen League goals two years earlier.

Not until their eighth game of that season did Rovers get off the mark, and although they escaped from last place they were unable to ward off relegation. Defeat at Luton in their final game sent them down with Brighton. Swansea edged above Rovers with a home draw that put paid to Sunderland's hopes of promotion. On his recovery, the stocky Hillard was a key figure as Rovers set about rebuilding. Twice he had an ever-present record, and twice he was voted the club's Player of the Year, but Second Division status was not to be regained until four years after he had left.

On a free transfer in 1968 he moved to Taunton Town, the Somerset club he led to the Western League title in the first of his five seasons as their player-manager. For several years afterwards he managed another local club, Mangotsfield United, combining that with running a sports equipment shop not far from Bristol Rovers' ground. Mangotsfield were newly elected to the Western League when he joined them, and in the following season they won the League Cup. He was in his 62nd year when he died in Frenchay Hospital after a short illness early in 1997.

Brian Doyle, a fully qualified FA coach, stayed on at Eastville for a while after being forced to give up playing. Appointed to succeed Jackie Pitt as trainer of the Colts team in the Western League, he also assisted Pitt, who had become chief coach, in the training and coaching of young players at evening sessions, while also having a job in the offices of the Douglas firm in the Kingswood area of Bristol. He later coached at Cambridge and Carlisle, went into management at Workington and Stockport, and was Bob Stokoe's assistant manager at Blackpool when the seaside club won the Anglo-Italian Cup in 1971. After that he coached in Kuwait and Finland before retiring in 1990, two years before his death.

CHAPTER 22

Bradford and the Strike Threat

Of all the players who were with Bristol Rovers during Bert Tann's time at the club, Geoff Bradford was surely just about the last one who could be expected to have to face the threat of being ostracised by his team-mates. Yet that is precisely what happened when the Professional Footballers' Association, popularly known as the Players' Union, proposed strike action in their attempt to do away with the maximum wage at the beginning of the 1960s.

There was 100 per cent membership of the union at Eastville, where all the players were prepared to support a strike – except for Bradford and Ray Mabbutt, who both felt that the maximum wage should be raised but could see the dangers of abolishing it altogether. When, however, it came to every-one stating firmly whether to strike or not, Mabbutt decided he would sup-port the union's action if it became necessary. Bradford was therefore left out on a limb, and that was when he was told that if it came to a strike, and he still kept the same attitude, the other players would refuse to play with him in the same team.

'There weren't many of the old brigade left at Eastville by then,' he said in recalling that unpleasant incident many years later. 'Two new generations of players had come into the team, and they had a different approach to football than I did. Our attitudes became so far apart that I was called a "blackleg". I was 33, and all I wanted to do was to go on playing football. But I was also concerned about what the changes could do to the game, not just to older players like myself but to the youngsters as well. Obviously, I didn't like being called a blackleg, but it didn't worry me, and in the end my firm stand gave some of the younger players second thoughts. They began to see what I was driving at.'

Alfie Biggs was the union's representative at Eastville. He used to come back from meetings and keep his colleagues up to date with what was hap-pening. What he had to say made Bradford feel that decisions were being made without sufficient thought being given to the consequences. He explained: 'My concern was not so much what a player could earn in the course of a season or two, but with what his life span in the game was going to be. The post-war boom was over. If clubs were going to have to pay play-ers a lot more money then there would be room for fewer players in the game. It was as simple as that to me, and I have been proved right. I saw it affecting players at both ends of the scale. The older player kept on to help bring on young players in the Reserves – he would go. And so would the younger players who had ability but needed to be given time for it to be brought out. Clubs wouldn't be able to afford to give them time.

'I was also concerned about what too much money would do to the game itself. I could see it bringing an end to artistry in football. The game has become a means of earning big money. Players can't afford to lose games, so they can't afford to let great players express their talents. I could see it wrecking the kind of team spirit we had known at Eastville. Football is a team game, so everyone in the team should be paid the same.'

That was a sentiment with which a great many would no doubt agree. Although players were well paid compared with the wage of the average working man, there was an obvious need for a further increase in the maximum, which had risen to £20 a week, but the obscene heights to which pay packets, and transfer fees, have escalated since the abandonment of a limit have had the undesired effect of concentrating power into the hands of a select few of the wealthiest clubs. The pendulum has swung grotesquely too far the other way, and players at the highest levels have become over-glamorised figures remote from the public who pay so much to see them in action. In recent years Bob Wilson, the former Arsenal and Scotland goalkeeper, expressed the view, widely held it seems safe to say, that 'the game is such big business that it is spiralling out of control; it has lost a great deal of its charm'.

It is also interesting to note what Jimmy Greaves, the England sharpshooter who scored more than 350 First Division goals, had to say on this subject in his autobiography: 'I lived in the same neighbourhood as many Chelsea supporters. I met them socially at Supporters' Club functions. Quite often on the train home from an away match my team-mates and I would have a natter with Chelsea fans who were also journeying home. We'd share a beer or a cup of tea. We got to know them and they got to know us. There was an affinity and understanding that I don't think exists today because players don't have that level of contact with supporters. Perhaps it still exists in the lower divisions, but sadly not in the Premiership, where too many players have erected barriers to separate them from supporters.'

How right Geoff Bradford was in seeing that Bristol Rovers would be among the clubs particularly hard hit by the release of the purse strings. No Buy, No Sell was doomed from the moment – on 18 January 1961, only three days before the threatened strike – when players were no longer all bound by the maximum. Loyalties that had got to the stage of being taken for granted were tested to the limit, and it was no mere coincidence that the first full season after the introduction of the New Deal ended with Rovers' loss of their hard-won Second Division status.

Biggs himself was the first to jump ship. He readily used the new-found freedom to seek higher wages, but Rovers were not prepared to meet his demands and put him on offer. His transfer to Preston on 17 July 1961 brought them what was then their top fee of £18,000, but on 5 October 1962, after 49 League games and 22 goals for the Lancashire club, Biggs was back in the Eastville fold with a price tag reduced to £12,000. That still made him Rovers' record signing up to that time. The pull of his home city and his old club had proved too strong.

Biggs, nicknamed 'The Baron' among his clubmates because of his natty dress sense, first joined Rovers as a junior in 1952 after playing for Connaught Road School, Bristol Boys and Eagle House Youth Club. He turned professional early in 1953 on turning seventeen, and totted up 77 goals in 214 League games before his departure to Deepdale. While in the Army on National Service he had the good fortune to remain available to Rovers while stationed at Corsham in Wiltshire, and he also gained valuable experience in Army teams – on one occasion against the Royal Navy at Eastville in the company of such established First Division players as Manchester United's Duncan Edwards, Eddie Colman and Bill Foulkes. It was in another Army game that he first made Preston fully aware of his scoring potential, scoring a couple of goals in the defeat of an Irish FA side at Deepdale.

On his return to Bristol Rovers from Preston he was appointed captain and embarked upon the most successful phase of his career. His 210 games and 101 goals in his second spell with Rovers took him to League totals for the club of 424 and 178, putting him second only to Bradford in their all-time scoring list. With Cup goals included he was not far off 200, and in 1963-64, when he was an ever-present for the second time, his overall total of 37 goals broke the Rovers' record for one season that Bradford had held for eleven years. Bradford, whose last season that was, retained the League best with his 1952-53 tally of 33 to the 30 of Biggs.

In 1966-67 Biggs was voted Rovers' Player of the Year, but he had only one more season with the club before leaving again, this time to Walsall on transfer deadline day in 1968, priced at £8,500. Towards the end of that year he moved to Swansea in exchange for a small fee and Jimmy McMorran, a forward who was later with Notts County and Halifax Town. Then, in May 1970, at the age of 34, Biggs ended sixteen seasons in the Football League by joining Doug Hillard at Taunton Town, with whom he wound up his playing career. After that, besides pursuing his favourite pastimes of snooker, dancing, race-going and socialising, he had a varied life as a car salesman, postman, baker, and with a business parcel delivery service. He also had a stint on the maintenance staff back at Eastville, where he continued to be a regular visitor on match days.

The record transfer fee Rovers received was boosted to £50,000 when another Bristolian, Larry Lloyd, a 6ft 2in, 12st centre-half who had joined straight from Lockleaze School, moved to Liverpool in April 1969. He went as a ready-made replacement for Ron Yeats, 'the colossus,' as manager Bill Shankly termed him, who moved on as Tranmere's player-manager after 450 games at the heart of the Anfield club's defence.

With Bristol Rovers, Lloyd, a Gloucestershire and England Youth player, took over from David Stone, also Bristol-born, who had been in the Bristol Boys side that won the English Schools Shield in 1958. Whereas Stone had just over 150 games behind him when he left Eastville for Southend with Ronnie Briggs (a former Manchester United goalkeeper twice capped by Northern Ireland while with Swansea before his brief stay with Rovers), Lloyd played in just under 50 games. During that short time, however, he struck up a daunting 'Twin Towers' partnership at centre-back with 6ft 5in Stuart Taylor.

Taylor, a former Bristol City amateur, might well have followed Lloyd to success in the First Division, but he soldiered on to set Rovers' appearances record of 546 League games – 207 of them in succession. He ended his fifteen seasons with the club by rejecting a one-year contract with Chelsea to become Bath City's player-manager for a couple of seasons at the beginning of the 1980s. He then returned to Eastville as commercial manager, but soon left again to turn his hand at being a publican, night-club owner and a plumber – his original trade..

In just over 200 games for Liverpool, Larry Lloyd was an ever-present in the 1972-73 season during which the Reds carried off the First Division title and the UEFA Cup (he scored in the first leg of the final against Borussia Moenchengladbach), and he was in the side that lost the FA Cup to Arsenal in extra-time, and after leading, at Wembley in 1971. Injuries and loss of form led to his transfer to Coventry at the start of the 1974-75 season, but the £240,000 fee plunged the Midlands club into a financial crisis and Lloyd, failing to justify it in looking slow and cumbersome, was in danger of seeing his career in ruins. It was revitalised under the dynamic management of Brian Clough with a move to Nottingham Forest, his price tag devalued to £60,000 – and that only after a 'test' period on loan.

Striking up another formidable defensive partnership, this time with Scottish international Kenny Burns, Lloyd promptly helped these other Reds to promotion from the Second Division, then to an immediate title in the First (though he was out of a number of matches through injury), as well as victory over Liverpool in a replayed League Cup final. Forest were really on fire in the most sustained period of success in their history. They were also League Cup finalists in both the next two seasons, Lloyd picking up another winner's medal against Southampton in 1979 but missing the Wembley defeat by Wolverhampton Wanderers in 1980 after again being in a winning team against Liverpool over the two legs of the semi-final.

A medal treble was denied Lloyd because on the Thursday before the final with Wolves he was suspended for one match by an FA Disciplinary Commission for exceeding twenty penalty points with six bookings. It was a decision that Bert Millichip, chairman of the Commission, said was the most difficult of that kind he had ever had to make, one that made him 'feel depressed and disappointed at having to put a player out of a Cup final at Wembley'. Lloyd described it as the biggest disappointment of his career, adding: 'I could have cheated my way out of suspension. The fifth booking that took me to eighteen points was on January 26, and the sixth didn't come until five weeks later. If I had gone out of my way to get it earlier I could have served the ban by now and been able to play at Wembley.'

For Lloyd, reprieve of a very different kind awaited, one that brought the greatest club honours the game has to offer. At the end of that 1979-80 season he was a member of a European Cup-winning team for the second consecutive year. And even that was not all. In that season he also earned the Forest fans' vote as their Player of the Year and added another England cap to the three he had won while with Liverpool – though the less said about that the better. Well below his best, he was substituted in a heavy defeat by Wales at Wrexham.

In March 1981, Lloyd became, at 32, the then youngest manager in the League in leaving Forest to join Wigan as player-manager, but despite leading them to promotion to Division Three the following season he was often at loggerheads with the directors and had an especially stormy relationship with chairman Freddie Pye, mainly because of his repeated refusal to move home from Nottingham. It culminated in his sacking in April 1983, only a few weeks before Pye also left, forced out by the boo boys. Lloyd quickly found his next job on his doorstep, as manager of Notts County, but he lost it when a slide from fleeting leadership of the First Division led to relegation. He had to contend with crowd abuse before the axe fell. 'One supporter immediately behind my touchline seat began shouting filthy remarks concerning my wife and kids. I jumped up and went towards the bloke, but he quickly ran off. I'd have snapped him in two if I'd got my hands on him.' Lloyd was afterwards proprietor of The Stage Door Club in Nottingham and was a regular contributor to local radio.

In the post-Tann era, the costliest player to leave Bristol Rovers after Lloyd was Phil Roberts, a full-back or wing-half whose consistency was reflected in the 150 consecutive League appearances he made in falling not far short of 200 overall before his £55,000 move to Portsmouth in May 1973. While at Fratton Park he added four full Welsh caps to those he had gained at Under-23 level along with his Rovers team-mates Frankie Prince, a combative ball-winner who was a substitute, but unused, for one full international against England, and Wayne Jones.

The next two outgoing transfers to break the Rovers record involved strikers who rejoined the club. Paul Randall went to Stoke for £180,000, but was bought back for £50,000, the Supporters' Club making a sizeable contribution; Steve White went to Luton for £200,000 and was re-signed from Charlton for £35,000. In 1989, goalkeeper Nigel Martyn became the first Rovers player to bring in £1 million, plus an extra £100,000 when he first played for England, when he moved to Crystal Palace. Other million-pound men to leave Rovers have been Marcus Stewart, Barry Hayles and Jason Roberts, the last two of those three strikers both costing £2,100,000 in their respective moves to Fulham and West Bromwich Albion. Stewart, later with Bristol City, went to Huddersfield for £1,200,000.

As buyers, Rovers were almost at the end of the second decade of the no-maximum era that had unhinged the financial floodgates before they negotiated a deal involving as much as a six-figure sum. Until then, their record expenditure on a player progressed from the fee that brought Biggs back from Preston to the forging of the 'Smash and Grab' forward partnership of Bruce Bannister (£22,000 from Bradford City) and Alan Warboys (£38,000 from Sheffield United).

After that the biggest fee forked out by Rovers rose to £50,000 for midfielder Gary Emmanuel from Birmingham City, and double that amount for winger Stewart Barrowclough from the same club. Not for more than a dozen years was that record broken – and then new highs were set three times in successive seasons: £130,000 to Fulham for midfielder Justin Skinner, £160,000 to Sunderland for full-back Paul Hardyman, £375,000 to QPR for Andy Tillson, a 6ft 2in central defender.

CHAPTER 23

Back to the Third Division

Londoner John Gummow wore himself out in the service of Bristol Rovers, and after he had left he cut himself off from the club completely. He had been secretary at Eastville for over fourteen years when he resigned five days before Christmas in 1960 because he 'could no longer stand the strain' after an illness that had put him in hospital for several weeks during the summer.

Delicate as his health then was, he outlived his successor, the younger and crew-cropped Ron Moules who had been his assistant. When he took over, Ron told me that 'after so many years' association with John G, both as friends and colleagues, I regretted the reasons for his departure, but I cannot disguise the fact that I am delighted at a promotion which at one time never seemed possible, and I eagerly look forward to the future.' Sadly, however, Ron did not have much of a future. He died within seven years, at the early age of 45.

There was one player who was no stranger to John Gummow when he became Rovers' secretary, for he had got to know Harry Bamford quite well while both were in the same Burma campaign during the Second World War. As already noted, Bamford got to Eastville in a rather roundabout way, and Gummow's own arrival was made in unusual circumstances. He was in the main stand at Bristol City's ground, waiting for a match to begin, when he read in a local paper that Rovers' secretary had resigned. Turning to the friend who accompanied him, he said: 'I'm going to apply for that job,' whereupon he immediately left the stand and phoned the Eastville ground. John Hare was the only director there, but he promised to make a note of Gummow's name and told him to apply in writing. This he did, and within a fortnight, on 8 December 1946, he was appointed.

Of his resignation, he said: 'Some people will read into this that I am leaving the Rovers because they are having a bad time, or that I have had disagreements or reservations about policy. This is emphatically not the case. The simple truth is that, after my recent illness, this season's playing record and its consequent worries have given rise to some anxiety about the duodenal ulcer from which I suffered in the summer. I shall always be terribly grateful to Bristol Rovers for the chance they gave me fourteen years ago.'

John Gummow's Rovers duties were only part of an extremely busy schedule. He was a member of the Management Committee of the Western League for ten years, and its chairman for four. For many years he was secretary of the Kingswood club in the Bristol and District League. He was also on the committee of the Friends of Frenchay Hospital, and chairman of the

City and County of Bristol Playing Fields Association. It was after address-ing a meeting of the National PFA at Clifton that he was taken ill in his office at Eastville in July 1960.

Bristol Rovers were indeed in sad decline when he left them. They ended that 1960-61 season in their lowest position, seventeenth out of 22, since their promotion to the Second Division, and the season after that they did go down. They got off to a dreadful start, failing to score in each of their first four games and going without a win for seven before suddenly gaining four in a row.

Geoff Bradford, the only survivor from the early days of the Tann regime still a regular, had struck up a useful partnership with Alfie Biggs the previous season, but now, with Biggs transferred to Preston, he found it much harder going. At one stage later on, as the team continued to struggle, never higher than seventeenth place, he was even tried at full-back.

The opening sequence of defeats ended with a home win in the League Cup against Hartlepools United, who were heading for a third successive application for re-election in the fourth season of the Fourth Division. Any hopes of further success in that direction were dashed in the next round by Blackburn, for whom Eddie Thomas scored all four goals in an Ewood Park replay. Blackburn, of the First Division, were unlikely semi-final losers to another Division Four side, Rochdale, who were beaten by Norwich in both legs of the final. In the FA Cup, Bristol Rovers fell at the first hurdle, losing at Oldham in another replay.

Defeat at Preston, where Biggs scored the only goal against his former team-mates, plunged Rovers back into one of the relegation places after their mini revival, and their problems were intensified when Norman Sykes tem-porarily became a pay rebel. An attempt to strengthen the side in his absence brought in David Bumpstead, a wing-half or inside-forward who was one of seven footballing brothers. He had won an amateur international cap while with Tooting and Mitcham's Isthmian League champions of 1957-58 before becoming a Millwall professional, but here was another player who was to detract from the Rovers' reputation for harmony. He left Millwall because of a dispute over terms, listed at £4,500, and within two years he walked out on Rovers, also because of a contractual disagreement.

After playing in two dozen games in the 1961-62 relegation season, Bumpstead was injured in training for the return to Division Three and did not return to the team until October. He then made only a dozen more appearances before he was dropped, and asked for a transfer. There were few further first-team chances for him while he remained on the list, but in the summer of 1963 he reached agreement with the club again and was rein-stated in the League side – but for only three matches. At that point he and Sykes were dropped from the wing-half positions in favour of Ray Mabbutt and Terry Oldfield, a former Bristol Boys player and Bristol City amateur. It was then that Bumpstead packed his bags, moved out of a club house and took his wife and family back to London. The only time he was seen at Eastville again was to collect his employment cards.

Rovers imposed a ban on Bumpstead that lasted for two years before it was partly lifted, enabling him to be paid for coaching Wingate, an Athenian League club, instead of doing so in an honorary capacity. It also allowed him to have a permit to play as an amateur for a Sunday League side at Rainham, his birthplace to which he had returned after obtaining work as a cost accountant with the Ford Motor Company at Dagenham. 'I have no regrets,' he said after watching Millwall and Rovers draw 3-3 at The Den on a Monday evening in October 1965 – only the fifth League game he had attended since leaving Eastville. 'I no longer have any big playing ambitions, but I miss Bristol. My football there may not have been much of a success, but I enjoyed living in the city very much.'

Bumpstead was afterwards manager of Brentwood, the Essex club he guided to the Southern League's First Division title in 1968-69, and for which he signed goalkeeper Ray White from Bristol Rovers. White, a League debutant for Southend against Reading only three months after his sixteenth birthday, had the horror of conceding nine goals at Brighton in 1965. He was restricted to mainly a reserve role at Eastville as understudy to Laurie Taylor, who later was with Chelmsford City while Bumpstead was manager there. After leaving that post, Bumpstead ran an off-licence at Romford.

In the 1961-62 season that was to be Bristol Rovers' last in the Second Division until 1974, hopes of avoiding relegation lingered right through to their final two games – but both were away from home, and both were lost. In the first of them, against Charlton – who had been the only club below Rovers as late as February – the score was 1-1 in the dying minutes when a fluke goal by Stuart Leary gave Athletic both points. This was how Geoff Bradford recalled it: 'Stuart had the ball on the right and intended to pull back a centre from the by-line. But he mis-hit it, and Howard Radford, taken by surprise, was beaten as the ball squeezed between himself and the near post. Stuart was very apologetic, upset that a goal like that had probably put us down.'

There was still a chance of survival, however, when Rovers went to Luton for their final match. They needed to win, and then for Leeds to go down instead of them by losing at Newcastle. But Rovers had no answer to the two goals they conceded at Kenilworth Road, and neither had Newcastle to the three they let in to Leeds.

Although Rovers gained eleven wins at home in the League that season, one of them in the return with Preston despite another Biggs goal, they were beaten seven times by visitors. Among those setbacks was one by an only goal at the hands of Brighton, who completed a Christmas double by the same score on a late December day when the Football League programme was cut to twelve games by a record number of postponements due to snow and ice. Brighton were the club that went down with Rovers. Swansea, who finished directly above the relegation trapdoor, three points ahead of Rovers, five above Brighton, and just behind Leeds on goal-average, were one of the clubs most soundly beaten at Eastville, victims of a Bobby Jones hat-trick.

Away from home, Rovers suffered some sobering defeats – most notably in the North-East, where they lost 1-6 at Sunderland, 0-5 at Middlesbrough and 2-5 at Newcastle. Only twice were they successful on their travels – at Southampton, where Bradford showed something of his old form with two goals, and, most unexpectedly, against Orient, who had gained nine wins in a row and were set to reach the First Division for the first time as runners-up to Liverpool.

With the loss of Second Division status that closed the door on one of the most entertaining and memorable periods in Rovers' history, it was far from being the best of times for two more of their outstanding local finds to establish themselves in League football. But Bobby Jones and Harold Jarman both survived the trauma to make over 400 appearances apiece for the club, and not far off a joint total of 1,000 when cup-ties were taken into account. Ironically, in view of the prominent part they played in Rovers' return to more winning ways, they both dropped out of the team in the season before Second Division status was regained in 1974.

Like Bradford, Jones was with the Soundwell club in the Bristol & Suburban League before becoming a Rover. Like Biggs, he had two spells at Eastville (and a third). First signed in May 1956, the year after playing for the Suburban League against the Downs League at the age of seventeen, he had to wait until the second day of November 1957 for his Second Division debut, but then took less than two minutes to score the first of his two goals in a 5-0 home win against Middlesbrough. That was one of the occasions when Rovers were seen at their most home-grown with this team: Nicholls; Bamford, Watling; Sykes, Hale, Sampson; Petherbridge, Jones, Bradford, Biggs, Hooper. All except Sampson were born in the West Country.

Despite his flying start, it was as late as the spring of 1961 before Jones began to command a regular place. His speed and skill brought him two goals in each of successive games against Liverpool and Norwich, who finished the season third and fourth behind promoted Ipswich and Sheffield United. In the next season, the one that was to be the ninth and last of Rovers' original stint in the Second Division, his thirteen goals made him the team's top scorer. He also got into double figures in three of the following four seasons before leaving for Northampton Town in September 1966. Within five months he moved again, to Swindon, and six months after that he was back at Eastville, re-signed for £9,000 less than the £17,000 Northampton had paid for him.

Over the following two seasons Jones missed only eight League games, and, although his appearances then gradually began to tail off, he played a prominent part in Rovers' run to the League Cup quarter-finals in 1970 – especially as scorer of both their goals in the home defeat of Newcastle United that set them on their way. It was only after a replay with Aston Villa that they failed to reach the last four along with Bristol City, who lost over the two legs to Tottenham, the Wembley winners. Two seasons later, Jones was awarded the Harry Bamford Memorial trophy for his sportsmanship, and in the following year his long service was rewarded with a testimonial match against West Ham United.

His second departure from Rovers, in August 1973, left Bryn Jones as the only player with that surname on the books, whereas there had been as many as four – and there were others to come in the years after the times of Tann who are beyond the scope of this book. Glynfor Jones (known as Gwyn), who had captained his school at cricket, rugby and soccer, went back to Wales, with Porthmadog, in 1966. He had repaid a £5,000 outlay to Wolves with more than 150 games at full-back, many of them in partnership with Doug Hillard. The injury-hit Wayne Jones left shortly before Bobby.

Bryn Jones, bearer of a name made famous by his fellow countryman who hit the headlines in a then record £14,000 move from Wolves to Arsenal the year before the Second World War broke out, was a midfielder who had played for Wales as a schoolboy and in one Under-23 international. By the time Bobby and Wayne Jones left Rovers he had lost his place to Frankie Prince, but he stayed on for two more seasons before going to Yeovil Town. His friendship with Phil Roberts influenced his decision to prefer Rovers to Fulham, and he got close to a century of first-team games after having had only rare opportunities with his previous clubs, Cardiff and Newport. He had, however, played in a European competition, for one of his four Cardiff outings (two as a sub) was in the home leg of a Cup-Winners' Cup quarter-final against Moscow Torpedo in 1968. After winning the first leg with a goal scored by their other Jones, Barrie, Cardiff lost the return match (without Bryn) by the same score, but won the play-off, also 1-0, to reach a semi-final. There they were beaten by S V Hamburg at Ninian Park after appearing to have put themselves in a favourable position by drawing in Germany.

Bobby Jones' second Eastville exit took him to Minehead. After 100 games he stayed in Somerset as player-manager of Paulton Rovers, then as Bath City's assistant manager, before joining Bristol Rovers, as youth coach, for a third time in January 1980. Two and a half years later he returned to Bath as manager, which lasted six seasons. He stayed near Bristol in his subsequent posts, managing Mangotsfield United and coaching at Yate Town.

CHAPTER 24

Eastville's only Bristolian Manager

As with Bobby Jones, Harold Jarman had a career with Bristol Rovers that was split into three parts. The first one, as a player whose entertaining wing play and powerful shooting so delighted the Eastville faithful that he became something of a cult figure, lasted for fourteen seasons from 1959 to 1973. Then he was youth coach and caretaker manager during the years 1978 to 1980. And finally he was youth coach again, and also coach to the reserve team, from 1984 to 1986.

In their excellent *Pirates in Profile*, Mike Jay and Stephen Byrne state that 'chants of "Harold, Harold" were commonplace during 1969-70, and his special relationship with those fans who primarily came to watch Jarman's skills provided memorable moments. No player since that era has captured the interest of the supporters to such an extent.'

Jarman's 452 League games, a dozen of them as sub, put him fourth, equal with Petherbridge, behind Bamford (486), Pitt (467) and Bradford (461) in the club's all-time list. Then came Warren (450) and Biggs (424) ahead of Bobby Jones, who was in eighth position with 421, eleven as a sub. All have since been pushed down a place by Stuart Taylor's rise to the top with 546. For League goals, Jarman climbed ten clear of Lambden's 117 to become the club's highest scoring winger. He has only Bradford (242) and Biggs (178) ahead of him, Hooper and Bobby Jones coming next, with 101.

Yet Jarman, who rose to the captaincy, might never have had the chance to delight Rovers fans if West Bromwich Albion had recognised his potential in the trial they gave him after he had been playing in local football for Hotwells Boys' Club and Clifton Villa. He was then also with Chippenham United and Victoria Athletic before his original signing for Bristol Rovers. His first move away from Eastville, after a total of 502 games and 143 goals and his rejection of a £4,000 transfer to Oldham, was to Newport County, after which he was briefly with New York Cosmos until he lost his place to the legendary Pele, no less.

Back home, Jarman rejoined Rovers after assisting Mangotsfield United and, as player-manager, the Portway club. He became the only Bristolian to be manager at Eastville, if only in a caretaker capacity, when he was promoted from youth coach to plug the gap caused by the dismissal of Bobby Campbell as Rovers struggled near the foot of the Second Division shortly before Christmas in 1979.

Jarman got the job only after chairman Graham Holmes and vice-chairman Alan Seager had made a second unsuccessful attempt to lobby sufficient support for it to be given to Terry Cooper, the former Leeds and England full-back who had moved across to Eastville on a free transfer from Bristol City the previous August, originally as player-coach. Seager, a solicitor, resigned in protest at the board's decision to block the managerial appointment of Cooper, who had stayed on as a player after a row with Campbell over tactics had shorn him of his coaching role. 'The views of these two,' said Holmes, 'are so diametrically opposed there is no way they could ever get together in a hundred years.'

At the third attempt, Cooper was made manager on 24 April 1980, only a couple of games from the end of the season with Rovers still perilously placed. Relegation was avoided even though both those games were lost, the club finishing immediately above the three relegation places, but six points clear of the dreaded drop. There was, however, to be no escape the following season, the one in which the club's troubles were intensified by the burning down of the main stand at Eastville.

How distant then, indeed, were the days when Bristol had the prospect of two teams in the First Division, for City it was who went down with Rovers on that occasion. How distant, too, were those happy 'family' times at Eastville. More discord was delayed for only a few weeks into the season that followed relegation. Cooper had left nobody in doubt that he wanted his own men to work with him, so out went Jarman, who had been made his assistant, and also Campbell, who had become chief scout.

And for Cooper himself time was fast running out. His dismissal came after only ten games of the first season back in the Third Division, with results continuing to disappoint and home gates down into four figures. Off he went to Doncaster, but very soon back he bounced in Bristol with City, piloting them to promotion and two Freight Rover Trophy finals at Wembley (one won, against Bolton, the other lost, to Mansfield, but only on penalties).

While Campbell went off to manage Gloucester City, Jarman also soon found new employment in being taken on as chief scout by Blackburn. Neither was it long before he was back in Bristol, coaching at the university before his final return to Eastville. That unfortunately ended with his becoming a victim of an economy drive as preparations were made for the club's move to share Bath City's ground. He afterwards preceded Bobby Jones as manager of Mangotsfield United, and after resigning from there he scouted for Norwich and Manchester City.

Cricket was Harold Jarman's other strong suit. From the Optimists, one of the leading clubs in Bristol and district, he graduated to playing for Gloucestershire, captaining the county's second team and scoring just over 1,000 runs in some 40 matches with the Championship side. Rovers tolerated his double sporting life because he was not required for cricket as regularly as Ron Nicholls and Barrie Meyer had been. At that time, making a total of seven, Gloucestershire had on their playing staff two other current Football League professionals, Bristol City's David Smith (who also played for Millwall) and Bob Etheridge, and two others who had been with League clubs, Arthur Milton (City) and Syd Russell, a former Middlesex batsman who had played for Brentford. Milton, while with Arsenal before assisting City to promotion, had been the last to play for England at both cricket and soccer.

Back in the years before the increasing overlap of the seasons, when players were able to indulge in a double career, Rovers had fielded a batsman who became England's best, and captain of the Test team – though in his case there was no serious clash of interests because he last played in League football after only one season of regular county cricket.

Shortly after the First World War, Bert Williams, then the groundsman at Eastville, was sent by Rovers to meet eighteen-year-old Walter Hammond, who had already joined the Gloucestershire CCC ground staff after leaving Cirencester Grammar School, and had also been showing some footballing ability that had attracted the Southampton club's interest. Hammond, whose father, an Army officer, was killed in the last year of the war, had by then played in only three County Championship matches – and none at all in 1921 – after qualifying by residence (he was born in Kent, at Dover), but a three-year agreement was reached for him to play for Rovers with the stipulation that Gloucestershire would have first claim on his services.

It was Captain Cecil Wills, a Rovers director and vice-chairman, and a member of the Gloucestershire club, who did most to persuade Hammond to sign for Rovers. Cricket, however, very soon became the obvious priority. 'All the Rovers directors really helped to persuade Walter to make cricket a full-time job as soon as he showed his great promise,' said Capt Wills. 'My opinion was, and still is, that he would also have been an international footballer had he chosen soccer – but what a loss to cricket that would have been.'

The fact that Bert Williams considered Hammond to be the fastest footballer he ever saw might well make strange reading to those who remember the thicker, stately figure of the master batsman's later cricketing years, but his biographer Ronald Mason has written of the 'slender, modest stripling' who in youth was 'lissom and supple-jointed'. Rovers, however, did not take full advantage of Hammond's ability in the twenty League games he played for them in the three seasons from 1921 to 1924. Instead of fielding him at inside-forward, his preferred position, he was put on the wing. Only once was he on the winning side, in December 1922 against a Brentford team that included Patsy Hendren, the Middlesex batsman who became a Test colleague. Hendren, a winger who played for England against Wales in a Victory celebration match just after the war, was also with Manchester City and

Coventry City, but, as with Hammond, cricket quickly became the game on which he concentrated.

Through an introduction by Hammond, Bert Williams attended the County Ground in Bristol to give treatment to Gloucestershire players when needed, a duty he carried out for many years. He also helped rugby players, and was in particular demand from famous lawn tennis players who competed at the tournament held annually in the city ahead of Wimbledon – among them Maria Bueno, Althea Gibson, Sandra Reynolds and Lew Hoad and his wife Jennifer. In fact, Bert was kept so busy that he often had Wally McArthur along to assist. On top of all that, he was appointed to look after the British Davis Cup team for a match against Chile, and in Prince-Cox's days at Eastville he helped to keep stage folk in trim.

In addition to Hammond, Nicholls, Meyer and Jarman, Bristol Rovers players associated with the Gloucestershire cricket club have included Phil Taylor, Geoff Fox and Johnny Watkins. Taylor turned out just the once in the county's first team. Fox and Watkins were on the ground staff.

One appearance in Rovers' League side, as an amateur, was made by Hubert Ashton, later Sir Hubert, one of three brothers who won their cricket Blue at Cambridge and, in turn, captained the side in successive years. Another brother, Percy, played for Essex as a batsman despite the loss of an eye in the First World war, during which Hubert was awarded the Military Cross while serving on the Western Front. Hubert, a full-back, played his lone game for Rovers in the season after Hammond left the club – in a team well beaten by Reading, whose centre-forward did the hat-trick. He afterwards also turned out in a few League matches for Clapton Orient, with whom his clubmates included two other former Rovers players, right-winger Jimmy Gardner and Jack Townrow.

Bert Blake, a schoolmaster at Eastville Boys' School who was a Rovers centre-half in the early 1930s, after being an amateur with Bristol City, played for Gloucestershire at both cricket and football, but only for the county's second team in the summer game. Two players who spent a short time at Eastville after being with Southampton in their Third Division South title-winning season of 1921-22, also had a county cricket connection. It was a vague connection in the case of Joe Barratt, an inside-forward signed from Lincoln City in exchange for full-back Harold Armitage. Barratt, reputed to have the quirky habit of playing with a piece of straw in his mouth, did not progress beyond a trial with Warwickshire. Ken Boyes, a free-transfer left-winger confined mainly to the second team in his one season on Rovers' books, was a member of the ground staff with Hampshire, but it was his brother Stuart who best represented the family for that county, as an all-rounder in 474 County Championship matches through most of the seasons between the two world wars.

In the middle of that inter-war period, Bristol Rovers possessed a first-class cricketer who went on to share with Wally Hammond the distinction of having a record aggregate of over 30,000 runs for his county, although Hammond totalled 20,000 more than he did with the inclusion of Tests and other representative matches. Leslie George Berry never played for England, or even for the Players, but, as Wisden said, he was a 'good county cricketer' in 21 years with his adopted county of Leicestershire (he was born at Dorking), a consistent and durable opening batsman who took on the additional responsibilities of captaincy for three seasons after the war. He later coached at Uppingham School, where he was so successful that he carried out those duties until he reached the age of 73, five years before his death early in 1985. For many years he was a director of a sports shop in Leicester.

Berry was goalkeeping understudy to England's Jack Brown while with the Wednesday at Sheffield. He had previously been an amateur with Market Harborough, where he moved with his family at the age of eight. Berry had a big act to follow in taking over after the retirement of Jesse Whatley, and, although he kept his place for 39 consecutive League and Cup games in his only season with Rovers, 1930-31, he had a most unenviable time behind a leaky defence. No fewer than eight hat-tricks were scored against him, the first of them by Ted Bowen, then of Northampton Town and later Bristol City, when he made his League debut.

Berry lost his place for the last eight games of that season to Tom Boyce, a Scot who had previously been with Southend, and after refusing terms for a renewal of his contract he left for Swindon Town. From there he went to Nuneaton, and as late as the mid-1930s was with Leicestershire Nomads as player-coach. Cricket, however, was always his main interest.

CHAPTER 25

Bribery Scandal Lifts Lid
off Betting Syndicate

On the morning of Saturday, 27 April 1963, Bristol Rovers blew the lid off a match-fixing bribery scandal that caused a sensation in English football. It involved two of their own players, and ten from other clubs, two of them England internationals. Some were imprisoned with the consequent exposure of a betting syndicate.

'It is never a pleasant task exposing events of an unsavoury nature,' said Bert Tann in looking back on it. 'This club came in for a fair amount of criticism within the game for the actions taken on that day, but I genuinely feel that, as a direct result of the decisions we took, people can go through turnstiles knowing they will be able to see an honest game again. There has been a lot of talk about the risks taken by *The People* newspaper in exposing the whole business, but it was our action that gave them the opportunity to make accusations.

'We lost the services of players valued at £11,000, and, remember, at that time we were in danger of being relegated to the Fourth Division. Events have taken a considerable turn for the better for us since we made that decision, but whatever had been the outcome I would have known that what we did was right. We were told from various quarters that it was not the first time that this had happened in professional football. It was said we should have hushed the whole thing up until the end of the season and then got rid of the players concerned. That was not the answer, and never will be. We did what we felt was the proper thing, and we are even more convinced now that it was the right thing.'

The Rovers players involved were Esmond Million, a goalkeeper in his first season after costing £5,000 from Middlesbrough, and Keith Williams, an inside-forward signed a few months earlier from Plymouth Argyle for £6,000. They were accused of accepting bribes to 'throw' a Third Division relegation clash with Bradford at Park Avenue. Both were suspended by the club for seven days, later fined a nominal amount by Doncaster magistrates, and eventually barred from football for life following an FA inquiry. Million was found guilty of accepting a £300 bribe with the object of ensuring victory for Bradford; Williams admitted trying to fix the outcome. As it turned out, the points were shared in a 2-2 draw.

Million, a Northumbrian from the Ashington hot-bed of football that most notably produced Newcastle's Jackie Milburn and his nephews the

Charlton brothers, had been signed by Rovers in the wake of an Eastville exodus in the summer of 1962. That left Geoff Bradford as the last of the old brigade in the aftermath of relegation from the Second Division. Two of those who went were goalkeepers he had been bought to replace – Malcolm Norman, who went out of the League to Welton Rovers via Kidderminster Harriers, and Howard Radford, forced out by his knee trouble. George Petherbridge and 'Josser' Watling were released (the Supporters' Club put Watling in their first full-time post as chief agent), Peter Hooper was transferred to Cardiff City, Bert Williams retired as first-team trainer, and Jackie Pitt gave way to Bobby Campbell as chief coach.

Million did well enough for Rovers before so rashly throwing his League career away only the month after his 25th birthday, though he had been far from efficiently protected by a suspect defence that leaked seven goals at Shrewsbury and five against Coventry, Hull and Wrexham. One of his first associations with Eastville, when in goal for Middlesbrough, had also been a painful one, but in the physical sense, for he had had to leave the field through injury.

To the 53 appearances he made in Boro's first team – after playing two of his games for their Reserves without knowing he had fractured a bone in his right hand – he appended 38 for Rovers before his inglorious exit. He went back to Middlesbrough to work as a bus driver.

The fee Rovers paid for Keith Williams was raised by the Supporters' Club. He first turned professional with Everton, but had no chance to break into their senior side before making the short journey to Tranmere on a free transfer. In four seasons with the Birkenhead club he scored nearly 90 goals in about 160 League matches, then was transferred to Plymouth after a descent into Division Four. He failed to make any impact during his short stay in Devon, and, although he got off to a scoring start for Bristol Rovers in an away victory over Leyton Orient, that was the only goal he managed in a dozen other games on the club's way out of the Second Division. There were to be seventeen more as he held a regular place in the lower section until his suspension, his League appearances for Rovers falling just one short of the half-century.

By January 1965, nearly two years after Rovers had triggered the investigations that culminated in the imprisonment of ten of the 33 players summoned to court at Nottingham Assizes, Williams was playing football again despite the world-wide ban imposed by the FA and FIFA. He was with Johannesburg Rangers, a club coached by his brother Reg, who had also played for Tranmere. Efforts made the previous summer to get Keith Williams' registration with the Jo'burg club accepted had failed because the suspension was effective in all member countries of FIFA, but now South Africa were out of that organisation, expelled because of the racialism in their sport. So the way was clear for Williams to combine the business he set up out there with the pleasure of kicking a ball again – something he had planned to do at the end of his League career in England even if he had been able to play on for as long as he had wished.

The England players caught in the web when *The People* Sunday newspaper exposed the betting scandal arising from Bristol Rovers' initiative were Peter Swan, the Sheffield Wednesday centre-half, and Tony Kay, who had been transferred from Wednesday to Everton for £55,000 – then a British record for a wing-half – as recently as December 1962. They were both jailed for four months, as also was another Wednesday player, the free-scoring David ('Bronco') Layne. They placed £50 bets that their team would lose at Ipswich in December 1962, and when Ipswich, then champions, won, they each collected £100.

Layne, who had been in the same Sheffield Boys team as Gordon Banks, England's goalkeeper in their World Cup win of 1966, said he had been lured into betting by Jimmy Gauld, a former Charlton, Everton, Plymouth and Swindon forward who, exposed as ringleader, incurred the severest prison sentence of four years and was ordered to pay £5,000 costs. 'There was never any question of our throwing the match,' said Layne. 'Our side was never in a position to win that day. All we had done was send off our £50. Only later did we realise what a big thing it was.'

Gauld developed a betting syndicate, allegedly involving far more players than the number prosecuted, while recovering from a broken leg suffered when he was playing for Mansfield Town. At its peak, from early 1961 to mid-1963, it was earning £1,000 a week, but professional gamblers behind the operation were said to be raking in ten times as much. Life bans from football were also imposed on all the convicted players, though eventually lifted under a new rule that enabled players to appeal after seven years.

The suspensions of Swan and Layne ended in June 1972, too late for them to be successful in their attempted comebacks with Wednesday. Both also failed to revive their careers with other Football League clubs – Layne at Hereford, Swan at Bury – but Swan did get to play again at Wembley. Thirteen years after winning the last of his nineteen caps there as England's centre-half against Switzerland, he was player-manager of the Matlock Town team that defeated Scarborough in the FA Challenge Trophy Final in 1975.

Tony Kay, the ban on whom was lifted from the first day of March in 1974, emigrated to Spain after turning out for Skelmersdale in the Northern Premier League. He returned to play in the testimonial match at Goodison Park for Harry Catterick, the former Everton manager. Brian Phillips, who was with Middlesbrough before Mansfield, became player-coach with Clipstone Colliery Welfare Reserves after being freed to play again in 1971, but suffered a dislocated knee and chipped bone in a Notts Alliance game.

Bristol Rovers' draw at Bradford – on the day in April 1963 when Million and Williams transgressed – left both clubs on the brink of the drop. The Big Freeze that year extended the season into May, and, after taking only one point from six games when it was over, Rovers did not pull to safety until winning a delayed visit to Halifax for their penultimate match. Halifax, who had conceded five goals when the clubs had met at Eastville, were already doomed to go down. Bobby Jones and Ian Hamilton gave Rovers an early two-goal lead that could have been increased to five by half-time. Jones had chances to complete a hat-trick, and Bradford missed what he admitted was an easy opportunity. In the second half Halifax quickly scored twice to equalise, but Hamilton half-headed, half-shouldered the winner.

On the following Monday evening Rovers lost their final game 0-2 at Port Vale, who thus clinched third place, but four points behind Swindon, the club promoted as runners-up to Northampton's champions. Rovers finished nineteenth with 41 points, one ahead of Reading, who survived only because of a goal-average that was superior to Bradford's. Relegated with Brighton, Carlisle and Halifax, Bradford six years later dropped out of the League altogether, failing to gain re-election after a third successive season at the foot of Division Four.

Ian Hamilton, scorer of the goal that saved Bristol Rovers from a second consecutive demotion, was the son of John (or 'Jock,' as he was generally known) who was a Rovers regular for most of the two seasons he spent with the club from 1929 to 1931. Another son, David, also seemed set to make the League grade after joining Rovers from Thornbury, but he was the tragic victim of a bungalow fire while still a teenager.

'Jock' Hamilton also played in local football for Thornbury after leaving Eastville. He made his debut at wing-half for Rovers Reserves in the same match as Willie Gillespie, a full-back who had been in the East Fife side beaten by Celtic in the 1927 Scottish Cup final, and had also played a few times for Newcastle in the First Division. With Rovers, Gillespie played in only two League games, whereas Hamilton Senior just exceeded 60 – in one of which he became the club's first player to score for both sides, his own goal giving Newport County victory.

Ian Hamilton, dubbed 'Chico,' and also 'Sir Laurence' by those unkind enough to see his winning of penalties as play-acting, also provided Rovers with a scoring curio. One of his hat-tricks made him the first to perform that feat for the club yet finish on the losing side, in a 3-6 defeat at Southend. He scored four goals in a 6-2 win against Shrewsbury in the League Cup early in the season after Rovers' narrow escape from the Fourth Division, and in one reserve game he found the net three times inside seven minutes. In the 1964-65 season, he was Rovers' top scorer despite missing several matches because of the knee trouble that shortened his League career.

After just over 150 games and 60 goals, he joined Newport County following a spell on loan at Exeter, then was with Weston-super-Mare – originally as a player, afterwards as assistant manage – either side of being in the Welton Rovers team that won the Western League championship for a fourth time, by one point from Taunton Town, in 1973-74.

The goalkeeper in that Welton team, and also in the side that landed the club's Western League title treble of 1964-67, was Malcolm Norman, one of the men Esmond Million was bought to replace. Norman, who at one stage was near a Welsh cap while at Eastville, interrupted his days at Welton with other Somerset spells at Bath and Radstock. He was made to feel really at home with Welton, for his team-mates there included four other former Bristol Rovers players – Trevor Rhodes, Mike Slocombe. David Stone, and John Watkins. The Southend-born Rhodes, a junior lawn tennis finalist at Wimbledon, played only two of his six League games with Bristol Rovers (the others with Millwall), and was never on the winning side. Slocombe, another of the local discoveries, had the misfortune to be introduced into a relegation-bound Bristol Rovers team, and after doing the rounds of several other clubs in the Bristol area he ran into the further bad luck of suffering a broken leg that forced him to give up the game.

Peter Hooper, priced at £10,500, joined Cardiff City, who had just fallen out of the First Division. He went as replacement for Derek Hogg, a former Leicester and West Bromwich left-winger the Welsh club had released along with Dai Ward. Hooper had an eventful start to both the next two seasons, first helping Cardiff to come from two goals down to force a 4-4 draw with Newcastle at Ninian Park, then returning to Bristol, with City, for a fee of just over £11,000, and scoring on his debut in their 3-0 home victory over, of all clubs, Bristol Rovers. He altogether exceeded 400 games and scored some 150 goals, a good number of them from penalties, before leaving the League for turns with Worcester, Glastonbury and Barnstaple. He became the licensee of a public house near Barnstaple, and afterward was a probation officer in that part of Devon.

CHAPTER 26

The Brave and Fearless Bernard Hall

The career of the player who took over from Esmond Million in Bristol Rovers' goal was also brought to a sudden and sad end, but in his case – as with Bert Hoyle and Bob Anderson – it was because of serious injury.

Bernard Hall was unconscious for sixteen days in Frenchay Hospital after colliding heavily with John O'Rourke, Middlesbrough's centre-forward, in the 54th minute of a Third Division match at Eastville on the last day of 1966 as he moved out to collect a back pass from Johnny Williams that slowed in the mud. O'Rourke limped away rubbing his hip while Hall lay motionless. The late John Parsons, a former *Daily Telegraph* colleague of mine who was then with the *Daily Mail*, recalled: 'First reports to the press box spoke of a fractured jaw. Only when we saw the grim faces of manager Bert Tann and director Douglas Mearns Milne in the tea room later did we realise how serious it was.'

Ray Mabbutt, though on the small side for a goalkeeper at 5ft 6in, was deputed to go between the posts, as he also had done on one previous occasion at Swansea when Howard Radford had required treatment off the field. He did not let the side down as Rovers earned a 2-2 draw.

Recovery for Hall, described as a 'brave and fearless' goalkeeper in reports of his many impressive displays, was slow and painful, and although he did attempt a comeback it was never even a remote possibility. He was out of the game at the early age of 25, after being an ever-present in two consecutive seasons, missing only three games in a third, and making 136 of just over 180 League and Cup appearances in succession.

It was Fred Ford, while assistant manager at Eastville, who spotted Hall's potential. He was in charge of an FA youth coaching course at Taunton which the goalkeeper attended as a member of the West Twerton Youth Club team in his home city of Bath – the club that also produced Alan Skirton, a winger who entered League football with Arsenal after coming into prominence in a Bath City side that included former internationals Stan Mortensen and Charlie Fleming. Despite being taken ill with pleurisy and pneumonia soon after joining Arsenal, and being discharged from National Service in the Army on medical grounds, Skirton played in more than 150 games for the Gunners before moving to Blackpool. From there he returned to the West Country with Bristol City, who had released him to Bath as 'not good enough'.

Fred Ford, his attention swiftly caught by Bernard Hall's ability and courage during that coaching course at Taunton, wasted no time in signing him on amateur forms. The disregard for danger that was so tragically to be Hall's undoing was immediately evident when, at the age of sixteen, he was knocked out in his first game for the Reserves. The fact that his indomitable spirit remained undimmed was also made very clear, however, when he readily stepped up to fill the vacancy left at such short notice by Million's expulsion despite not having been considered fit enough to play in the second team that afternoon.

Hall, who was put in the care of an orphanage at the age of seven, moved to a new foster home in Bristol shortly before signing as a part-time professional on turning seventeen while learning to be a bricklayer. By the time he became a full-timer three years later on completing the apprenticeship as a stonemason to which he had switched, he had made his first-team debut in a Good Friday home match with Charlton Athletic in 1962. He deputised for the injured Radford while Rovers were immersed in the grim battle against the relegation they were unable to avoid. He gave a good account of himself in a 2-2 draw, and again did well in the next match with Walsall, which had the same result, before having to give way to Radford for the last two games. With Radford announcing his retirement the following summer, Million was signed because Hall was then considered too short of experience.

Not until Million missed one match through injury only weeks before being banned did Hall get another chance in the first team. His future looked bleak when he gave what he himself described as 'a terrible display' in a 1-2 home defeat by Southend. 'I remember kicking six successive clearances straight into touch,' he said. 'I felt so depressed.' But what a different story it was when he had to be so abruptly promoted to first choice after Million's departure. The pick of his many daring and agile saves during the next three and a bit seasons before his alarming accident was the one he made from a penalty in an FA Cup-tie at Bournemouth. Rovers took play straight back to the other end and were themselves awarded a spot-kick from which they did score on the way to a 3-1 win. Victories in the next two rounds, at Coventry and at home to Norwich, earned them the visit to Old Trafford. Although that was where their run ended, Hall still had a happy memory to take away. 'Denis Law came up to me after the game, shook my hand, and said "Well done." I shall never forget that moment.'

After his enforced retirement from football, Hall became groundsman at the Imperial club's ground in the Knowle area of Bristol. In October 1967 Rovers granted him a testimonial match against West Ham United.

To replace Hall for their remaining 28 games of the 1966-67 season, Rovers looked to Ronnie Briggs and, mainly, Laurie Taylor. Briggs, who had guested for Rovers on their tour of Eire before being signed, was a Northern Ireland international who had kept goal for Manchester United. Openings for him at Eastville were restricted by Taylor, and, after being loaned to

Minehead and having a trial at Southend, he found more scope at Frome and Glastonbury.

Taylor, a former Exeter Boys goalkeeper, was soon showing his good positional sense, if in defeat, in a third-round FA Cup-tie with Arsenal in front of an Eastville crowd of nearly 35,500. In the 1968-69 season, in which he was absent from only three matches, he excelled before some 55,000 fans in a fifth-round tie that Everton won at Goodison Park by only one goal. Soon after that, however, with 90 League games behind him, he was on his way out to Chelmsford City, and a Southern League championship medal, after himself coming up against a rival whose challenge he was unable to ward off.

This newcomer was Dick Sheppard, who, although born in Bristol, was first a professional with West Bromwich Albion before Rovers snapped him up on a free transfer. With the Baggies he played in the first League Cup final to be staged at Wembley, though that was the match in which the First Division club, holders of the trophy, lost 2-3 to Third Division Queen's Park Rangers after leading at half-time with two goals by winger Clive Clark, a former QPR player.

Among Sheppard's clubmates at the Hawthorns was a fellow Bristolian who also became one of his clubmates at Eastville – on his recommendation. Kenny Stephens, a blond-haired winger who had been in the Bristol Downs League XI while in his teens, would almost certainly have been lost to the Football League if Sheppard had not tipped off Bill Dodgin, then Rovers' manager, about him. Disillusioned after being released by Albion and then having few chances at Walsall, Stephens had lost hope of finding a new club and become a newsagent. Given a trial by Rovers, he was soon offered a contract and proved a real bargain for more than 200 League games over eight seasons, featuring strongly in the return to Division Two in 1974, before a move to Hereford made him one of those who played in all four of the divisions the League then comprised. Not a bad record for somebody who had not been wanted.

Sheppard also appeared in all four divisions, but completed the set only through playing a couple of times on loan to Torquay – and that after becoming another Bristol Rovers goalkeeper to have his career cut short by a major injury. On 13 January 1973, he suffered a depressed fracture of the skull in challenging for the ball with Tranmere's Eddie Loyden at Eastville. He did get to play again in Rovers' first team, but for just one match, his 151st for the club in the League, on the last Saturday of December in 1974. Bristol City were the visitors that afternoon, and they came away convincing winners with four second-half goals after being behind at the interval. Sheppard was also loaned to Fulham after Torquay, but did not make their senior side and soon afterwards went to Weymouth on a free transfer. He was later with the Portway club in Bristol and Paulton Rovers in Somerset before rejoining Rovers as goalkeeping coach.

Tom Stanton, a versatile former Scottish schoolboy international, was brought on as substitute to take over in goal when Sheppard had to be carried off against Tranmere and preserved a clean sheet as Rovers took both points. Stanton, previously in the background as a full-back or midfielder with Liverpool and Arsenal, had been signed on a free transfer from Mansfield nearly five years earlier. He did not, however, become a regular choice until the promotion season of 1973-74 in which he was an ever-present. Not long after that, however, he too was forced out by injury and left for Weymouth. His subsequent moves also included returning to Rovers as a coach, of the Reserves and with schoolboys.

For their first few games after losing Sheppard, Rovers relied on Malcolm Dalrymple, another free-transfer man. Capped by England at youth level, he arrived from Luton following a trial with Cambridge United, but was not seen as a long-term prospect. He had had the misfortune to be Sheppard's deputy earlier in the season when non-League Hayes had sprung an FA Cup shock by knocking out Rovers in the first round. Within two months he was on his way out to Watford via Margate.

The answer to the goalkeeping problem was splendidly supplied by big Jim Eadie, who, most remarkably considering he had gained experience of European football with Cardiff City, was also obtained without payment of a fee after the Welsh club had loaned him to Chester. Right from his debut in a scoreless draw at Blackburn it was obvious that Don Megson had picked up one of his biggest bargains as manager of Bristol Rovers.

Alarming as the injuries suffered by Bernard Hall and Dick Sheppard were, there was another concerning a Rovers player that very nearly resulted in a fatality. On the evening of Monday, 2 April 1984. Aiden McCaffery, the club's captain and their 1982-83 Player of the Year, was only a minute away from dying when he swallowed his tongue as a crashed to the ground in an accidental collision with his own goalkeeper, Phil Kite, during an Associate Members Cup game Rovers won 2-1 at Southend. 'You have got four minutes to work on someone because of oxygen to the brain,' said Roy Dolling, Rovers' physiotherapist, who was on the spot immediately, 'and it must have taken us all of three minutes to get him round.'

Dolling claimed it was the accuracy of Southend striker Greg Shepherd that helped to save McCaffery's life. 'Southend scored during the incident,' he said, 'and that was the luckiest thing that happened. The referee, Alan Gunn, waved me on instantly. Had the ball not gone in, he would probably have had to play on. Every second was vital. When I got to Aiden his body was dead still and his eyes were fluttering. There was blood form his nose and mouth and he had swallowed his tongue.' Dolling tried to force open the player's mouth, but succeeded only when the Southend club's doctor, Monty Lubel, joined him on the pitch. They forced open McCaffery's clenched teeth with a small pair of scissors, just in time to keep him alive.

After being discharged from hospital, the former Newcastle and Derby central defender could remember nothing of the penalty-area collision that went so desperately close to costing him his life. He recovered to have one more season with Rovers, even doing the hat-trick only six months later against Shirehampton in one of the memorial matches Rovers played for Mike Barrett. The Bristol-born winger died from cancer at the age of 24, not long after snatching a last-minute winner against Millwall in what was to be his last home game. His widow gave birth to a son six weeks after his death.

Epilogue

The firmer footing – after several more lean years since relegation in 1962 – on which Bristol Rovers were placed during the last three of Bert Tann's 22 full seasons with the club was amply demonstrated when they finished each of them among the Third Division's top six clubs. They then took only two more seasons to gain promotion again.

Indeed, in 1969-70, the first season in which Bill Dodgin was team manager – with Tann continuing in the dual role of general manager and secretary to which he had switched with Fred Ford's appointment as team manager in April 1968 – Rovers took third place behind Orient and Luton. They would have gone up with them if the increase to three up and three down had not been rejected at the League's annual meeting. That change was to be delayed until 1973-74, the season in which Rovers did regain their lost status as runners-up to Oldham, edging York into the new third promotion place with superior goals figures.

Bill Dodgin brought about the improvement with a settled defence in which Phil Roberts and Lindsay Parsons formed a fine full-back partnership in front of Dick Sheppard (until his injury). Stuart Taylor was the centre-half rock on which so many opposing forwards foundered. Up front, Dodgin added speed, flair and punch first by making Ray Graydon his regular choice on the right wing, then by bringing in Bruce Bannister, the 'Grab' half of the strike force he was soon to form with the 'Smash' of Alan Warboys.

It was inevitable that a talent as obvious as Graydon's would attract attention from higher up, but when he left for Aston Villa the acquisition of Welsh international Brian Godfrey in part exchange gave Rovers a forceful midfielder who rendered two seasons of excellent service before leaving for Newport County. Graydon was a key member of the Villa team that carried off the Third Division championship in 1971-72 while Rovers took sixth place for the second successive year. Two seasons later he was their leading scorer when they accompanied Manchester United back to the First Division. He was also twice a League Cup winner with Villa, and for a third time with Oxford United.

During the post-Tann period, Bristol Rovers have also possessed a goalkeeper, Brian Parkin, whose League and Cup appearances for the club put him second only to Jesse Whatley, and a forward, Paul Miller, a £100,000 signing from Wimbledon, who became one of their four-goal men in an FA Cup-tie with Bath City that gave the setters of sports quizzes the curio of an away win gained at home (Twerton Park, which Rovers were then sharing with the Somerset club). Parkin, who joined Rovers from Crystal Palace when Nigel Martyn went in the opposite direction, finished three League games behind Howard Radford's 244, but ahead of him overall with a total of almost 270. The 5-0 defeat of Bath in 1994 left Rovers one goal short of equalling their record victory for the FA Cup proper, gained on the back of a Gary Penrice hat-trick in the first round against Merthyr Tydfil in 1987, although Weymouth Town had been beaten 1-15 in the third qualifying round in 1900.

The winning of the short-lived Watney Cup in 1972 was an encouraging prelude for Rovers to the promotion they gained two years later under the management of Don Megson. But they had to do it the hard way to claim a trophy competed for by the two highest-scoring clubs from each of the previous season's four divisions of the League who had not won promotion and were not involved in Europe. After a scoreless draw with Sheffield United in the final at Eastville, they converted seven penalties in the shoot-out before Ted Hemsley, another of the footballing cricketers, was the first not to be sharp enough for the Blades. 'What has happened to Bristol Rovers is absolutely marvellous,' enthused Alan Hardaker, the Football League's normally more reticent secretary. 'This competition has brought a taste of soccer success to an area that is crying out for it.'

Life back in Division Two was an unremitting struggle for Rovers, however, seven seasons in its lower reaches leading to the relegation they shared with their City neighbours. After Bobby Gould, a man of many clubs, had twice been put in charge without the desired results, the next promotion was achieved in 1989-90 under the direction of Gerry Francis, former captain of QPR and England, but there were to be two more relegations as the League rang its sponsorship changes with Barclays, Endsleigh Insurance, Nationwide and Coca-Cola.

Neither did Rovers have much more good fortune in penalty shoot-outs, although in 2000-01 there was a notable exception when they knocked one Premiership club, Everton, out of the Worthington Cup in that manner before losing to another, Sunderland, in the next round.

A mistake was made in parting with Bristol-born Keith Curle, a central defender who was sold to Torquay for £5,000 but played for England after costing Manchester City £2.5m. And, among the strikers who made good elsewhere, the departure of another Bristolian, Jamie Cureton, coupled with that of Jason Roberts, had an important bearing on the club's return to the Third Division (equivalent to the old Fourth) in 2001.

The escape from there in 2007 came under the fresh direction of Lennie Lawrence, Director of Football, and Paul Trollope, the chief coach responsible for team selection. Lawrence arrived as a manager who had seen it all in eight years at Charlton before being with Middlesbrough as they rose to, but fell out of, the Premier League – promotion, relegation, dramatic play-off survival with two extra-time goals, near bankruptcy, and even the loss of the Valley ground that drove the club into temporary exile as Crystal Palace's tenants at Selhurst Park. Trollope, whose father, John, broke the appearance record for one club with 770 League games (three as a substitute) for Swindon Town, had had his appetite for success whetted by being with Derby County when they reached the Premiership for the first time.

Only after a remarkable transformation was promotion again achieved, for as late as March Rovers were in sixteenth place with only eleven games to go following defeat away to Boston, the club heading for the drop with Torquay under the burden of a ten-point penalty for a breach of rule. Of those remaining matches, however, Rovers lost only one, at home to a Wrexham goal scored just three minutes from time. Two were drawn and the eight others won – three of them, each by the odd goal, in a final surge that hoisted them from ninth to the third play-off position of sixth.

Their last two opponents were two of the teams automatically promoted behind champions Walsall – Swindon Town at home, Hartlepool United away. It was so close that if Rovers had not won in the North-East on the final day, after being a goal down at half-time, they would have been denied their play-off place by Stockport County, who ended with a 5-0 victory at Darlington. As it was, Stockport were foiled of qualification by Shrewsbury on goal-difference, both one point behind Rovers.

Rovers' previous experience of the play-offs had been a losing one, but this time they battled through in completing a feat only costly Chelsea were able to achieve – that of playing in finals at the Millennium Stadium in Cardiff and the new Wembley in the same season. In Wales, Rovers lost to their namesakes from Doncaster in the Johnstone's Paint Trophy competition before an Associate Members' record crowd of 59,024 (nearly two-thirds of whom travelled from Bristol), but only in extra time after a gallant fight-back from falling two goals behind within five minutes of the kick-off. At Wembley, where they again had huge support in an attendance of 61,589, they recovered from conceding a goal in the third minute to defeat a Shrewsbury side that had to replace one defender who injured a knee in the warm-up and then lost another through a sending-off.

So Rovers were up to the third tier of soccer's pyramid six years after dropping out of it. Their City neighbours were back in the Championship as Division One runners-up to Scunthorpe after eight years of under-achieving. And Bristol's rugby club, one of the best in the country during most of Bert Tann's years at Eastville, were third in their Premiership. Not all that much to shout about in comparison with the money-mad chasers after Champions League glory, but something of another overdue boom time for that part of the West Country.